In Search of New Horizons
Epic Tales of Travel and Exploration

In Search of New Horizons
Epic Tales of Travel and Exploration

Robert B. Downs

American Library Association   Chicago 1978

LIBRARY OF CONGRESS CATALOGING IN PUBLICATION DATA
Downs, Robert Bingham, 1903-
   In search of new horizons.
   Bibliography: p.
   1. Adventure and adventurers. 2. Explorers.
I. Title.
G525.D64   910'.92'2 [B]   78-13656
ISBN 0-8389-0269-3

Printed in the United States of America

Contents

Contents

Illustrations

Preface

The choice of books qualifying for the classification "epic tales" in my title was difficult and, in the end, highly personal, though a majority of those chosen were almost automatic; they could hardly have been omitted. Advice on inclusions came from many sources, both actual and armchair travelers. Scores of works were considered before a final consensus was reached. Among those left out—perhaps saved for a second volume—were the following:

Charles Doughty, *Travels in Arabic Deserts*
Julian Duguid, *Green Hell*
George Featherstonbaugh, *Excursion through the Slave States*
Harry Franck, *Vagabonding down the Andes*
Peter Freuchen, *Arctic Adventure*
Sven Hedin, *Through Asia*
William Hudson, *Naturalist in La Plata*
Samuel Johnson, *Journey to the Hebrides*
T. E. Lawrence, *Seven Pillars of Wisdom*
Anne Morrow Lindbergh, *North to the Orient*
David Livingstone, *Missionary Travels*
Alexander Mackenzie, *Voyages from Montreal*
Douglas Mawson, *Home of the Blizzard*
Alan Moorehead, *White Nile* and *Blue Nile*
Frederick Olmsted, *The Cotton Kingdom*
Robert F. Scott, *Voyage of the Discovery*

Vilhjalmur Stefansson, *The Friendly Arctic*
Aurel Stein, *Innermost Asia*
Lowell Thomas, *With Lawrence in Arabia*
George Vancouver, *Voyage of Discovery to the North Pacific Ocean*

I am grateful to the University of North Carolina Press for permission to include the chapter on William Bartram's *Travels through North and South Carolina,* from *Books That Changed the South* (Chapel Hill: Univ. of North Carolina Press, 1977). Included here, too, are revised and expanded discussions of Amerigo Vespucci's *Four Voyages,* Richard Henry Dana, Jr.'s *Two Years before the Mast,* and Francis Parkman's *Oregon Trail,* from my *Famous American Books* (New York: McGraw-Hill, 1971); and Lewis and Clark's *History of the Expedition,* from my *Books That Changed America* (New York: Macmillan, 1970).

For permission to use an illustration of *Kon-Tiki* from the book of that name, acknowledgment is made to Rand McNally and to Allen & Unwin, and for the illustration from *Annapurna* to E. P. Dutton and to the Federation Française de la Montagne.

The arrangement of IN SEARCH OF NEW HORIZONS is strictly chronological (except for Francis Parkman's *Oregon Trail*), without regard to the area being explored. The chronological plan is most useful in revealing the state of geographical knowledge in each era of history. By coincidence, this scheme brings together Peary and Amundsen's accounts of the discovery of the North and South Poles, and Herzog and Hunt's gripping tales of Annapurna and Everest. In every case except for Ferdinand Magellan, the chapters dealing with twenty-four individuals are based on the explorers' own narratives.

In the actual creation of the book, I feel a deep sense of appreciation to Elizabeth C. Downs, who did much of the preliminary research on each title included, and to Deloris Holiman, who prepared the manuscript for publication. Their assistance was indispensable.

1
Outward Bound—
Why Travel?

Why do so many men—and some women, such as Amelia Earhart and Anne Morrow Lindbergh—travel and explore? In fact and in fancy, travelers have been wandering over the earth and sea since time immemorial.

The travel epics of the ancient world include those of Moses, leading the Israelites out of bondage in Egypt and wandering through the wilderness for forty years; Homer's Odysseus, who experiences varied adventures on his return from the Trojan War; Xenophon's incredible retreat, leading a defeated Greek army home through a thousand miles of enemy territory; and Herodotus' wanderings throughout the known world following the Greco-Persian wars. In 221 B.C. Hannibal, the Carthaginian general, led his army, including war elephants, in a remarkable march across the Alps, invaded Italy, and defeated three Roman armies.

Religion and war have, in fact, frequently been the compelling motives for travel. St. Paul, most traveled of the early Christians, completed four extensive journeys in the first century A.D.: first, to Antioch of Syria, Cyprus, and southeastern Asia Minor; second, to Asia Minor, Ephesus, Athens, and Corinth; third, revisiting churches in Asia Minor, Ephesus, Corinth, and Jerusalem; and, finally, to Rome. Later, in the seventh century, Mohammed's *Hegira*, the story of his flight from Mecca to Yathrib to escape persecution and possible death and his establishment of the Islam faith, was recorded. The Pilgrims and Puritans came to New England in the seventeenth century to escape religious persecution in England; more than 400,-

000 Huguenots, or French Protestants, fled France in the seventeenth century because of ruthless governmental harassment; and the Mormons, members of the Church of Jesus Christ of Latter-Day Saints, migrated in the 1840s from Illinois to the barren desert of Utah. A celebrated instance in the military sphere was the "Long March" made by Mao Tse-tung and his hard-pressed Communists, a tortuous 6,000-mile trek through northern China; only 20,000 of the more than 100,000 original participants survived.

Economic pressures have also motivated great migrations. A striking instance was the mass immigration of the Irish to America as a result of the Great Potato Famine in the mid-nineteenth century. As a consequence of starvation and emigration, the population of Ireland dropped from more than 8,000,000 in 1841 to 6,500,000 in 1848.

Economics was a major factor, too, in the 1835–37 migration of the Boers, or Afrikaners, of South Africa. These people, attempting to escape British rule, migrated by the thousands with their slaves and herds, traveling north and east from the cape in the Great Trek, and eventually founding the Orange Free State and the Transvaal.

Paul Herrman, in his *The Great Age of Discovery,* discussed Henry M. Stanley's African explorations. He offered these comments:

> This was a task requiring an almost superhuman resistance to fatigue and exertion, and glancing through the pages of Stanley's travel reports, we are puzzled about what it was in Stanley's make-up that enabled him to bear all these dangers, rigours and deprivations. Time and time again we have asked similar questions and although the name of the protagonist changes from Columbus to Vasco da Gama or Magellan, Mungo Park, Caillié, Barth, etc., the question remains each time in the same form. Within certain limits, we can offer a partial solution of the motives that urged these men on, such as incentives of trade, glory or religious convictions, but the core of the question remains untouched. We can glibly state that all these men were endowed with exceptional natures and that they marched towards their goal as if under a spell, insensitive to all suffering, but this facile answer brings us no nearer the crux of the problem.

Explorers apparently typify the human need for freedom from the safety and routine provided by a predictable and stable existence in society. Maurice Herzog, who led the French expedition on one of the most memorable adventures of modern times, the conquest of the great Himalayan peak Annapurna, attempted to analyze explorers' psychology. Why, he asked, would men want to scale Mt. Everest, plumb eerie ocean bottoms, grope farther and farther down into the underground darkness of caves? "The answer," Herzok concluded, "it the spirit of adventure—a yearning for the unknown, for risks, that moves Western men who live in modern 'comfort,' the heaven and hell of our days. As life has grown progressively easier over the centuries, with adventure disappearing from the face of the earth, man's physical organism has protested," leading him to an intense desire "to recapture the great primeval satisfaction of his forebears" in such ways as running, jumping, striking, swimming, and climbing.

In reviewing Herzog's book *Annapurna,* Philip Hamburger observed,

> Mountain climbers are a mysterious lot. They seem to the rest of us to belong less than half to this earth and more than half to the high hills above. One often wonders, reading an account of their unbelievable exploits, among the dangerous, wind-blown, dizzying heights, whether they are more intent upon conquering mountains or being conquered by them.... It would seem that mountaineers, being supreme gamblers, often let themselves go when they are climbing great peaks and take a chance on fate to guide both their steps and their thoughts.... Their goal can only be the summit.

The old cliché that men climb mountains "because they are there" is a superficial explanation, valid to a point, but falling short of full understanding.

A foremost Japanese explorer, Naomi Uemura, was a member of an expedition to the top of Mt. Everest, and also reached the peaks of the highest mountains in five continents, drove a dog sled 12,000 frigidly cold kilometers from Greenland to Alaska, and sailed solo 6,000 kilometers down the Amazon River on a raft. Asked what motivated him to embark on such challenging, nearly impossible missions, he replied that, in the case of the Greenland-Alaska trek, he was curious about the origins of the Eskimo; he wished to discover possible links between them and Asian peoples, especially the Mongolians. Otherwise, he stated, he wanted to challenge the elements and added: "You achieve something, then you want to try and surpass it."

A perceptive critic of American culture, Carl Bode, in a discussion entitled "Foreign Ports and Exotic Places," pays particular attention to Americans as travelers and explorers. Among a complex of our national characteristics, he notes, is restlessness. As Tocqueville observed in his *Democracy in America*, Americans are "in constant motion," demonstrating a high degree of mobility. This meant, according to Bode, "that a family had relatively few qualms about picking up and moving away to improve its situation. The American seldom felt a compulsion to endure misery when he could alleviate it by settling somewhere else, preferably in the West. If times grew bad in New England and rocks seemed to multiply in the field, the Yankee farmer heeded Ohio's call or Iowa's." Recreational travel also came early into vogue. The riverboats and packets were crowded, the trains were full, and the rough-riding stages and carriages did a thriving business. Other aspects of American restlessness noted by foreign visitors, Bode points out, were "the habit of walking fast, of being unable to sit still, of erupting into all sorts of brisk motions from drumming our fingers to tapping our feet."

An entire tribe of eternal travelers are the gypsies, a wandering, dark-skinned people living in Europe, the Near East, North Africa, and the Americas. The gypsies first appeared in Europe in the fourteenth century, and nothing has induced them to settle down as they wander over the face of the earth.

Robert Louis Stevenson, in his *Travels with a Donkey in the Cevennes,* observed: "But we are all travellers in what John Bunyan calls the wilderness of this world—all, too, travellers with a donkey; and the best that we find in our travels is an honest friend. He is a fortunate voyager who finds many. We travel, indeed, to find them. They are the end and the reward of life. They keep us worthy of ourselves; and when we are alone, we are only nearer to the absent."

One of the most searching examinations of the motivations for travel is presented in M. A. Michael's *Traveller's Quest.* In this symposium, a contributor, Freya Stark, suggests that all travel is a quest, a conscious or unconscious searching for something that is lacking in our lives or in ourselves. Michael adds, "I have always thought that the urges which drove the early travellers out on their wanderings must have been in essence violent, rather than quiet and compelling; that these were men avid for riches, covetous of fame, striving to be first to visit distant places, craving to know more than their fellows." By contrast, the true traveler today, in Michael's view, is concerned with "simplicity, solitude, beauty, instead of riches and fame; knowledge of self instead of self-aggrandisement; fulfillment instead of conquest."

From a historical standpoint—and virtually all essays in the present work are historical in nature—the great travelers have been driven by one or more of several aims or impulses. First are patriotic and religious reasons, such as stirred the medieval crusaders from 1096 to 1272, carrying on holy wars designed to free Palestine from the infidels, and incidentally to win military glory and material wealth for themselves; the voyages of Columbus, Magellan, Vasco da Gama, Hernando Cortes, Francisco Pizarro, and other explorers and conquerors, to add new territory, gold, and riches to their mother lands, occasionally mixed with efforts to convert primitive peoples to Christianity; and the world-wide activities of religious missionaries of all faiths to spread their doctrines.

Second in importance, perhaps, among the incentives for travel and exploration is simply a craving, sometimes verging upon madness, for material wealth—an explanation for the gold rushes to California in the 1840s and to Alaska in the 1890s; the search for gold in the American Southwest, so graphically described by J. Frank Dobie in his *Coronado's Children*; and Cecil Rhodes's pursuit of diamonds and diamond mines in southern Africa. Essentially, the westward movement of the American people, described in Frederick Jackson Turner's *The Significance of the Frontier in American History*, was materialistic; starting with the foundation of Jamestown in 1607, a great land, comprising more than three million square miles, was conquered, fierce nomadic Indian tribes were defeated, and innumerable natural obstacles were overcome in an irresistible surge toward the Pacific Ocean.

The spirit of adventure is undoubtedly the third major factor in many of the most famous narratives of travel, exploration, and discovery. Thus Amundsen and Scott went to extreme limits to be first at the South Pole, Peary to discover the North Pole, Hillary and Tensing to surmount Mt. Everest after earlier expeditions had failed, Maurice Herzog to be the first climber to reach the crest of a mountain exceeding 8,000 meters in height, Magellan to be first to circumnavigate the world, and, in the twentieth century, American astronauts to be the first men on the moon.

The phenomenon of migration and travel is by no means confined to mankind, but is found throughout the animal, bird, and fish kingdoms. There are innumerable examples. Among birds, golden plovers nest in the Arctic and then travel to Brazil and Argentina. Arctic terns nest in an area only a few degrees from the North Pole, and several months later appear on the borders of Antarctica, 11,000 miles away. Bobolinks nest in northern states and spend the winter in Brazil. Migratory mammals travel shorter distances, but certain species have well-established patterns of travel: caribou move in immense herds from summer to winter quarters; gray whales frequent the coast of California from early winter to late spring and then spend the summer in the Arctic Ocean; fur seals breed off the west coast of Alaska in the spring, then travel 3,000 miles to winter in southern California. Various species of fish are also migratory, including salmon, herring, shad, and eels. The most remarkable migrants among invertebrate animals are monarch butterflies, which assemble in vast hordes in Canada and the northern United States during the late summer and early fall and fly to spend the winter in the southern United States, from Florida to California.

But in his avid desire to explore every corner of the world—and indeed the universe—man has far outstripped any other member of the animal kingdom. New worlds remain to be discovered.

2
The First Sightseer

Herodotus' History of the Persian Wars, 464–447 B.C.

Cicero called Herodotus the "Father of History," Plutarch rated him as the "Father of Liars," and others have designated him as the "Father of Tourists." The classical historian Edith Hamilton, in her *The Great Age of Greek Literature,* describes Herodotus as "the first sight-seer." He was also a master storyteller. His travels grew out of both his intellectual curiosity and his simple enjoyment in seeing strange lands and meeting different peoples. Moses and the Israelites were famous travelers perhaps a thousand years before Herodotus, but they traveled to escape death and destruction. Herodotus is the first person on record to go touring for personal satisfaction; in fact, an estimated twenty of his approximately sixty years were thus employed.

Neither the exact date of Herodotus' birth or death is known. He was a native of Halicarnassus in Asia Minor, located on the southeastern shore of the Aegean Sea within easy reach of Athens by galley, almost in sight of the Grecian archipelago. His birth date was about 484 B.C. He was an omnivorous reader, thoroughly acquainted with classical and contemporary Greek literature—which made him one of the most instructive, as well as one of the most charming, of ancient writers. He was intimately familiar with and deeply influenced by the writings of Homer. His foremost English translator, George Rawlinson, comments: "It may be questioned whether there was a single work of importance in the whole range of Greek literature accessible to him, with the contents of which he was not fairly acquainted." Included in this range of literature were works of Greek and Persian historians, now lost.

Apparently Herodotus' peregrinations were undertaken chiefly between his twentieth and thirty-seventh years, that is, between 464 and 447 B.C. He crisscrossed Asia Minor and European Greece on more than one occasion. All the important islands of the archipelago were visited: Rhodes, Cyprus, Delos, Paros, Thasos, Samothrace, Crete, Samos, Cythera, and Aegina. One of his long and perilous journeys took him from Sardis to the Persian capital Susa. He saw Babylon, Colchis, and the western shores of the Black Sea as far as the estuary of the Dnieper; he traveled in Scythia and in Thrace; visited Sante and Magna Graecia; explored the antiquities of Tyre; coasted along the shores of Palestine; saw Gaza; and made a long stay in Egypt. A conservative estimate calculates that his travels took him 1,700 miles from east to west and 1,600 miles from north to south.

Herodotus was not a superficial tourist. Whenever he came to a place that excited his interest, he settled down to live for a period, during which he investigated, made inquiries, measured those items that aroused his curiosity—such as the pyramids—and accumulated material. With his future great *History* in mind, he thus undertook by personal observation to obtain full knowledge of the various regions he visited.

Edith Hamilton provides a vivid description of Herodotus' observations, as seen through his writings:

> Everything everywhere in the world of men was of interest to him. He tells us how the homely girls in Illyria get husbands, how the lake dwellers keep their children from falling into the water, what Egyptian mosquito nets are like, that the king of Persia when travelling drinks only boiled water, what the Adrymachidae do to fleas, how the Arabians cut their hair, that the Danube islanders get drunk on smells, how the Scythians milk their mares, that in Libya the woman with the most lovers is honored, how the streets of Babylon are laid out, that physicians in Egypt specialize in diseases, and so on, and so on. Bits of information that have nothing to do with what he is writing about keep straying in.

Travel conditions in Herodotus' day were truly hazardous. The stark realities are provided by Plutarch: "It was at that time very dangerous to go by land on the road to Athens, no part of it being free from robbers and murderers. That age produced a sort of men, in force of hand, and swiftness of foot, and strength of body, excelling the ordinary race and wholly incapable of fatigue; making use, however, of these gifts of nature to no good or profitable purpose for mankind, but rejoicing and priding themselves in insolence, and taking the benefit of their superior strength in the exercise of inhumanity and cruelty." Travelers like Herodotus had to contend with vicious characters such as these on the highways and byways in the fifth century B.C. Herodotus evidently possessed a rugged physique; no one could have spent twenty years in arduous and often perilous travel without one.

To travel even short distances was an adventure at that time. The saddle, the wheel, the oar, and the sail were the only means of transportation for those who could not walk. Four hundred years after Herodotus, under similar conditions, St. Paul's journey to Rome provides an idea of the hazards to be faced by sea, while Xenophon's description of the endless miles on foot or horseback across the blazing heat of Asia Minor to Babylon is a comparable picture of land travel. Only the most dedicated seeker of knowledge or one with strong instincts for exploration would undertake any except the most essential travel. At least in his writings, Herodotus strangely ignored discomforts, difficulties, and dangers, evidently too much absorbed in other matters.

Critics have accused Herodotus of being overly credulous and naïve, accepting as true everything that he was told, no matter how incredible. This charge is only partially justified. In fact, he was skeptical of many of the tales related to him. His attitude was that of the born investigator. "For myself," he commented, "my duty is to report all that is said, but I am not obliged to believe it all—a remark which applies to my whole History."

That Herodotus was willing to record mixtures of fact and fiction, however, is demonstrated in the following account of some small winged snakes, described as occupying certain trees in Arabia:

> The Arabians say that the whole world would swarm with these serpents if they were not kept in check in the way in which I know that vipers are. Of a truth Divine Providence does appear to be as one might expect beforehand, a wise contriver. For timid animals which are a prey to others are all made to produce

young abundantly, so that the species may not be entirely eaten up and lost; while savage and noxious creatures are made very unfruitful. The hare, for instance, which is hunted alike by beasts, birds, and men, breeds so abundantly, as even to super-foetate, a thing which is true of no other animal. You find in a hare's belly, at one and the same time, some of the young all covered with fur, others quite naked, others again just fully formed in the womb, while the hare, perhaps, has lately conceived afresh. The lioness, on the other hand, which is one of the strongest and boldest of brutes, brings forth young but once in her lifetime, and then a single cub; she cannot possibly conceive again since she closes her womb at the same time she drops her young.

Both an inclination to doubt and a willingness to believe, however, crop up repeatedly in Herodotus' narrative. The holy women at Dodona insisted that doves speak, but Herodotus was certain that they did not; at the same time, he did not question the story told him that a mare gave birth to a rabbit. He doubted the Egyptian priests who asserted that the phoenix wraps up the dead body of his parent in a mass of myrrh and carries it from Arabia to the Temple of the Sun in Heliopolis where he buries it, but accepted the folklore that headless creatures with eyes in their breasts live in Libya, and that Egyptian cats have a strange habit of jumping into fire.

Herodotus' principal concern, as he roamed the earth, was to observe the customs of various non-Greek peoples: Lydians, Babylonians, Indians, Persians, Arabians, Massagetae, Egyptians, Libyans, Scythians, Thracians, and others. He investigated the effects of geography and climate upon the physical appearances, mores, and the institutions of peoples, their progress in the arts and sciences, their religions and laws. He was no less interested in legendary and historical accounts of the past, especially as these may have affected their contemporary attitudes and political behavior.

Herodotus' first major expedition was to Egypt. "I speak at length about Egypt," he wrote, "because it contains more marvelous things than any other country—things too strange for words. Not only is the climate different from that of the rest of the world and the rivers unlike any other rivers, but the people also, in most of their manners and customs, reverse the common practice of mankind."

The First Sightseer

Herodotus then proceeded to list seventeen ways in which the Egyptians were distinguished from the Greeks and other people: women buy and sell in the market place; men weave at home. Other men push the woof up; Egyptians down. Men carry burdens on their heads; women on their shoulders. Women urinate standing up; men sitting down. They relieve themselves in their homes; they eat out in the street. No woman is a priestess; men are priests of both male and female gods. Sons are not compelled to take care of their parents; daughters are so compelled. Priests elsewhere let their hair grow; Egyptian priests are shorn. In grief other men shave their heads; Egptians let their hair and beard grow. Other men live apart from animals; Egyptians live with them. Other men eat wheat and barley; Egyptians eat only spelt. They knead dough with their feet; mud and dung with their hands. Other men leave their genitals as they are; Egyptians are circumcised. Each man wears two garments; each woman one. Others fasten the rings and ropes of sails on the outside; Egyptians on the inside. Greeks write and count from left to right; Egyptians from right to left. Egyptians have two kinds of letters: sacred and demotic.

Note that six of these customs concern different practices for men and women; three deal with change in direction, such as the direction of writing; most of the remainder deal with bodily functions. The Egyptians defended their practices, especially as relating to the human body, with the statement, "Whatever is shameful though necessary must be done in secret, but whatever is not shameful openly." In short, only that which is clean should be seen publicly, all that is not should be hidden. In particular, sacred things must be kept clean, which is why, for example, the Egyptian priests shaved their whole body every second day, washed twice at night and twice during the day.

Herodotus noted that the Egptians were excessively religious. The priests' dress was entirely of linen and their shoes made from the papyrus plant; they were not permitted to wear clothing of any other materials. Every day bread made of the "sacred corn" was baked for them, and they were well supplied with beef, goose flesh, and wine, but fish and beans were forbidden foods. Every day, according to Herodotus, the priests "observe thousands of ceremonies." Any animal marked for sacrifice to the gods was meticulously examined to make certain that there was not a single black hair on its body, and an elaborate ritual was followed in the actual sacrifice. As Egyptians venerated the cow more highly than any other animal, female cattle were sacred and therefore not sacrificed. The Greeks, on the contrary, had no such restriction. "This is the reason," Herodotus stated, "why no native of Egypt, whether man or woman, will give a Greek a kiss, or use the knife of a Greek, or his spit, or his cauldron, or taste the flesh of an ox, known to be pure, if it has been cut with a Greek knife."

The pig was regarded by the Egyptians as an unclean animal, to such a degree that "if a man in passing accidentally touch a pig, he instantly hurries to the river, and plunges in with all his clothes on." Swineherds were forbidden to enter any temple and could not intermarry with other Egyptians.

The art of embalming the dead had grown to be a science in Egypt centuries before Herodotus' time. He found it of sufficient interest to provide detailed descriptions of the process. He also noted that three separate levels of embalming, based on the survivors' ability to pay, were used: one for the rich; another for persons of moderate means, and a quick, simple method for the poor.

Herodotus found that Egypt did not abound with wild animals, and those that did exist were all held to be sacred. If a man purposely killed one of the sacred animals, he was punished with death; if by accident, he was required to pay such fine as the priests chose to impose. More severe was the penalty for slaying an ibis or a hawk; whether done with malice or by chance, the perpetrator had to die.

Two pieces of folklore emerge in Herodotus' account of Egypt's control of the cat population. After a mother cat had kittens, she shunned the males. The latter seized the kittens, carried them off and killed them, whereupon the females once more accepted attention from the males. Again, in the presence of a fire, cats would rush headlong into the flames and be destroyed.

Other animals and birds discussed by Herodotus include the crocodile, the hippopotamus, otters, and the ibis. Another sacred bird was the fabled phoenix, which Herodotus admits that he had never seen, "except in pictures," though he appeared to believe in its reality. In the Egyptian religion, the phoenix was a miraculous bird, the embodiment of the sun god. It lived for 500 years, was then consumed by fire through its own act, only to rise in youthful freshness from its own ashes. Herodotus describes the phoenix's plumage as "partly red, partly golden, while the general make and size are almost exactly that of the eagle."

Medicine, as practiced among the Egyptians, was specialized. Each physician treated a single ailment or disorder, and no others. The country swarmed with medical practitioners, Herodotus noted, "some undertaking to cure diseases of the eye, others of the head, others again of the teeth, others of the intestines, and some those which are not local."

Herodotus was fascinated by the Egyptian pyramids, especially the manner in which these tremendous monuments had been constructed. As Aubrey de Sélincourt points out in his *The World of Herodotus,* "the belief in the actual divinity of the Pharaoh rendered intelligible the building of the pyramids: the pyramids were not the tombs of men, raised by slaves to flatter the pride of a tyrant; they were the tombs of gods, who had died to be born again, and they were raised by their worshippers." This view is different from that presented by Herodotus, who was convinced that the pyramids were built by ruthless despots, who sacrificed untold thousands of slaves during the period of more than a century in which the largest were constructed.

In addition to the pyramids, Herodotus provided accounts, often eyewitness descriptions, of other Egyptian building and engineering feats, notably the marvelous labyrinth near the City of Crocodiles, with its 12 covered bridges and 3,000 rooms; the room hollowed by the order of Amasis from a single block of stone; and the canal, begun in the days of Neco and completed by Darius, the Persian king, which stretched from the Nile to the Arabian Gulf, a distance of four days' journey by boat.

The mysterious Nile was also a subject of keen interest and speculation. Herodotus sailed for some 700 miles up the river from the coast, past Heliopolis, the once-famous city of ancient Egypt, past Memphis, the former capital, past Thebes, with its hundred gates, to Elephantine, the "ivory island," opposite to what is now Aswan. Herodotus was deeply puzzled about the Nile's course and the reason for its periodical floods. "Concerning the nature of the river," he wrote, "I was not able to gain any information from the priests. I was particularly anxious to learn from them why the Nile, at the commencement of the summer solstice, begins to rise and continues for a hundred days—and why, as soon as that number is past, it forthwith retires and contracts its stream, continuing low during the whole of the winter until the summer solstice comes around again. On none of these points could I obtain any explanation from the inhabitants, though I made every inquiry." Herodotus rejected the theory that the Nile's annual flooding was caused by the melting snow on distant mountains, but came up with no sensible explanation of his own. The source of the great river remained hidden, of course, for many centuries after Herodotus' time.

From Egypt, Herodotus traveled to Libya for a brief time, though he little realized the vast size of the continent of which that land was a part. The customs of various tribes were described: in one, the warriors used ostrich skins for shields, in another a leather anklet was given a woman by each of her lovers, and her popularity was measured by the number of such anklets worn on the leg; there was a tribe which hunted with four-horse chariots, and—a tall tale—whose oxen walked backward as they grazed, because their horns curved outward in front of their heads, and if they moved forward the horns would stick in the ground. As Herodotus crossed the desolate sandy desert of the north, he told of seeing antelopes, gazelles, asses, foxes, wild sheep, jackals, and leopards. Further odd tribal customs are reported. In one tribe the wives drove the chariots to battle; in another the people painted themselves red and ate honey and monkeys; a third grew their hair long on the right side of their heads and shaved it close on the left.

In his description of Babylon, which he called Assyria, Herodotus was chiefly interested in the city's size and wealth, but he also noted certain unusual customs. One that greatly intrigued him was the Babylonian marriage market. Once a year the girls of the surrounding villages were assembled for inspection, with an auctioneer in charge. The auctioneer began by offering the prettiest girls, who would be bid off to the richest buyers. When all the pretty ones were sold, the homely ones were told to stand up, and the bidding process was reversed. The poor men present were asked which of them would take the smallest sum to accept them as wives. "The money," Herodotus explains, "came from the sale of the beauties, who in this way provided dowries for their ugly or misshapen sisters." Another practice that took his fancy was the treatment of disease. Since there were no doctors in Babylon, invalids were carried out into the street, and anyone passing by was expected to stop and offer advice about their complaints. An equally odd custom prevailed among Babylonian husbands and wives—they sat over incense to fumigate themselves after intercourse.

Herodotus' work is entitled *History of the Persian Wars*, but only the last part is concerned with that famous conflict. The first two-thirds of the book contain his accounts of his journeys and what he learned from them. His travels into many lands and among diverse peoples were in the nature of a stage setting. As the wealth and apparently invincible power of the huge Persian empire under Cyrus is displayed, the drama of a few impoverished Greek city states, armed chiefly by courage and love of liberty, winning victory and remaining free, is tremendously enhanced.

Questions concerning the reliability of Herodotus' information about the lands visited are numerous. Modern historians generally agree that he is accurate and trustworthy when he describes what he saw with his own eyes. Much of his historical matter is, however, hearsay. For example, he quotes verbatim speeches by and conversations among historical personages when he could not have been present or have possessed written documents. Thus, Herodotus' account is a mixture of first-hand reporting, of great interest and value, mixed with numerous folktales and legends. A perceptive comment, again from Edith Hamilton: "Herodotus is a shining instance of the strong Greek bent to examine and prove or disprove. He had a passion for finding out. The task that he set himself was nothing less than to find out all about everything in the world."

Herodotus possessed one of the prime requisites of a great historian—objectivity. He was remarkably free of national prejudice and racial bias. He had a broad appreciation of all nations and invariably found something to praise even among the most uncivilized people. His *History* remains one of the great travel narratives of all time.

3
Quest for Cathay

Marco Polo's Travels, 1271–1295

A span of seventeen hundred years separates two celebrated travelers of the ancient and medieval worlds—Herodotus in the fifth century B.C. and Marco Polo in the thirteenth century A.D. Yet they share striking similarities in their avid interest in exotic lands and strange customs, and in their faithful recording of every detail of what they had seen or heard.

To thirteenth-century Europe, the East was a land of mystery—strange, remote, and completely alien. Direct contacts were restricted to the periphery, although for millennia active commerce had flowed back and forth among the sister continents of Europe, Asia, and Africa. In Byzantium, and elsewhere in the Mediterranean area, European merchants bartered with Orientals for porcelain, silk, jade, jewels, spices, and precious balms, brought in caravans across great deserts from a largely unknown world.

By the middle of the thirteenth century the Mongols had ended their destructive rampages in Europe and Asia, and ruled in reasonably tolerant fashion from the Black Sea to the Pacific Ocean. Thus, after a complete break extending over more than four hundred years, some mutual knowledge and communication were beginning to percolate between Europe and China, due largely to the journeys of a few traders, especially the Polos.

Marco Polo was born in Venice about 1254. At the time, Venice was the greatest trading power of the age. From India she obtained the pearls, diamonds, and sapphires that made her the jeweler of Europe; from Siberia came the ermines for the doges' robes and sables for the wives of wealthy merchants; from Cathay (China) came spices, camphor, and silk. Transportation was by camel train across the deserts of central Asia, or by the sea route in Chinese junks and Arab feluccas. No Venetian had ever seen the lands from which these riches came.

The curtain was parted by two brothers, Nicolo and Maffeo Polo, who were Marco's father and uncle and prominent Venetian merchants, trading up and down the Levant and beyond into the Black Sea region. Another brother, Marco, established himself as a merchant prince in Constantinople. Nicolo and Maffeo dreamed up a new venture that would blaze the trail some years later for Nicolo's son Marco, then a small lad. In an unexpectedly long journey, begun about 1260, they proceeded on a trading mission from Constantinople into the Crimean peninsula, thence far north along the Volga. The brothers seem to have prospered greatly, dealing in furs, amber, and other products. While trading in southern Russia they found their return route cut off by a local war. Since they could not go forward, they boldly decided to push on into the unknown Orient. Eventually they reached Bokhara, in the heart of central Asia, 3,000 miles from home, and settled there for three years, buying and selling and learning languages. They described Bokhara as "the finest city in the whole of Persia." It has in fact, remained one of the great cities of central Asia, surrounded by high walls and famous for its silks, tiles, and furs.

The Polo brothers were now within the domain of the great Kublai Khan, ruler of the Tartars, whose domain stretched from the Arctic Sea to the Indian Ocean, and from the shores of the Pacific to the borders of central Europe—the largest empire of all time. The Khan had never seen any western Europeans, and was curious to meet some in person. Through his emissaries, an invitation was extended to the Polo brothers to visit the Khan in his remote capital of Peking. Willingly accepting the invitation, the intrepid Polos continued their journey eastward to Samarkand and, continuing stage by stage for about a year, often enduring hunger and cold, they came at last to Kublai Khan's court.

According to young Marco's account, the emperor was deeply interested in the two brothers: "Many questions he asked them, first about their emperors, how they governed their lands according to justice and how they went out to battle. After that, he questioned them concerning the Lord Pope and all the affairs of the Roman Church, and all the customs of the Latins." The Polos had considerable knowledge of Asian languages, and answered Kublai Khan "well and wisely as befits wise men like them who well knew the Tartar and Turkish languages."

So pleased was the emperor with Nicolo and Maffeo that he decided to send them as his envoys to the pope, for he had been deeply impressed by what they had to tell him of Christendom. Loaded with gifts and furnished with "golden tablets" (passports to ensure them safe passage through all parts of Kublai Khan's dominions), the brothers began the long return journey westward to Europe. They carried letters requesting that the Venetians might be allowed to return to China accompanied by a hundred learned teachers, "intelligent men acquainted with the Seven Arts, able to enter into controversy, and able clearly to prove to idolators and other kinds of folk that the Law of Christ was best."

No details are given as to the route followed on the Polos' return journey, but it took three years to accomplish and, when they finally reached Venice, they had been absent for nine years. While they had been away, Pope Clement IV had died and his successor had not yet been chosen. In order to comply with Kublai Khan's wishes, they decided to await the election of a new pope; after a two year delay, Gregory X was chosen. Instead of a hundred teachers, however, the Polos were offered the services of only two young, inexperienced Dominican friars. Even this pair had little interest in their mission; at the first hint of danger, the two monks refused to proceed farther than Palestine.

When the Polos left Venice for their first long trek to China, Nicolo's son Marco was six years of age. By the time they returned, Marco was an upstanding lad of fifteen, full of an adventurous spirit. The brothers readily agreed to his entreaties to be permitted to accompany them back to China.

The second journey eastward started by way of Jerusalem, because the Great Khan had been promised some oil from the lamp which burned in the holy sepulcher. The travelers then made their way through what is now Turkey, Iraq, Iran, Afghanistan, the Pamir Mountains, the Gobi Desert, the frontiers of the great steppes of

Mongolia, and northwest China to Peking. Marco, a keen observer, stored up in a retentive memory everything that he saw and heard. He brought to life for the reader the eccentric customs, the market-places, the eating habits, the costumes, and other colorful characteristics of Arabs, Persians, Turks, Tartars, Kurds, Mongols, Russians, and Chinese. Adventures en route were many. The Polos struggled through torrential rains, rivers in flood, sandstorms, and avalanches. They went past Mount Ararat, on top of which, Marco heard, Noah's Ark rested; the oil wells of Baku and the great inland Caspian Sea; past Mosul and Bagdad through Persia. At Hormuz, on the Persian Gulf, they had planned to take ship, but decided instead to make the remainder of the journey by land because of unseaworthy vessels.

Farther on, the travelers came to the Pamir Mountains, a land of icy cold, where they crossed deep gorges on swaying rope bridges over "the roof of the world." It was there that Marco saw and described the great horned sheep which naturalists have since named for him, the *ovis Poli*, "whose horns are a good six palms in length." After descending from the mountains and reaching Khotan, they were confronted by the great Gobi Desert. For thirty days they journeyed over the sandy wastes of the silent wilderness. Marco gave a vivid description of its terrors, including voices which seem to call the traveler by name; mirages in which were seen the march of phantom cavalacades, luring them off the road at night; spirits which filled the air with sounds of music, drums and gongs and the clash of arms—all typical desert illusions.

At last the Polos arrived safely at Tangut in the extreme northwest of China. Skirting the frontier across the steppes of Mongolia, they were met by agents of the Khan, who had learned of their approach and had sent guides to escort them for the last forty days of their journey. When they were greeted by the Khan in May of 1275, they had been en route three and a half years. The potentate received his old friends with sincere delight, and young Marco, now twenty-one, was also given a cordial welcome. As reported in the *Travels*, "His Majesty entertained him with a friendly countenance, and taught him to write among others of his honorable courtiers; whereupon he was much esteemed of all the Court, and in a little space learned the customs of all the Tartars, and four languages, being able to read and write them all." Their linguistic abilities proved a valuable asset to the Polos in dealing with the Khan and his people.

For Marco Polo, the arrival in Peking was the beginning of a long and close association with the Chinese emperor, who enrolled him among his personal attendants. Kublai Khan found that Marco was both discreet and intelligent and began to send him on various missions. Marco soon noted that the Khan had much curiosity and was always desiring to learn more about the manners and customs of the many tribes over whom he ruled. Thus Marco noted:

> Perceiving that the Great Khan took a pleasure in hearing accounts of whatever was new to him respecting the customs and manners of people, and the peculiar circumstances of distant countries, he [Marco Polo] endeavored, wherever he went, to obtain correct information on these subjects and made notes of all he saw and heard, in order to gratify the curiosity of his master. In short, during seventeen years that he continued in his service, he rendered himself so useful, that he was employed on confidential missions to every part of the empire and its dependencies and sometimes also he traveled on his own private account, but always with the consent and sanctioned by the authority of the Great Khan. In such circumstances it was that Marco Polo had the opportunity of acquiring a knowledge, either by his own observation or by what he collected from others, of so many things until his time unknown respecting the Eastern ports of the world, and these he diligently and regularly committed to writing.

Eventually, these travel notes, originally collected for the Khan's delectation, were incorporated in Marco's *Travels*.

On various missions for the emperor Marco Polo journeyed through the provinces of Shansi, Shensi, and Szechuan and followed the borders of Tibet to Yunnan to enter Northern Burma, lands unknown to the West until the second half of the nineteenth century. For three years, by appointment of the Khan, Polo was governor of the city of Yangchow, which was overrun with traders and makers of arms. He was also sent on a mission to visit Karakorum in Mongolia, the old Tartar capital, and with his Uncle Maffeo spent three years in Torgut. He was also sent to Cochin China and went by sea to the southern states of India; he left a graphic description of the great trading cities of Malabar.

Marco's account of the wonders of Cathay begins with a vivid picture of the summer palace at Shangtu. Here, the Great Khan "caused a palace to be erected, of marble and other handsome stones, with halls and rooms all gilt and adorned with figures of beasts and birds, and pictures of trees and flowers of different kinds. It is most wondrously beautiful and marvelously decorated. On one side it is bounded by the city-wall, and from that point another wall runs out enclosing a space of no less than sixteen miles, with numerous springs and rivers and meadows. And the Great Khan keeps a variety of animals in it, of the deer and goat kind, to serve as food for the hawks and other birds employed in the chase, whose pens are also in the grounds."

The Khan's real palace, however, was at Peking, described by Marco as "the largest that ever was seen. It has no upper floor, but the roof is very lofty. The paved foundation on which it stands is raised ten spans above the level of the ground, and a wall of marble, two paces wide, is built on all sides. This wall serves as a terrace; along the exterior edge is a handsome balustrade, with pillars. The sides of the great halls and the apartments are ornamented with dragons in carved work and gilt, figures of warriors, of birds, and of beasts, with representations of battles. The great hall is extremely long and wide, and admits of dinners being served there to great multitudes of people." Many other marvels of the palace, its surrounding area, and the capital are also pictured in detail by Marco.

The capital city had been newly rebuilt in the form of a square, six miles on each side, surrounded by earthen walls and with a dozen gates. "The streets are so broad and so straight," Marco wrote, "that from one gate another is visible. It contains many beautiful houses and palaces, and a very large one in its midst, containing a steeple with a large bell which at night sounds three times, after which no man must leave the city. At each gate a thousand men keep guard, not from dread of any enemy, but in reverence of the monarch who dwells within it, and to prevent robberies."

Even greater than Peking was the city of Hangtcheou-feu, the "City of Heaven," in south China, which had lately been conquered by Kublai Khan. "It is without doubt the largest city in the world,"

Marco stated. "The city is one hundred miles in circumference and has twelve thousand stone bridges, and beneath the greater part of these a ship may pass. The city is wholly on the water and surrounded by it like Venice. The merchants are so numerous and rich that their wealth can neither be told nor believed. In the city, too, were 4,000 baths, the largest and most beautiful to be found anywhere, each capable of accommodating a hundred persons at a time."

The Khan's female companions seemed to be legion in number. He had four wives of first rank and the eldest son of any one of these might succeed to the empire, upon the decease of the Great Khan. All four wives were designated as empresses and had separate courts. Each had no less than three hundred young female attendants of great beauty, together with a multitude of youths serving as pages, eunuchs, and ladies of the bedchamber; thus, there were 10,000 persons belonging to each court. The emperor also had many concubines. The inhabitants of Ungut were noted for their beauty of features and fairness of complexion. Consequently, the Khan sent his officers every second year to that province to collect for him one hundred or more of the handsomest of the young women. In making their selection, the Khan's agents inspected the girls' hair, faces, eyebrows, mouths, lips, and other features. Further selection occurred upon arrival at the emperor's court to insure against any hidden imperfections; the girls had to sleep tranquilly, not snore, have a sweet breath, and be free of any unpleasant scent. Thirty or forty were retained by the Khan, and the remainder were divided among lords of the household. The people of the province, Marco claimed, regarded the selection of their daughters for the imperial court as a favor and an honor.

Prostitution was common in Peking. Marco estimated that "the number of public women who prostituted themselves for money in the city and its suburbs was 25,000." Visiting ambassadors had courtesans furnished to them every night of their stay in the capital.

Marco's inclination to deal in superlatives eventually won him the nickname "Marco Millions" from skeptics in Venice. Among his possibly true, but seemingly improbable, statements were that the Khan kept "up a stud of ten thousand horses and mares, which are white as snow"; that at the Khan's splendid festivals, 40,000 people were served on each occasion; as well as that the emperor's personal bodyguards numbered 12,000 horsemen. Presents received by the Khan were on an equally colossal scale: "It was no rare occurrence for him to receive five thousand camels, one hundred thousand beautiful horses, and five thousand elephants covered with cloth of gold and silver."

Marco's reporting was more in the realm of the tall tale when he related the following wonder: "A large lion is led into the Great Khan's presence, which, as soon as it sees him, drops down and makes a sign of deep humility, owning him its lord and moving along without any chain." More unlikely still are the wonders performed by the court astrologers or magicians: "If it should happen that the sky becomes cloudy and threatens rain, they ascend the roof of the palace where the Great Khan resides at the time, and by force of their magic they prevent the rain from falling and stay the tempest."

An elaborate system of mail delivery was used to expedite communication of messages from all areas of the empire—a scheme reminiscent of the American "Pony Express." Marco noted that there were many roads leading in all directions to the different provinces. On each of these, at distances of twenty-five or thirty miles apart, were post-houses. "At each station, four hundred good horses are kept in constant readiness, in order that all messengers going and coming upon the business of the Great Khan, and all ambassadors, may have relays of fresh horses." Between the post-houses, about every three miles, were foot messengers wearing girdles with several small bells around their waists to announce their coming. So effective was the postal system that messages could be delivered to distant provinces, which would take weeks or months to reach in ordinary travel, in a matter of days.

The Khan's favorite sport was hunting and for that purpose he kept many leopards and lynxes for chasing deer, and also many large lions. The lions were active in seizing boars, wild asses, and oxen, bears, stags, roebucks, and other beasts that were the objects of sport. Further, the emperor kept large eagles which were trained to catch wolves. Two noblemen, called "keepers of the mastiffs," had charge of the hounds and mastiffs, numbering some 5,000. The keepers were charged with supplying the court daily with a thousand pieces of game and also with as large a quantity of fish as could be provided.

Reminiscent of the biblical story of Joseph, who directed the storing of grain against seven years of famine, was Kublai Khan's similar plan, described by Marco: "In times of great plenty, he caused large purchases to be made of such grains as are most serviceable, which are stored in granaries provided for the purpose in the several provinces, and managed with such care as to ensure its keeping for three or four years without damage. It is his command that these granaries be always kept full, in order to provide against times of scarcity." If any of his subjects suffered crop failures, loss of cattle, or other misfortunes, the Khan would forego collecting taxes or tribute and send aid to the unfortunate ones.

Repeatedly, Marco refers to the immense wealth of the Mongol dynasty under Kublai Khan. The method used for the manufacture of money is described as follows:

> The Great Khan has the bark stripped from mulberry trees, the leaves of which are used for feeding silkworms, and takes from it that thin inner rind which lies between the coarser bark and the wood of the tree. This being steeped, and afterward pounded in a mortar, until reduced to a pulp, is made into paper, resembling in substance that which is manufactured from cotton, but quite black. When ready for use, he has it cut into pieces of money of different sizes and different values. And all these sheets bear the Great Lord's seal and authenticated as if they were actually pure gold or silver.

The issue of paper money in China dates back to at least the ninth century. Marco made no reference to printing, though the art in China existed long before his time.

The use of coal was apparently unknown to Marco or to his part of Europe, despite the fact that it had been burned by Roman legionnaires in Britain twelve hundred years earlier. He stated:

> You must know that all over the province of Cathay there is a kind of black stone, which is dug out of the mountains like any other kind of stone, and burns like wood. These stones make no flames, except a little at the beginning when they are lit, like charcoal, and by merely remaining red-hot they give out great heat. They keep alight better than wood. If you put them into the fire at night and kindle them well, I assure you

that they remain alight all night, so that you will still find the fire burning in the morning. And you must know that these stones are burnt all over the province of Cathay.

As previously noted, Marco's travels, usually on missions for the Khan, were extensive. By following the western highway, he traversed a rich, densely populated area to Tai-yuan-fu, the only district in China that produced wine. Next he described Caichu, home of the celebrated Golden King, who was said to be served only by beautiful girls. Marco admired the Yellow River, which he said "no bridge can span, for truly it is very broad and deep and swift," a constant source of danger due to its devastating floods. Days of travel through mountains, valleys, and forests brought the tireless traveler to Acbaluc, "the white city on the frontier of Manji." Farther west he came to Sindufu and the Upper Yangtse river, where he was impressed by the tremendous volume of shipping and trading. "So big is the river, that you would rather think it a sea than a river." Entering Tibet, Marco wrote: "This is an extremely large province, with a language of its own. They are a barbarous people. They have very large mastiffs, as big as donkeys."

Other highlights of Marco's western explorations included visits to the province of Chiung-tu, where blocks of salt served as money; the province of Yung-chang fu, where the people "make a gold case fitted to their teeth, and cover both the upper and lower ones"; and the province of Chuju, where Marco provided a lively account of how tigers were hunted by an archer and two dogs, and also described the custom of tattooing.

Natural history was a subject of keen interest to Marco. He had a sharp eye for observing natural phenomena such as wild flowers and trees, rugged mountains and wide plains, the great horned sheep of the Pamir highlands, bird life, and trout streams. In the first section of the travels he made twenty references to birds, and throughout he described animals, trees, and various forms of vegetation, and also different fruits, nuts, and seeds. In the province of Karazan, he "found snakes and huge crocodiles ten paces in length, and ten spans in the girt of the body. At the fore part, near the head, they have two short legs, having three claws with eyes larger than a fourpenny loaf and very glaring. The jaws are wide enough to swallow a man, the teeth are large and sharp, and their whole appearance is so formidable, that neither man, nor any kind of animal, can approach them without terror."

Numerous signs of an advanced civilization in the China of his day were described by Marco. Admirable and new to him were such features as broad avenues, paper money, police patrols at night, public carriages providing taxi service, high bridges, drains under the streets, roadsides beautified with plantings of double rows of trees, and elevated highways.

For seventeen years Marco served the Khan, while his father and uncle grew rich in trade. At last the Polos longed to return home to Venice. Furthermore, Kublai Khan was growing old and they feared what might happen to them from jealous courtiers when he died. But the emperor was adamant in refusing them permission to depart. They were being given wealth and honors, which the Khan considered sufficient compensation. Finally, a chance circumstance gave them their opportunity. A mission came to the Khan from Arghun, the ruler of Persia, whose wife had just died. Her last wish was that he should choose for his new bride a member of her own family at the court in China. A "very pretty and charming girl" of seventeen was selected. The Persian ambassador asked that the Polos, famous as seasoned travelers, be allowed to escort the party back to Persia. Reluctantly, the Khan was prevailed upon to let them go.

Thirteen ships were fitted out. The voyage was a long and difficult one, with lengthy delays in Sumatra, Ceylon, and Southern India. The journey, in fact, was full of disasters, during which several ships and many of the company were lost. Thus it was more than two years before the Persian court was reached and the princess safely delivered. While still in Persia, the Polos received news of the death of the Great Khan whom they had served for so long. This, Marco wrote, "entirely put an end to all prospects of our revisiting those regions." And so the three Polos continued by way of Tabriz, Trebizond, and Constantinople to Venice, arriving home late in 1295.

According to legend, when the Polos knocked on the door of their Venetian house neither relatives nor friends recognized them. They had been believed dead for many years. Their identity was established when they gave a large banquet and displayed an extraordinary quantity of jewels and precious stones from China.

The transcription of Marco Polo's memoirs came about through a curious circumstance. In a war between the city-states of Venice and Genoa, Marco was taken prisoner by the Genoese. His prison cell was shared by a Pisan writer of romances, Rusticano. In him, Marco found a skilled and talented scribe, who wrote down the adventures as they were dictated from Marco's memory or notes. The work was barely completed when the prisoners were freed. The original manuscript has vanished, but it was frequently copied by hand before the invention of printing 150 years later.

Marco Polo's contemporaries always remained highly skeptical of his account. They were particularly incredulous about such yarns as black stones that burned, sheep with tails weighing thirty pounds, mountains of salt, snakes thirty feet in length, liquid that burns (Baku oil), and the singing sands of the desert.

Following Marco Polo, growing numbers of merchants and missionaries traveled eastward by land and sea to China. The curtain fell again in the mid-fourteenth century with the overturn of the Tartar dynasty, reversion to the old antiforeign policy by the new rulers of China, and the conquest of central Asia by Islam, setting up a nearly impassable barrier between the West and the Far East.

A momentous consequence of Marco Polo's travels was its influence on Christopher Columbus. As noted in Washington Irving's *Life of Columbus,* "the travels of Marco Polo furnish a key to many parts of the voyages and speculations of Columbus, without which it would hardly be comprehensible; it was evidently an oracular work with him." Marco's account was avidly studied by Columbus, who made marginal notes on his copy and carried it with him on his first voyage to the New World. The Orient could be reached, Columbus concluded, by traveling west across the Atlantic, as well as east by Marco Polo's route.

Marco Polo's *Travels* has remained for nearly seven centuries one of the great travel records, its authenticity confirmed and reconfirmed by many later explorers and writers. The narrative is as readable, fresh, and exciting today as when it was delivered orally to the author's fellow prisoner in medieval Genoa.

Marco Polo

4
Discoverer of Continental America

Amerigo Vespucci's Four Voyages, 1497–1504

Doubtless the most controversial figure in American history is a Florentine citizen for whom, early in the sixteenth century, two new continents were named. The fundamental issue is whether or not Amerigo Vespucci discovered mainland America, or whether the naming of the New World was an invention based upon misleading information, thus bestowing a great honor upon the wrong man.

In his own time, it was widely accepted that Vespucci was the actual discoverer of continental America and his fame exceeded that of Columbus. The campaign of character assassination against him began with Bartolomé de Las Casas, Spanish priest and historian, who accompanied Columbus on his fourth voyage to America. An ardent supporter of Columbus, Las Casas's writings damned Vespucci as a sly thief who cunningly robbed Columbus of his rightful glory. "And it is well to give thought here," he declared in his *Historia de las Indias,* "to the injustice and offense that Amerigo Vespucci seems to have done the Admiral, or those who first printed his four voyages, attributing to himself, or alluding only to him, the discovery of this mainland." Taking their cue from Las Casas, some later writers have concluded that Vespucci's accounts of his voyages are fictitious. Most virulent of the critics was Ralph Waldo Emerson, who has long represented the popular viewpoint: "Strange that broad America must wear the name of a thief, Amerigo Vespucci, a pickle dealer at Seville, whose highest naval rank was boatswain of an expedition that never sailed, who managed in this lying world to supplant Columbus and baptize half the earth with his dishonest name." Only in recent years have efforts been made to examine all surviving records objectively and to set the record straight. In the process, Vespucci's reputation has been rehabilitated and his rightful place in American history established.

Amerigo Vespucci was born in Florence in 1451 and died in Seville in 1512. He belonged to a family that had been prominent and powerful in the fourteenth century. His early studies had emphasized cosmography, astronomy, and mathematics. From 1478 to 1480 he served as secretary to an uncle who was Florentine ambassador to France. Beginning in 1480, Vespucci was an agent of the Medici family in Florence. Late in 1491 he was sent to Seville to assist in overseeing the Medici shipping interests, then engaged in building a fleet of ships for the Spanish government. When the firm's chief representative, Juanoto Berardi, died, Vespucci was appointed to complete the royal contract "to outfit twelve ships for the next trip of the Admiral Christopher Columbus to the island of Hispaniola." It was this assignment, apparently, which led Emerson to apply the epithet "pickle dealer," since the provisions supplied for seagoing vessels usually included barrels of pickles.

Vespucci soon arrived at the decision that outfitting ships for other men's adventures on the high seas was too tame an occupation. He proposed to abandon commercial pursuits and devote himself henceforth to the life of a navigator. What were his qualifications? Until now, his knowledge of sailing was vicarious and secondhand, acquired by talking to pilots, going on board caravels with shipmasters, observing preparations for voyages, and buying and selling ships. On the other hand, he was also a member of a family long active in maritime affairs, was of a mature age (about forty), had a robust constitution, had proven his ability in the complex business of equipping ships, possessed practical knowledge of the materials and supplies needed for a long sea voyage, was skilled in cosmography, cartography, mathematics, and astronomy, and acquainted with all the aids to navigation then known. His qualifications were strengthened by the fact that he had become an expert on maps, charts, and globes, was an avid map collector, and a good map maker.

The facts of Vespucci's first voyage have been frequently disputed. In a letter to the Gonfalonier of Florence, Piero Soderini, Vespucci

A sixteenth-century engraving (by de Bry) showed Vespucci aboard ship off the coast of South America

states that he was chosen by King Ferdinand of Castile to go with a fleet of four ships "to discover new lands to the west," and the expedition left Cádiz on May 10. 1497. Vespucci was supposedly sent for a double purpose: as an astronomer "who knew cosmography and matters pertaining to the sea," and to represent commercial interests, to report back later on any commercial opportunities discovered. The commanding officer and the names of individual captains are not known with any certainty. The fleet's first call was the Canary Islands, where several days were spent taking on a fresh supply of wood, water, beef, pigs, and chickens.

As the voyage resumed, a southerly course was set, instead of heading for Hispaniola or Cuba, Columbus's farthest point west until his third voyage. The mainland was reached thirty-seven days later. Here Vespucci's expedition entered the Gulf of Honduras, skirted the Yucatán peninsula, and ascended the Mexican coast to

Florida, or perhaps even as far north as Georgia. If the date is accurate, Vespucci was on the mainland a year before Columbus. Vespucci reports that several boats filled with armed men went ashore from the fleet. They could see "hordes of naked people running along the shore," but as the boats approached, the natives fled to the nearby hills and refused to respond to the sailors' overtures. As no protection against rough seas existed in the area where the ships first anchored, early next morning they set sail, seeking a safe harbor. After two days, following a northern route, "a place quite suited to our needs" was discovered and the ships anchored a half-league from shore. Again the voyagers "saw countless hordes of people." At first the natives would not respond to advances, but eventually "they received us kindly, and in fact mingled among us with as complete assurance as if we had often met before."

The customs of the natives and their modes of life were described in detail by Vespucci—their complete nudity, excellent physical condition, weapons, perpetual wars with neighboring tribes, uninhibited sexual mores, food, habitations, ornaments, treatment of the ill, and burial customs. Among one tribe Vespucci noted a strange serpent with huge claws (an iguana) being roasted and eaten. The natives generally were friendly, but on several occasions the voyagers were attacked by warlike tribes, and once lost two sailors to cannibals.

Continuing their explorations, the ships sailed around the curve of the Gulf of Mexico, and from "Lariab" in the Mexican state of Tabasco the ships passed south of Florida and followed a northern route. "And since by that time," Vespucci wrote, "we had already been thirteen months on our voyage, and since the tackle and rigging were very much the worse for wear and the men were reduced by fatigue, we unanimously agreed to repair our small boats (which were leaking at every point) and to return to Spain." A safe landing was made at Cádiz on October 15, 1498.

The only account extant of this first voyage of discovery is Ves-
_____ Nevertheless, his report is confirmed by the maps drawn
_____ showing the complete outline of the Gulf of
_____ e peninsula of Florida, and the profile
_____ appears as an island, instead of a part
_____ ed by Columbus. No other recorded

Amerigo Vespucci

voyage accounts for these new cartographic features, and thus the veracity of Vespucci's report is supported. Records of Vespucci's latitudes and longitudes prove that he reached Tampico.

The famous Cantino map, made in Portugal before 1502 and now in the Modena Library in Italy, shows the Gulf of Mexico and the coast of Mexico, and outlines the southern coastline of the United States. No less than twenty-nine capes, bays, and rivers are shown for Florida alone. The place names are Spanish; since no other Spaniard was ever near Florida before the date of the map, the obvious conclusion is that the work was based on descriptions supplied by Vespucci from his 1497 expedition. Ponce de León did not land in Florida until fifteen years after Vespucci's voyage; Hernández de Córdoba explored the coast of Yucatán some twenty years after Vespucci.

Vespucci's discoveries in the course of his 1497 explorations were naturally limited to maritime and coastal features, but they supplied sufficient data for another famous cartographer, Juan de la Cosa, to draw up a map in 1500 showing Cuba as an island and the ocean between Cuba and the Mexican coast. A map drawn in 1503 by Bartholomew Columbus, the admiral's brother, summarizing Christopher's discoveries to that point, omits Florida, though it represents the coastlines of the Guianas and Venezuela as far as Panama.

The letter written by Vespucci to Piero Soderini in 1504, seven years after the 1497 journey, is the only written relation of the voyage to have survived. Two prime concerns were revealed by the account: a keen interest in the scientific aspects of the expedition and a desire to learn the art of navigation. Most of Vespucci's time aboard ship was spent in the company of the pilots. He mentioned the degrees of the globe's circumference, measured distances by leagues, knew the names of all the winds, and the quarter from which they blew. Clearly, his abilities as a practical pilot were developing rapidly.

There is less dispute concerning Vespucci's second voyage than his first; the independent testimony of Alonso de Hojeda, the commander, verifies the voyage. When Hojeda sailed in 1499 to follow up on the discoveries made by Columbus in his third voyage of 1498, he stated that he was accompanied by Vespucci. According to Vespucci, the expedition first touched land in June of 1499 near the present boundary between Brazil and French Guiana. The fleet of four ships steered along the coast and the great river mouth that had been discovered by Columbus. The equator was crossed and the coast of Brazil, near Cape St. Vincent, where the continent bulges out toward Africa, was skirted. This was the first European expedition to cross the equator in the New World sea. About June 27 a landing was made, the first to touch the territory of Brazil.

On the homeward voyage, Vespucci and his companions covered all the northern coast of Brazil, the Guianas, and Venezuela up to Cabo de la Vela in Colombia. His description of the Guiana coast, with its half-drowned lands, is accurate. A report prepared by Hojeda stated that 600 leagues of new coast had been explored. The native tribes encountered ranged from excessively friendly and hospitable to hostile and warlike. In Venezuela, the travelers saw Indian villages built on piles in the water, giving them a resemblance to the city of Venice. The country was therefore given the name of Venezuela, "Little Venice," which it still bears.

During the second voyage, Vespucci was much occupied with his astronomical researches, and he made an extraordinary discovery concerning the coordinates of latitude. Jesuit Father T. W. Stern, director of the Vatican Observatory, in a study published in 1950, concluded: "Until there is proof to the contrary, we must consider Vespucci as the inventor of the method of lunar distances. He was the first to employ it, measuring the distance between the moon and Mars at midnight of August 23, 1499. He lacked only exact information to have given an exact longitude." In 1501, Vespucci calculated almost exactly the earth's circumference. His figure for the circumference at the equator was 24,832 miles; modern science places it at 24,902. Columbus's estimate was 6,125 miles short.

Back in Seville, "resting and recovering from the many hardships suffered on the last two voyages," as he wrote to Piero Soderini, Vespucci received a message from King Manuel of Portugal asking him to come to Lisbon. The king had determined to send an expedition to explore the South American coast farther south, in order to strengthen Portuguese claims. For the purpose he engaged the services of Vespucci as cosmographer to accompany a fleet of three ships under the command of Nuno Manoel or Gonzala Coelho. This, Vespucci's most important voyage and the one most thoroughly documented as to dates and distances, was his third to the New World.

Leaving Lisbon on May 13, 1501, the expedition landed on August 7 on the northern coast of Brazil after a long and dangerous crossing. For most of sixty-seven days Vespucci reported that "rain, thunder and lightening so darkened the sky that we never saw the sun by day or fair sky by night." The route followed was the one most familiar to the Portuguese: by way of the Canary Islands, along the coast of Africa to the Cape Verde Islands, and then across the Atlantic at its narrowest point. The extended period spent in the crossing was caused by the extremely rough weather and, according to Vespucci, by the ignorance of the pilots. None of the pilots "could chart our bearings within five hundred leagues," and all depended on Vespucci's knowledge to help them find their way.

After the first landfall, the coast was followed east and then south until a point was reached where, in Vespucci's words, "it was no longer possible to see the Small Bear, and the Great Bear was on the line of the horizon"; that is, south of the Tropic of Capricorn. The landscape had previously been seen by Vespucci but, as before, he was fascinated by the exotic odors, the flowers of such varied shapes and colors, and the differently flavored fruits and tubers. Strange birds and animals also held his rapt attention—lynxes, jaguars, wolves, monkeys, wild boars, goats, deer, and hares—all wild. The natives went about naked and were human flesh eaters, mainly of enemies taken as prisoners of war. A Portuguese sailor who had ventured ashore alone was slain and eaten by the cannibals. The savages were remarkably healthy; "a doctor would die of starvation here," Vespucci noted.

As the navigators proceeded down the coast, they discovered capes, bays, river mouths, and islands. Each conspicuous geographical feature was given the name of a saint taken from the saints' calendar carried by the ship. By February 1502 the expedition had been wandering over sea and land for ten months without seeing an end to the trip, and the question of whether or not to continue leaders of the crew realized that they had reached in 1494, dividing any new land discovered between tugal; to proceed further would, in effect, be en- n Spanish territory. Command was turned over to

America

Vespucci, who decided to press forward. The weatherbeaten ships penetrated south as far as the ridge of Montevideo, the mouth of the Plata River, and the coast of Patagonia. A terrible storm forced the explorers to turn back before Vespucci could attain his main objective, the search for a water passage to Asia, but not before he determined the probability of the route later followed by Ferdinand Magellan.

The final point reached by Vespucci was the farthest south ever penetrated by a European. Information supplied by Vespucci for the maps issued shortly after his return shows that he was not far from the strait opening into the Pacific. But the "mountainous" waves, violent gales, intense cold, and long nights, experienced by later voyagers along the Patagonian coast as well, were obstacles too great for small ships to surmount. Outrunning the storm, the little fleet moved northward toward the equator. On May 10, 1502, the expedition reached Sierra Leone in West Africa, spent a fortnight there, proceeded to the Canary Islands, and finally arrived in Lisbon in September 1502 with only two ships. The third had been set afire because it was no longer seaworthy.

Before the third voyage, Vespucci had accepted with little question Columbus's belief that the lands being explored were part of Asia. In a long letter to Lorenzo di Pier Francesco dé Medici in 1503 (later published under the title *Mundus Novus*) Vespucci reached the conclusion that a new continent had been discovered: "These new regions which we found and explored," he declared, "we may rightly call a new world." Continuing, he stated: "It is lawful to call it a new world, because none of these countries were known to our ancestors. We knew that land to be a continent, and not an island, from its long beaches extending without trending round, the infinite number of inhabitants, the numerous tribes and peoples, the numerous kinds of wild animals unknown in our country, and many others never before seen by us."

The *Mundus Novus,* issued in 1504, became a literary sensation and in various translations was widely circulated in Europe. Two ideas caught the popular fancy and brought fame to Vespucci among his contemporaries: first, the fact that a new continent had been discovered, and second, that the antipodes existed and were habitable, refuting long-held beliefs to the contrary. "Without doubt,"

Amerigo Vespucci

Vespucci commented concerning the lands he had visited, "if the Garden of Eden exists anywhere on earth, it is my opinion that it cannot be far from those countries."

A Vespucci biographer, Stefan Zweig, points out:

> The actual event of this letter consists oddly enough not in the letter itself, but in its title—*Mundus Novus*—two words, four syllables, which revolutionize the conception of the cosmos as had nothing before. . . . Columbus, up to the hour of his death, blindly entangled in the delusion that by landing in Guanahani and Cuba he had set foot in India, has with this illusion actually decreased the size of the cosmos for his contemporaries. Only Vespucci, by destroying the hypothesis that this new continent is India and insisting on its being a new continent, provides the new dimensions which have remained valid to this day.

Vespucci's fourth voyage to the New World, lasting from June 1503 to June 1504 in a fleet of six ships, possibly under the command of Gonzalo Coelho, had as its principal aim a continuation of the earlier discoveries and finding a passage that he believed to exist at the extremity of the South American continent. Midway across the Atlantic the fleet broke up and only two ships reached Brazil. After a brief exploration of the coast, construction of a fort, and the landing of twenty-four persons to establish a new settlement, Vespucci turned homeward. Vespucci judged the expedition a failure; it was also, probably, his last.

In 1505 Vespucci left the service of King Manuel and went back to Spain. There he met Columbus, who had recently returned from his last voyage. It is significant, in view of later controversies, that Columbus and Vespucci remained firm friends until the former's death in 1506, with no indications of rivalry. In his letters Columbus speaks highly of Vespucci as a man constant in his devotion, "a true man of his word," and "a man of good will." Columbus's sons, so jealous of their father's fame, never voiced even the slightest complaint against the Florentine. As Frederick J. Pohl points out in his excellent biography, *Amerigo Vespucci, Pilot Major:* "Between Columbus and Vespucci there need to be no recriminations in Hades. Columbus destroyed the conception that the western ocean was a vast and impassable barrier. . . . On the other hand, Amerigo

Which did more to enlarge man's conception of the earth? Here was
their only rivalry."

To keep the record straight, however, it should be noted that
Columbus never set foot on any part of the present United States.
His first voyage touched at the Bahamas, Cuba, and Haiti. His second
added Jamaica, his third Trinidad and Brazil, and his fourth
and last Honduras and Panama.

Following his return to Spain, Vespucci was granted Castilian
citizenship by King Ferdinand and appointed to the newly created
post of pilot major of Spain. In that capacity, held until his death
in 1512, he supervised Spanish pilots and held the responsibility for
approving new maps before they were issued. Navigators were expected to report all new discoveries to him. His appointment to
such a position is evidence of Vespucci's reputation as an able
cosmographer.

Vespucci's travel narratives are generally straightforward, without
any inclination to let his imagination run away with him, as other
writers of the period (including Columbus) frequently did. His
accounts, for example, feature no countries populated by monsters,
kingdoms inhabited only by women, dog-headed men, or fountains
of youth.

A curious series of events led to the attachment of Amerigo Vespucci's name to the newly discovered continents. The ancient monastery of Saint-Dié in France was the birthplace of the name *America*.
The monks there had received a copy of Vespucci's *Four Voyages,*
one now regarded by scholars as a forgery. Martin Waldseemüller,
one of the monks, was then engaged in writing *Cosmographiae In-
troductio,* "Introduction to Cosmography," an updating of Ptolemy's
work. A Latin translation of the Vespucci letters, under the title
Quattuor Americi Vesputti Navigationes, was appended to the Waldseemüller geography when it was published in 1507. After discussing
the older, better-known areas of the world, Waldseemüller wrote:

> Now, these parts of the earth have been more extensively ex-
> plored and a fourth part has been discovered by Amerigo
> Vespucci. Inasmuch as both Europe and Asia received their
> names from women, I see no reason why any one should justly
> object to call this part Amerige, i.e., the land of Amerigo, or

America, after Amerigo, its discoverer, a man of great ability. Its position and the customs of its inhabitants may be clearly understood from the four voyages of Amerigo, which are subjoined.

Here was the first suggestion that the New World should bear the name of Amerigo Vespucci. Supplementing his geography, Waldseemüller drew a planisphere and a huge map of the world, beautiful works of cartography and design, on which the southern continent of the new hemisphere is labeled "America." Soon the word spread through Europe, where Vespucci's fame was already well established, and eventually won universal acceptance. The Waldseemüller map shows the general outlines of the northern and southern continents, the Antilles, Cuba as an island, the Gulf of Mexico, and the Yucatan Peninsula, though of course not the Pacific coast, which remained unexplored. Thus the naming of the New World was irretrievably accomplished. In 1538 Mercator applied the same name to the northern continent.

Actually Vespucci had no part in giving his name to the new continents; in fact, it is even doubtful that he knew of the honor. Though the name "America" appeared on Waldseemüller's map five years before Vespucci's death, it was never shown on any of Vespucci's own maps or those made by his nephew Giovanni, who was still drawing maps in 1525.

Thus, the naming of the New World for Vespucci, the first to recognize that a new continent had been discovered, was neither an error nor an injustice. Columbus denied until the day of his death that he had found a new part of the world, insisting that he had reached the mainland of Asia. As Pohl declares, "Columbus could not bring America to the knowledge of Europe, because he had not the faintest conception of what America was or that there was any such thing as a New World." Except for his mental fixation, Columbus might have recognized the truth. Men of science in Europe suspected from the first that the newly discovered lands had nothing to do with the East Indies, as indicated by the term "West Indies" which soon came into vogue. Geographers quickly agreed that this land was indeed a new world, without any resemblance in its natural or social aspects to Asia or Asiatic islands.

Discoverer of Continental America

Vespucci was probably the best cosmographer of his day. He was more expert than Columbus in plotting ocean routes, and his voyages along the coast of America went far beyond those of his predecessors, clearly indicating the continental nature of the new land. He prepared the way for Magellan's circumnavigation of South America, and his influence on the cartography of the sixteenth century was immense. Altogether, the weight of evidence supports Amerigo Vespucci as a man in whom Americans can take pride—one of the greatest in an age of great seamen, discoverers, and explorers.

5
Circling the Globe

*Antonio Pigafetta's The First Voyage around
the World by Magellan, 1519—1521*

When Ferdinand Magellan set out to circumnavigate the earth
in 1519, his command consisted of five ships. Magellan himself, four
of the five ships, and all but 18 of a crew numbering approximately
250 failed to return from the epochal voyage. The most complete
and reliable account of the history-making expedition was written
by an Italian traveler, Antonio Pigafetta, who accompanied Magellan
and survived to tell the tale.

Pigafetta came out of obscurity to join Magellan and slipped back
into the shadows soon after his return. A native of Vicenza, a city
in northern Italy, and member of a noble family, Pigafetta was
perhaps thirty years old when the voyage began. Shortly before, he
had been a gentleman-in-waiting to the pope's representative at the
Spanish court. When he heard of Magellan's preparations, his love
of travel and the glamorous prospect of seeing new worlds induced
him to ask permission of the papal nuncio and King Charles to enlist
with Magellan as a supernumerary, a kind of gentleman volunteer.
Magellan at once signed him on as aide to the admiral and as official
historian of the expedition, a most fortunate association. Magellan's
own records were lost or destroyed and documents relating to his
birth, life, and death are scattered and conflicting. It is, therefore,
only in the faithful, day-by-day record maintained by Pigafetta from
the moment that he began writing his account of the expedition,
that an accurate and reliable history of the three-year voyage has
survived.

Pigafetta was blessed with a reporter's keen eye; he was intrigued with everything that he saw and heard. His sharp observations led him to describe strange birds and fish, mysterious lights at sea, the dress and appearance of Indian men and women, their homes and tools, cannibalism, volcanoes, the rigors of long weeks at sea, and anything else that caught his interest.

Magellan lived in an age of exploration and discovery. Christopher Columbus had only recently returned from his first voyage to the New World; John Cabot, in 1497, had discovered the coast of North America; in four voyages, 1497–1503, Amerigo Vespucci had explored the coasts of North and South America from as far north as Chesapeake Bay and as far south at Patagonia; in 1497–98, Vasco da Gama had completed the first ocean voyage from Europe to the Orient; and in 1513, six years before Magellan's fleet left Spain, Balboa crossed the Isthmus of Panama to discover the Pacific Ocean west of the Americas.

Nevertheless, the geographers of Magellan's day, as indicated in their maps, assumed that everything between the limited area of South America that had been explored and Asia was a blurred, vague region of islands and ocean. The ocean, enormously wider than anyone imagined, was variously referred to as the South Sea, the Great Gulf, and the Eastern Ocean.

The question of who owned the newly discovered lands was a bitter source of controversy for centuries and one of the motives for the Magellan expedition. Spain and Portugal had pioneered in the early voyages of discovery and, on the basis of information submitted by Columbus and other douments, Pope Alexander VI was persuaded by King Ferdinand of Spain to issue a bull, dated May 4, 1493, establishing a line of demarcation dividing the world. Spain was assigned possession of all lands it might discover to the west of an imaginary line drawn from pole to pole; the world east of the line would be exclusively Portugal's to explore and navigate. By the Treaty of Tordesillas, 1494, the two nations agreed to a revision whereby everything found 1,500 miles or more west of the Cape Verde Islands belonged to Spain; everything east to Portugal. The line was never exactly drawn, and such an arrangement was not meekly accepted by England, France, and other maritime nations. The end result was generations of rivalry, friction, and strife.

Early in the sixteenth century, it became clear that Columbus'

Antonio Pigafetta

"Indies" had no connection with the Far Eastern Indies claimed by Portugal. Between the two, in fact, lay a great land barrier and an ocean of unmeasured and unknown extent. Here Spanish empire builders were confronted with a dilemma. How could they send ships to the spice-producing islands of the East without encroaching on the Portuguese side of the old line of demarcation? Spain still claimed everything west of the line to the other side of the earth, a claim not recognized by the Portuguese. Ferdinand Magellan's proposal for resolving the problem was to reach the Moluccas, or the "Spice Islands," by sailing westward through a strait which he hoped to discover at the southern tip of South America, cross the Pacific, and prove that the Moluccas lay within the Spanish sphere, because they were west of Spanish Peru. Spain's hope was to find rich spice islands not reached by Portugal from the Indian Ocean.

The importance of spices in sixteenth-century Europe can scarcely be overestimated. They were the source of fabulous fortunes; a markup value of 10,000 percent over the prices paid in the Indies was not uncommon. Cloves, cinnamon, ginger, and pepper took the place of modern refrigeration, preserving meat through long winters, covering up the odors of partially spoiled food, and lending savor to a monotonous diet. Lisbon became the leading port for this lucrative business. The spices loaded on the lone returning ship of Magellan's fleet more than repaid the total cost of outfitting the squadron.

Prior to the globe-circling expedition which established his permanent fame, Ferdinand Magellan had a series of noteworthy adventures. He was born about 1480 in northern Portugal; his parents were members of the petty nobility. At the age of twelve he became a page at the court of Queen Leonora in Lisbon, where he had an opportunity to study various subjects, including maritime science—map making and simple astronomy. As early as 1505, Magellan went to the East Indies in the king's service and was active for several years as a naval officer. The record shows that he was at Cochin in 1510, participated in the attack on Goa in that year, sailed as far east as the Moluccas, and was present at the fall of Malacca in 1511. When he returned home in 1512, Portugal was fighting the Moslems in Morocco. Magellan took part in the battle at Azamor, and received a wound in his knee that left him permanently lame.

After the end of his military career Magellan, in an audience with King Manuel, asked, as a reward for his services, to be raised to the rank of cavalier of the household. He further petitioned for an increase in his living allowance or pension, and requested that the king provide him with a new commission, cherishing the ambition to command a ship to return to the Moluccas. According to contemporaries, Manuel had hated Magellan for years; thus all of his petitions were summarily and brusquely rejected. Magellan was informed that no position awaited him in the service of the Portuguese crown; when he requested permission to serve another country, he was told to do as he pleased—it was a matter of complete indifference to the king.

Thoroughly incensed at his unjust treatment, Magellan renounced his Portuguese citizenship in 1517 and crossed the border to Spain. The news soon came back to Lisbon that he had gone to the court of Spain, offered his services, and been accepted as captain of a great westward sailing expedition, aimed at adding wealth and glory to the name of the Spanish king. King Manuel was filled with fury.

In Spain, Magellan managed to obtain the support of Juan Rodriguez de Fonseca, bishop of Burgos and president of the Council of the Indies, which was responsible for the management of colonial affairs. Through his influence, Magellan was granted an immediate audience with King Charles. At first suspicious of a Portuguese renegade, the king's interest and enthusiasm were quickly aroused as Magellan unfolded his plans for a westward expedition, recognizing that Magellan's experience in the Moluccas and his skill as a navigator were exactly the qualities needed for the daring enterprise.

A formal agreement was made. First, the captain was to assert the king's sovereignty in such East Indian lands as belonged within the Spanish sphere, but not to trespass on Portuguese rights. Next, the king agreed to furnish Magellan with a fleet and to allow him both one-twentieth part of the profits of the expedition and a one-fifteenth part of the profits gained from any two of the islands he might claim for Spain in perpetuity. A remarkable rapport was established between the twenty-year-old king and Magellan, perhaps twice his age; the king never failed to give his unstinting support through every difficulty.

Antonio Pigafetta

44   The five sailing vessels provided by the crown were old and unseaworthy, and Magellan had to overhaul them completely—a task requiring a full year. A surviving account reveals substantial amounts spent for beams, planks, carpenters' wages, the sawing of planks, iron work, wages for caulking the ships, for canvas, cables, splices, and hemp. Also needed were top-masts and yards, pumps, rudders, and anchors. The armament included various types of guns and 5,600 pounds of gunpowder. In the list of navigating appliances were compasses, astrolabes, charts, and hourglasses. A cargo of trading material was comprised of quicksilver, fishhooks, knives, basins, bracelets, glass beads, copper bars (for the coinage mints of the East), colored cotton cloth, brocade, velvet, lace, hand mirrors, ornamental combs, and tinkling little bells.

After their overhauling under Magellan's careful direction, the fleet of five vessels was ready for sea duty. The largest was the *San Antonio* (120 tons), followed by the *Trinidad* (110 tons), the *Victoria* (90 tons), the *Concepción* (90 tons), and the smallest, the *Santiago* (75 tons). The *Trinidad* was seleted by Magellan as his flagship.

Meanwhile, Portuguese saboteurs, acting under King Manuel's orders, employed every sort of device to undermine Magellan and prevent the expedition from sailing. The ringleader was the Portuguese consul in Serine, Dom Sebastian Alvarez, whose instructions were to stop Magellan at any price. He instigated a serious riot at the wharves by claiming that Magellan was a Portuguese spy planning to steal the fleet of Portugal. The ships' workers were routed and the captain wounded in the hand. The rioters were later punished by King Charles. More successful was a plot to cut the ships' food supplies. Those stocking the ships were bribed by Alvarez to cut the supplies by exactly one-half, a fact not discovered by Magellan until the expedition was on its way; the resulting food shortage led to starvation in the Pacific. As a last resort, if all else failed, a plot was concocted for three of the captains to murder Magellan at sea and take command of the fleet. Alvarez was able to obtain information about the course planned for the ships, and King Manuel ordered his navy to intercept and destroy the fleet at sea. All these gangster methods were resorted to by the Portuguese to protect their precious spice trade with the East.

graphically described by Antonio Pigafetta:

The situation confronting Magellan prior to his departure was graphically described by Antonio Pigafetta:

> The Captain-General, Ferdinand Magellan, had resolved on un-
> dertaking a long voyage over the ocean, where the winds blow
> with violence, and storms are very frequent. He had also deter-
> mined on taking a course as yet unexplored by any navigator.
> But this bold attempt he was cautious of disclosing lest any one
> should strive to dissuade him from it by magnifying the risk
> he would have to encounter, and thus dishearten his crew. To
> the perils naturally incident to the voyage was joined the un-
> favorable circumstances of the four other vessels he commanded,
> besides his own, being under the direction of captains who were
> inimical to himself, merely on account of his being a Portuguese,
> they themselves being Spaniards.

One of the most troublesome problems facing Magellan in the
organizing of his expedition was in recruiting a suitable crew, which
was to number about 250 (estimates range from 237 to 280). Low
pay made it difficult to find seamen for the voyage. Too, the route
and destination of the ships were a closely guarded secret and men
were told they had to sign on for not less than two years. In addition,
Spanish sailors were reluctant to serve under a Portuguese admiral.
Eventually Magellan put together a mixed crew of Spaniards, Portuguese, Italians, Basques, Frenchmen, Germans, Greeks, Moors, Negroes, and one Englishman, the master gunner of the fleet. At the
outset, the Council of the Indies had directed that Portuguese seamen be limited to five per ship. With the King's permission, however, Magellan was allowed to ignore the order; thirty-seven able
and experienced Portuguese sailors signed on, forming a dependable
nucleus of men on each vessel.

Filling the top positions was even more difficult. Bishop Fonseca
schemed to place his own followers in key places. He had supported
Magellan at first and wanted the expedition to succeed, hoping to
grab any profits for himself. He thought that the contract terms
granted Magellan by King Charles were too generous. His master
plot was to have Magellan replaced at sea by his "nephew" (actually
his illegitimate son), Juan de Cartagena. Three of the bishop's hench-
men, including Cartagena, were appointed ship captains. The one

faithful ship captain was Juan Serrano, Magellan's cousin. Another crucial post, that of chief pilot, was filled by Estevan Gomes, who was deeply resentful of Magellan because he himself had hoped to head the expedition. A further complication involved the council's political appointees, who insisted on bringing with them a retinue of personal servants. Cartagena, for example, brought no less than eight such aides, whose duties were to lay out his clothes and wait on him at table, but not to do ship duty. Fully one-sixth of the *San Antonio*'s crew, thertfore, were of no value in manning the ship.

It is interesting to note the foodstuffs taken aboard Magellan's fleet for its long sea voyage. Basic were ship's biscuit (213,800 pounds), salted beef (72,000 pounds), salted pork (57,000 pounds), cheeses (984 pounds), and dried and salted fish. These items were supplemented by anchovies, dried beans (5,600 pounds), chick peas (10,-080 pounds), and smaller amounts of onions, raisins, figs, nuts, honey, rice, lentils, olive oil, and flour. Little was provided to prevent scurvy or beriberi, the dread disease caused by poor nutrition during long voyages which was to prove a horrible curse to Magellan and his men. Long before Magellan, the Vikings and other experienced seafarers had discovered the importance of having onions, radishes, oranges, lemons, and raw sauerkraut on board. They learned that fresh food and vegetables, in particular, worked wonders with this strange deficiency disease.

Before sailing, on August 10, 1519, the entire fleet's company and their families attended a high mass in a church near the dockyard. Magellan was presented with the royal silken standard of the king. The four ship captains knelt before the altar and swore allegiance and loyalty to Magellan, despite the fact that three of them had entered into an agreement to murder him at the first opportunity.

The two years spent by Magellan in repairing, fitting out, and stocking the ships were worthwhile. The expedition which sailed out of Seville is said to have been the best equipped that had ever left Spain. A seventy-five-mile trip down the Guadalquivir River brought them to the ocean port of San Lúcar; this short trip was followed by a layover of more than a month while Magellan was having shortages checked and partially corrected. Even then the deficiencies in ship's biscuit, salt beef, salt pork, peas, honey, olives, and other food supplies, resulting from Alvarez's bribes, were not fully realized.

From Spain the fleet headed for the Canary Islands, reached after twelve days' easy sailing. The ship's crew were terrified by a volcano eruption on Tenerife Island, and were ready to return home. The fleet remained three days at Tenerife, taking on meat, wood, and water, and then proceeded to Punta Rasca at the southern end of the island and loaded pitch. While thus employed a caravel, flying the standard of Spain, anchored, carrying a message for the captain-general. A letter from Magellan's father-in-law, Diego Barbosa, warned: "Keep a good watch, since it has come to my knowledge that your Captains have told their friends and relatives here that if there is any trouble they will kill you . . . your Captains have resolved not to obey you, particularly Juan de Cartagena." The caravel returned to Spain. The message confirmed Magellan's previous suspicions of a plot and put him on guard against treachery.

One of the commander's hardest tasks was to keep together five ships of such varying tonnage and speed. One ship straying off the route could be lost in a vast ocean. Magellan's order was for all to follow in the wake of the *Trinidad,* the flagship. By day, this was not difficult. When darkness fell, a system of signals was arranged: at sunset a wooden torch was lighted in a lantern; two more lights on the flagship meant that the others were to sail slower or were to tack in case of an unfavorable wind; three indicated that a storm was brewing and all ships were to shorten sail; four signified that all sails were to be lowered. A flickering light or gunshots warned of shoals or sandbanks nearby. The signals were to be answered by the other ships to assure the captain-general that his directions had been understood and would be obeyed. Futhermore, the four ships had to steer close to the flagship and salute the commander. Thus was discipline enforced, though not without keen resentment on the part of the three disgruntled captains.

On leaving Tenerife off the northwest coast of Africa, the five vessels ran parallel to the African coast as far as Cape Verde, instead of steering directly across the Atlantic to Brazil, apparently to avoid encountering the Portuguese fleet sent out by King Manuel to intercept them. In the area of Sierra Leone Magellan struck west to

Antonio Pigafetta

the Brazilian coast. The game of hide and seek had cost him three weeks' time, added many miles, and brought bitter criticism from the Spanish captains. To show his displeasure, Juan de Cartagena had his ship, the *San Antonio,* begin to cruise on its own, sometimes circling the other ships, sometimes dropping out of sight and then catching up with them. When Cartagena announced that he no longer recognized Magellan as his commanding admiral and would refuse to follow his orders, Magellan had him arrested, placed in irons, and replaced by Antonio de Coca, a Spaniard, as captain of the *San Antonio.*

Two months passed before the ships sighted the Brazilian coast near the site of the future Rio de Janeiro. Pigafetta relates that they took on plentiful supplies of poultry, sweet potatoes, pineapples, tapir meat ("which tastes like beef"), sugarcane, and other foodstuffs. Trading objects such as fishhooks, knives, combs, mirrors, or scissors were exchanged for hens, fish, sweet potatoes, or other supplies.

Pigafetta's talents as an anthropologist were apparent in his descriptions of the natives of Brazil and Patagonia. He found that the Brazilian Indians were cannibals, eating the flesh of their enemies for ritualistic rather than utilitarian reasons. The naked Indians painted their bodies and faces "in a wonderful manner"; when dressed they adorned themselves with clothes made of parrot feathers in the shape of great wheels fastened around their middles. Pigafetta described in detail the Indians' appearance, food, houses, and language.

Magellan and his men spent thirteen days at the point of first landing and then sailed south to the Plata estuary. At first the wide mouth of the Rio de la Plata was assumed to be the entrance to the strait around South America sought by Magellan, but exploration brought disappointment. Sailing farther south along the coast of what is now Argentina toward the Antarctic, islands densely populated with penguins and seals were discovered, many of which were killed and eaten by Magellan's men.

When they reached the 49th latitude south of the equator, the ships entered a haven called Saint Julian to spend the winter and remained for five months, from March until August of 1520. It had taken them eight weeks to fight their way this far south. The ships

had been battered by hurricane winds, swamped by heavy seas,
struck by hail and sleet, and sometimes coated with ice. The crews
were nearing the limit of their endurance and yearned to return
home. For the first two months not a single human being was sighted;
then a number of Patagonian natives, the men gigantic in size, began
to appear on shore and visited the ships. Magellan coined the name
by which these Indians are still known, "Patagonians," a Portuguese
slang word for big feet. Pigafetta described the many curious customs, the language, and the beliefs of this primitive society, as he
had done for the Brazilian Indians; he may thus perhaps be one of
the founders of what is now called cultural anthropology.

Pigafetta was somewhat gullible, however, in his acceptance of
improbable facts. For example, he wrote that the female stormy
petrel lays her eggs on the back of the male and the eggs are hatched
there; that a certain species of jackdaw flies out to sea, is swallowed
alive by a whale, and then eats the whale's heart; he recorded that
in the Bay of China there are birds large enough to carry off grown
men and even the largest of animals; that one of the small Molucca
islands was inhabited by dwarfs barely two feet tall, whose ears were
large enough to cover them when they lay down; that in one place
women were made pregnant by the wind; that one type of sea bird
had no feet and another no rump; the peccaries seen in South America have their navel on their back (actually a sweat gland) ; and so
forth. The fictitious elements in Pigafetta's chronicle do not, however, detract from his factual account of day-to-day events during
the Magellan odyssey, but rather serve to add entertainment.

Due partially to boredom during the long wait in the freezing
cold and partly to accumulated resentments, a mutiny exploded
while the ships were anchored in the Bay of Saint Julian, on April 1,
1520. The aim of the leaders was to murder Magellan himself and
sail back to Spain. Thirty men, headed by Cartagena and Gaspar
de Quesada, capain of the *Concepción*, boarded the *San Antonio;*
mortally wounded the master of the ship, Juan de Elorriaga; imprisoned the captain, Alvarez de Mesquita; and turned the ship
against Magellan. The officers aboard the *San Antonio, Concepción,*
and *Victoria* then refused to obey Magellan's orders. In brief, three
of his five ships, with nearly two-thirds of his men and supplies, had

been captured by mutineers. His own ship, the *Trinidad*, was attacked the following evening. The end of the expedition was apparently at hand.

Magellan pretended to negotiate with the mutineers. He sent a letter by his sergeant at arms, Espinosa, to Captain Mendoza on the *Victoria*. Espinosa stabbed Mendoza, killing him; fifteen heavily armed men, sent by Magellan, boarded the ship and all resistance collapsed without another blow. The *Victoria* then joined the *Trinidad* and the *Santiago* at the entrance to Saint Julian to block the rebel escape. Cartagena on the *Concepción* surrendered, and the mutiny was over.

Magellan's punishment for the mutineers was swift and harsh. One of the ringleaders, Quesada, was beheaded. Juan de Cartagena and a priest (never identified) were left to starve on the Patagonian coast and not heard of again. Mendoza's corpse was taken ashore, drawn, and quartered.

During the dreary winter months Magellan sent out his ships, when weather permitted, to explore the coast farther south. One, the *Santiago*, met with disaster. Captain Juan Serrano, after battling head winds for two weeks, was hit by an easterly gale which smashed his rudder and hurled the *Santiago* onto a sand spit, where it broke up. The crew all reached shore in their lifeboats; usable supplies and other valuables were later salvaged from the wrecked ship.

After the loss of the *Santiago* and the rescue of the survivors, Magellan abandoned the winter quarters of Saint Julian to move farther south. For two months the fleet remained encamped at the Rio Santa Cruz. Further exploratory expeditions finally found the almost hidden entrance to the Strait of Magellan, the long-sought route around South America. However, Magellan's expedition met with another serious blow at this point. The *San Antonio*, piloted by Estevan Gomes, who, according to Pigafetta, "hated the captain-general exceedingly," deserted the fleet to sail back to Spain. The *San Antonio* was Magellan's largest ship and carried a good share of his supplies, especially food. The runaway ship arrived back in Spain six months later, where Gomes made bitter accusations against Magellan to justify his conduct.

Magellan's remaining three ships—the *Trinidad, Concepción,* and *Victoria*—were brought safely through the strait, a voyage of 360 miles lasting over a month. In November 28, 1520, the little fleet entered an unknown ocean. The water was so peaceful that Magellan named the vast sea the *Mar Pacifico,* the Pacific. To escape the cold he headed up the coast of Chile before heading west, an unfortunate decision; if he had gone diagonally across the Pacific from his southern starting point, he would have found a chain of islands from which food and water could have been obtained.

The fleet sailed two months without sighting land and three months without fresh fruit and vegetables, one of the most disastrous voyages in history. Pigafetta left a lurid account:

> We ate biscuits which were no longer biscuits, but powder of biscuits swarming with worms, for they had eaten the food. It stank strongly of the urine of rats. We drank yellow water that had been putrid for many days, We also ate some ox hides that covered the top of the mainyard. . . . Rats were sold for one-half ducat apiece, and even then we could not get them.

Nineteen men died of scurvy and almost the entire crew was ill from malnutrition or actual starvation. The first land touched by the starving mariners was a group of islands which they called the Ladrones, "Islands of Thieves," because the natives boarded Magellan's ships and stole whatever they could lay their hands on.

A more hospitable reception was found in the Philippines, where the fleet stayed from March 16 to April 14, 1521. Quantities of fresh fruit, bananas and coconuts, pigs and chickens, and pure water quickly restored the crew to good health.

A dramatic change came over Magellan at this point. Instead of pushing on to reap the wealth of the Spice Islands, he turned into an evangelist. Always a devout Catholic, he now became almost fanatical in his desire to convert the Philippine natives to Christianity. (Some historians have termed this a case of religious hysteria.) One of the powerful local kings, Rajah Humabon, his queen, and various subjects were converted, at least on the surface, but a neighboring ruler refused to submit. King Cilapulapu of the small island of Mactan declared: "I will not abandon our worship of the gods, and I will make war on any chief who does." To punish such defiance, Magellan led a detachment of about fifty marines to burn the chief's capital. An overwhelming force of 1,500 natives met them and, in the battle

Antonio Pigafetta

that followed, Magellan and eight of his men were killed and others wounded.

Under pressure from King Cilapulapu, Rajah Humabon turned against the Spaniards. He set up a trap, inviting twenty-four men to come ashore to dine with him and receive a gift of jewels from the king of Spain. The new leaders walked blindly into the trap, and twenty-two were murdered.

Through the treachery of King Humabon the fleet had lost its key men, including the experienced Serrano and Duarte Barbosa, who had been elected to succeed Magellan. The total crew was reduced to 115, less than half the men who had originally sailed from Spain.

The remainder of the voyage was almost an anticlimax. Because of the manpower shortage, the *Concepción* was scuttled. With her, by intent, went all of Magellan's papers—his diary, logs, charts, invoices, and personal letters. The fleet wandered aimlessly for weeks, finally ending up at the Spice Islands, where the two remaining ships were loaded for the return voyage. As they were preparing to depart, the *Trinidad* suddenly sprang a leak, indicating the need for a complete overhaul. To take advantage of the winter monsoon, the *Victoria* proceeded alone. Fifty-four men remained; forty-seven sailed on the *Victoria*. Later, following a different route, the *Trinidad* was captured by the Portuguese and its crew imprisoned.

The return voyage for the *Victoria* was as dreadful as the outgoing trip. More than nine months went by, during which the crew struggled to keep a leaky ship afloat and to survive on spoiled meat and a reduced diet of rice. Twenty-one men died. Thirteen were detained by the Portuguese in the Cape Verde Islands. On September 6, 1522, the *Victoria* entered the bay of San Lúcar with only eighteen men, all sick and half-starved. One of the survivors was Antonio Pigafetta, who presented his record of the epic expedition to King Charles, "a book written by my own hand," he stated, "concerning all the matters that had occurred from day to day during our voyage."

What, actually, did Magellan achieve? He became the first man to circumnavigate the world (earlier he had sailed from somewhere near the Philippines eastward to India, Africa, and Portugal); he demonstrated the globular nature of the earth, though the idea was already generally accepted in educated circles; he discovered the inside passage around South America, now known at the Strait of Magellan; his voyage across the Pacific revealed the vast extent of that ocean; he discovered the Philippine archipelago, which Spain was to hold for three centuries. Magellan accomplished what Columbus had attempted to do a generation earlier—to reach the East Indies by sailing west. The existence of two great oceans separated by a continent was proven. Seafaring merchants thereafter had a choice of two routes to the riches of the Orient: the Pacific-Atlantic route or the Indian-Atlantic route, even though the former was largely impracticable until the construction of the Panama Canal.

What kind of a man was Ferdinand Magellan? The deliberate destruction of his own records handicaps any objective evaluation. The Portuguese historians denounced him as a traitor, and Bishop Fonesca's disloyal Spanish officers accused him of high-handed conduct. Their testimony can, on the whole, be discounted. The few clues as to his personal appearance, including contemporary portraits, indicate that he was a short, thickset, bearded, and rugged-looking man, walking with a limp from the wound received fighting the Moslems. He was an extremely capable seaman and a born leader. His outstanding characteristic was courage, a physical bravery to the point of recklessness, as shown by the unnecessary tragedy of his death fighting the Philippine natives. He was also a man of tremendous determination; once he had set a goal for himself he never turned back. Magellan's achievements speak for themselves. The first circumnavigation of the globe was his most spectacular feat, marking the beginning of a new chapter in the history of the world. For more than fifty years his feat was not duplicated; the next circumnavigation was not accomplished until Drake's voyage of 1577.

Antonio Pigafetta

6
Navigator and Discoverer Par Excellence

Captain James Cook's Journals, 1768

In his own time, Captain James Cook was called "the ablest and most renowned navigator England or any other country has produced." Posterity is in full agreement.

Among Cook's phenomenal accomplishments, completed in the short period of ten years in an age of sail, were three world-circling voyages. In the course of these voyages he took possession of Australia's east coast for Britain; circumnavigated Antarctica; discovered the Hawaiian Islands; established the fact that New Zealand is two islands, and not a part of a mysterious "Southern Continent"; explored 2,000 miles of Australian coastline; charted the dangerous west coast of North America for 3,000 miles from Oregon to beyond Bering Strait; and won a notable victory over the dread disease of scurvy. Cook's leading modern biographer, Alan Villiers, comments that "in those ten years he charted more of the Pacific than had been recorded by more than twenty predecessors—Spanish, Portuguese, Dutch, French, English—over the previous 250 years."

Cook's initial prospects were meager. He was born in 1728, the second of nine children, son of a Scots farmhand living in a remote Yorkshire village. But even as a child he was unusually gifted and intelligent. His father recognized these qualities and employed a private tutor for him before sending him on to a church school. Cook's education lasted five or six years, during which he acquired the rudiments of reading, writing, and arithmetic, though he never learned to spell. He was apprenticed to a grocer and dry goods merchant at age sixteen. As the life of a tradesman seemed dull and with little future to Cook, he jumped his contract two years later and signed on as a cabin boy on the *Freelove*, a collier of 450 tons plying between Newcastle and London, belonging to a Quaker, John Walker, and his two sons.

Cook had neither family influence nor wealth, but his ability evidently pleased the Walkers; at the end of seven years he was appointed first mate of the *Friendship*, a ship newly built by the firm for sailing between England, Norway, and the Baltic. Along the rough and stormy North Sea coast the small barks were in greater peril than on the open sea. Cook learned early to handle a ship under the most adverse conditions.

At age twenty-seven, Cook left the merchant marine service to join the British Navy as an able seaman, foreseeing possibilities for rapid promotion. His expectations were justified. In a short time he reached the rank of master, a noncommissioned warrant officer in charge of sailing the ship. At age twenty-nine, he was named master of the *Pembroke*, a sixty-four gun ship being sent to fight the French in Cánada.

Cook's role in the British attack on French Canada was unspectacular but highly important. A naval squadron under the command of Admiral Sir Charles Saunders was navigating up the broad, winding, and unpredictable St. Lawrence River. Cook soon acquired the title of "master surveyor and master of the fleet," for he charted the turbulent river as far as Quebec. His accurate surveys of the difficult channel known as the Traverse made possible the successful amphibious assault on Quebec under General James Wolfe, an operation that dislodged the French as the dominant power in Canada. Cook's assignment was completed amid cut-and-run skirmishing with French boat patrols. When the fighting ended, he continued for five years, 1763–69, his charting of the Gulf of St. Lawrence close to Newfoundland, off the coast of Labrador. The charts remained in use for a century after Cook's time—the best available for an exceptionally difficult region. Grim hazards had to be overcome in completing the task, as the rapid Labrador Current carried floes, pack ice, and icebergs accompanied by fog, sunken rocks, and freezing gales.

On one of his trips to England, after a doubtless quick courtship,

Cook married the twenty-one-year-old daughter of a London merchant, Elizabeth Batts. Six children were born to the union; three died in infancy, two sons were drowned while serving as young naval officers, and a third died while a student at Cambridge University. Elizabeth Cook lived to be ninety-three.

Following his Canadian adventures, Cook's next opportunity for fame came in 1768. Edmund Halley, appointed royal astronomer in 1721, had predicted that the planet Venus would pass between the sun and the earth in 1761 and 1768. The observation of this phenomenon was important to scientists in their attempts to measure the earth's distance from the sun. Because weather conditions had prevented satisfactory viewing in 1761, elaborate plans were made for the next occasion, the last for another one hundred years. The Royal Society hoped to make arrangements for observations to be made in the south seas, where cloudless skies could be anticipated. King George III responded to the society's request for material assistance by directing the Admiralty to provide a suitable naval vessel for the proposed expedition to the Pacific. In April of 1768 a ship, the *Earl of Pembroke,* was renamed the *Endeavour* and assigned the task.

The *Endeavour* was a bark, a term applied generally to small ships and especially to those carrying three masts without a mizzen topsail. She was a typical east coast collier and, while certainly no thing of beauty, was of exceptionally strong construction, large storage capacity, and shallow draft. She was spacious, bluff-bowed, 105 feet in overall length and about 20 feet wide in the beam. Fully laden she would draw 13 feet. Altogether she was a slow, ponderous, massive beamed little vessel that could take an extraordinary amount of hard wear and buffeting.

The *Endeavour* remained at anchor for two months at Deptford while preparations were made for the voyage. Space had to be provided for such scientific equipment as botanists' tins, atlases, astronomical instruments, books, and charts, and also for ropes, sails, lumber, paints, spare rolls of canvas, and other items needed for a long voyage. Food supplies, naturally of first importance, included casks of biscuits, barrels of salted pork and beef, large cheeses, and barrels of beer. The British seamen's favorite food was "burgoo," a thin porridge with lumps of boiled meat floating in it, a delicacy carried in quantity.

While stocking the *Endeavour* with a variety of foodstuffs, Cook made a major contribution to the science of human nutrition, an achievement that later won him the Royal Society's gold medal. He was determined to avoid the scourge of the sea, scurvy, a deficiency disease that had killed crews by the hundreds, as in the case of Ferdinand Magellan and many other commanders over the centuries. Before Cook's pioneering efforts to prevent it, scurvy was common on long voyages—an ugly, frequently fatal affliction causing debility, depression, loss of teeth, hemorrhages, and death. Fresh fruits and vegetables, containing the essential vitamin C, were generally unavailable on ships. In his search for preventatives, Cook tried "portable soups," a thick brown meat broth issued by the Admiralty in concentrated slabs; barrels of sauerkraut in quantities sufficient to allow every crew member two pounds a week to be added to the soup; evaporated malt ("wort") ; large issues of vinegar; and limited amounts of lemon juice, which was in short supply. As opportunity offered in the course of the voyage, Cook bought or had gathered edible greens, onions, fruits, and fresh vegetables, all of which were added to the crew's diet. Further, vinegar and water were frequently used to scrub out the crew's quarters aboard ship, for Cook knew from experience that scurvy flourished in damp, dark, and unsanitary quarters. As a result of these drastic and strictly enforced measures, Cook lost not a single man to scurvy during his voyages.

Why Cook was given command of the *Endeavour* remains something of a mystery. He was still a warrant officer, only a master. He had never crossed the equator, had never commanded any kind of expedition. Apparently the officers of the Admiralty simply recognized his outstanding qualities. In any case, he was now commissioned a lieutenant and placed in charge of the *Endeavour,* bound for the South Seas.

When the *Endeavour* set sail on August 26, 1798, her limited quarters were jammed with ninety-four officers, scientists, seamen, and marines. The total consisted of seventy-one officers and sailors, twelve marines, and eleven passengers. The distinguished group of scientists aboard included Charles Green of Greenwich Observatory and his assistants; a young amateur botanist, Joseph Banks (later Sir Joseph Banks, president of the Royal Society), an extremely wealthy man who had persuaded the authorities to allow him to accompany the *Endeavour;* another botanist, Daniel Charles Solander; and two artists, Alexander Buchan and Sydney Parkinson, brought to sketch the scenery and plants.

Banks was an aristocratic, autocratic individual, apparently under the impression that the entire expedition had been arranged for his personal benefit and convenience, and he added considerably to Cook's burden. On the other hand, his presence on board widened the scope of the voyage, giving it increased significance in the eyes of the scientific world. It also set a precedent for including scientific observers on naval expeditions. As Villiers remarks, "had Banks not set the precedent, Charles Darwin might never have sailed aboard the *Beagle* 60 years later."

After crossing the Atlantic, the *Endeavour* sailed down the east coast of South America. At Rio de Janeiro, the Portuguese governor refused to permit anyone to land, suspecting that the ship was engaged in smuggling; he refused to believe that such an unprepossessing little vessel could belong to Britain's Royal Navy. Banks managed to slip ashore at night for some botanical collecting and Cook made an excellent surreptitious chart of the harbor before they continued on toward Cape Horn.

On January 11, 1769, while the *Endeavour* was off Tierra del Fuego, Cook undertook some charting while Banks and the other scientists landed to collect botanical specimens. Banks nearly lost his life while climbing a mountain with Solander and two Negro servants. A sudden snowstorm left them trapped on a ledge for hours. The two Negroes died of the cold, but Banks and Solander fought their way back.

The short but extremely dangerous task of rounding Cape Horn proved much less of an ordeal than Cook and his crew had anticipated. By this date the Horn had acquired a well-deserved reputation among mariners as a grim and treacherous passage. Consequently, ship captains often chose to go through the Strait of Magellan. For a number of reasons, however, experienced seamen argue that the open sea is preferable. The strait is narrow, with little room to maneuver; there are twisting channels; wild winds sweep down from the mountains; visibility is often almost zero; few anchorages are available; and charts in Cook's time were poor, causing ships to make wrong turns. The strait's chief advantage is quieter water and an absence of the enormous seas pounding ships rounding the Horn. In any event, Cook took the route most of the early skippers had found best: through the Strait of le Maire between Tierra del Fuego and Staten Island, and then bearing west as fast as possible. The westward passage around the Horn meant sailing at least 1,500 miles from the Atlantic to the Pacific, threading through a labyrinth of off-shore islands. The *Endeavour* traversed the distance in thirty-eight days, ocean to ocean, and emerged into the Pacific on February 12. This was astonishing luck, "a circumstance," Cook wrote, "which perhaps never happened before to any ship in those seas, so much dreaded for hard gales of wind, insomuch that the doubling of Cape Horn is thought by some to be a mighty thing and others to this day prefer the Strait of Magellan."

Cook sailed on to Tahiti, nearly 5,000 miles northwestward. The weather became milder, "like spring in England," Banks reported. The *Endeavour* anchored in Matavai Bay, Tahiti, on April 11, 1769. The island had been previously visited by English and French explorers, from whose accounts it had acquired the reputation of being a veritable paradise—lush green valleys, high peaks, and beautiful beaches. Its harbors were good and it had ample quantities of fresh food. Even more appealing to seamen were the island's fleshly attractions. The present of an iron nail would win a sailor a girl, and a spike would finance a harem for a month. The Tahitians were willing to trade almost anything for this wonderful metal. A previous British ship, the *Dolphin,* came close to sinking because the crew had extracted so many spikes and bolts from her construction. One consequence of the feminine favors was that a considerable number of the *Endeavour's* crew contracted venereal diseases—a legacy from the earlier French visitors.

On June 3, 1769, as Halley had predicted, a small dark point could be observed, through the smoked glass of the telescope, moving across the face of the sun. Cook and his scientists were ready and waiting when the astronomical phenomenon occurred. Observatories had been established at two points some fifteen miles distant from each other. Three telescopes of different magnifying powers were set up in the main observatory. The day was hot but cloudless, and thus, as Cook stated, "we had every advantage in observing the whole of the passage of the planet Venus over the sun's disc." Natives gathered around looked on in awe, expecting some kind of voodoo magic, and were disappointed when nothing spectacular happened.

Cook's main mission was now completed, and he was anxious to move on. The *Endeavour* remained in Tahiti three months, during which the ship sailed around the island and charts of the shoreline were prepared. Before departure, the vessel was thoroughly overhauled and fresh food and water were taken on board. Banks planted watermelon, orange, lemon, and lime seeds and gave the natives other seeds for planting.

After the Tahitian visit, the *Endeavour* sailed south and west into an unknown region, instead of following the safe route back to Europe around the north of New Guinea. The next port of call was the group of atolls called the Society Islands, over which the British flag was hoisted and the waters sounded and charted. Before leaving England, the Admiralty had handed Cook secret instructions to explore New Zealand before returning home. Also, if it existed, he was to find the vast "Unknown Southern Land" which, according to legend, extended far up into the Pacific. It was still to be determined whether New Zealand was a separate land mass or capes of the mysterious *terra australis*.

Cook spent six months disproving the notion that New Zealand might be part of the great southern continent. He charted 2,400 miles of the New Zealand coast and discovered the straits between the North and South Islands. Both islands were circumnavigated, often in the face of storms and gales at sea, while being opposed by hostile Maori aborigines on shore. The natives were graphically described by Cook as

> a strong, raw-boned, well made, active people rather above the common size, of a dark brown colour, with black hair, thin black beards, and white teeth. Both men and women paint their faces and bodies with red ochre mixed with fish oil. They wear ornaments of stone, bone, and shells at their ears and about their necks, and the men generally wear long white feathers stuck upright in their hair. They come off in canoes which will carry a hundred people; when within a stone's throw of the ship, the

chief of the party would brandish a battleaxe, calling out: "come ashore with us and we will kill you." They would certainly have eaten them too, for they were cannibals.

Nearly two centuries before Thor Heyerdahl's *Kon-Tiki* expedition Cook wondered about the origin of Polynesian peoples and the sources of their culture, questioning why a common language was spread over islands thousands of miles apart; reasons for the varying physical characteristics of the natives from island to island; the source of their religious beliefs and customs; how they had acquired the sweet potato and other indigenous American plants; and similar ethnological problems.

"As we have now circumnavigated the whole of this country," Cook reported, "it is time for me to think of quitting it." The *Endeavour* sailed away to the west and nineteen days later, on April 28, anchored on the east coast of New Holland, or Australia, at Botany Bay, named from the quantity of plants found in the area by Banks. Continuing north, Cook surveyed the coast as he passed and named various bays and capes.

Castastrophe struck as Cook sailed into the labyrinth of the Great Barrier Reef. This area is not a single reef or line of reefs but a huge zone of them, 80,000 square miles stretching from below the Tropic of Capricorn to the coast of New Guinea in a 1,200-mile line sometimes 100 miles wide. Despite the utmost precautions, the *Endeavour* struck the reefs at night as she was approaching the end of the reef area. All sails were taken in immediately, the boats lowered, and the ship was found to be caught on a reef of coral rocks. The vessel started to leak and seemed headed for total destruction. Everything possible was tossed overboard to lighten her—guns, iron and stone ballast, casks, and nonessential stores. On the second day, the ship floated off into deep water at high tide, but with about four feet of water in the hold. Slowly she was moved from the vicinity of the reef and headed for a harbor the master had found along the shore. There she was beached for repairs, a process that required two weeks. How close the *Endeavour* came to sinking was revealed when a large piece of coral broken from the reef was found jammed in the worst hole, effectively serving as a stopper.

Further narrow escapes and hair-raising adventures occurred before the *Endeavour* was finally able to steer clear of the Great Barrier

Reef. In his two subsequent Pacific voyages, Cook never again approached the area nor touched Australia.

With his food supplies down to three months, Cook directed his course to the East Indies and reached Java on October 10, 1770. The Dutch-Indonesian port turned out to be a pesthole, an almost unmitigated disaster for the *Endeavour*'s crew. Malaria and dysentery struck quickly; seven men died and many more succumbed to dysentery on the voyage to the Cape of Good Hope. Before reaching Batavia only five members of the crew had been lost, four by accident and one by tuberculosis, none from scurvy; when the *Endeavour* anchored in the Downs on Saturday, July 13, 1771, only fifty-six men and boys remained of the ninety-four who had left England nearly three years earlier.

The Admiralty showed its confidence in Captain Cook by asking him to lead a second expedition to the Pacific barely three months after returning from the first. Critics pointed out that the existence of New Zealand and Australia was previously known, but the possibility of an "Unknown Southern Land" remained. In an ocean as vast as the Pacific, they maintained, there was still room for a great continent between New Zealand and South America. And so Cook was directed to make a further search. His order was to circumnavigate the Antarctic and either find a new continent or prove conclusively that one did not exist.

Cook, now promoted to the rank of commander and without the complications of Joseph Banks and his retinue on board, was provided with two small ships for the expedition, the *Resolution* and the *Adventure*. The current theory held that two ships were better than one, because of the risk of losing one of them; in practice the idea did not work satisfactorily, as the two sloops were frequently separated. The *Adventure*, under the command of Tobias Furneaux, returned to England a year before the *Resolution*. Cook, commanding the latter vessel, was out for over three years.

The second expedition sailed July 13, 1772, with orders to sail past Madeira to the Cape of Good Hope and then south, exploring any land that might be discovered, and to return across the Pacific to Cape Horn on as southerly a course as possible. This would be the first circumnavigation of the earth from west to east. Cook thoroughly combed the southern ocean, going well below the Antarctic Circle in the Atlantic and in the Pacific. In fact, he circum-navigated Antarctica. The *Resolution* became the first ship to cross the Antarctic Circle and did so a total of three times in three separate expeditions, searching the frozen wastes during the short summer seasons of 1773–74. After sailing around the whole area, Cook disproved the myth of a huge, inhabited southern land. If such a continent existed, he reported, it lay too near the South Pole to be of practical use to man. Thousands of islands were discovered, but no continental land between the meridian of New Zealand and Cape Horn. In further sailing in the Pacific, Cook carried out extensive explorations on Easter Island, the New Hebrides, New Caledonia, Norfolk Island, the Marquesas, and the Isle of Pines.

When the *Resolution* anchored at Spithead on July 30, 1775, she had sailed between 60,000 and 70,000 miles, much of the time in icy seas and under arctic conditions. Only four men had been lost, again none by scurvy. Cook was promoted to the rank of captain.

Cook's third and last voyage, undertaken less than a year after his return to England, was planned as another effort to settle a long disputed matter of geography. The *Resolution* was refitted once more to search for a passage, or a sailing route between Britain and the East Indies. If a route could be found in the Northern Hemisphere, it would shorten voyages and expedite trade, even if it could be used during the summer months only. The idea was far from new. During the sixteenth and seventeenth centuries, many navigators had hunted vainly for a Northwest Passage from Britain to China. Cook's mission was slightly different—to approach the hypothetical passage from the Pacific, not the Atlantic. It seems that Cook himself believed in the existence of such an opening, at least at the outset. The Admiralty's order was to "search for and explore such rivers or inlets as may appear to be of considerable extent, and pointing towards Hudson's or Baffin's Bay." If no such passage existed, Cook should proceed to look for a Northeast Passage round northern Russia to European seas.

On July 12, 1776, Cook left Plymouth, again with the *Resolution*. A second ship, the *Discovery*, followed a month later. After once more visiting Tahiti, Tasmania, and New Zealand, a prolonged stay was made among Pacific islands before turning north in December of 1777. One of the discoveries, Christmas Island, produced a large supply of fresh turtle meat. A few days later the expedition came upon a hitherto unknown group of islands, named the Sandwich Islands by Cook after the earl of Sandwich, first lord of the Admiralty and inventor of the sandwich. The group formed the kingdom of Hawaii, the chief island. With a good supply of fresh provisions obtained there, Cook sailed on east, striking the American continent approximately in California and coasting northward to anchor in Nootka Sound on Vancouver Island, British Columbia. The weather was cold and stormy and the progress of the little English ships up the coast had been slow.

Cook left Nootka Sound on April 26, 1778, and on August 7 arrived at the most westerly point of America, which he named Cape Prince of Wales. Sailing on west, he was off the coast of Asia and then turned north to pass through Bering Strait. A solid wall of ice made further progress impossible. After a long and futile search for the mythical Northwest Passage, Cook returned to Hawaii. He had concluded that the idea of a passage was pure fantasy, but even if it existed, it would be so packed with ice as to have no commercial value. After months amid ice, snow, rocks, and fogs, Hawaii was a paradise.

At first, the Hawaiian natives were friendly, considering the English gods. A prolonged stay, however, changed their attitudes. There was jealousy among the Hawaiian men over the promiscuous relations between their women and the sailors; all the island's provisions were being consumed by the visitors; and brawls and killings occurred over petty thefts by the natives. Cook and some of his men went ashore to try to pacify the people, but they were attacked by a mob. Cook was hit by a large stone and repeatedly stabbed. Cook's body and those of some of his sailors were literally cut to pieces.

The date was February 14, 1779. Such was the end of England's greatest navigator, Captain James Cook, the man who had circumnavigated New Zealand and the Antarctic, who had explored the coast of New South Wales, discovered Hawaii, named various unknown islands in the Pacific, and charted large areas of the Pacific northwest. His great victory over the horrible disease of scurvy made long voyages possible without loss of life to the crew. In little more than a decade he had filled in more details of the map of the world than virtually all other explorers of the previous two centuries.

Navigator and Discoverer

James Cook's end is strikingly reminiscent of the death of Ferdinand Magellan, about two and half centuries earlier. Cook in Hawaii and Magellan in the Philippines were both killed by angry natives as they were retreating to their ships.

Until Cook's time, no one had any real idea of the size of the Pacific, nor the proportion of water to land. All of his predecessors, from Magellan onward, had left the chart of the vast ocean little altered. Cook changed all that; the present map of the Pacific was, in large measure, established by Cook's exploratory surveys in the ten years from 1769 to 1779.

A statement by Desmond Wilcox, in his *Ten Who Dared*, sums up the significance of Cook's career: "Both as a symbol of a time of transition and important in moving it forward, James Cook of England is a towering figure. He was at once the last of the old explorers concerned with great territorial problems, and the first of the new men interested in precise descriptions of what he found as well as its nature and its implications."

7
Terrestrial Paradise

*William Bartram's Travels through North and
South Carolina, Georgia, East and West Florida,
1773–1777*

America's first two great botanists were father and son, John and William Bartram. John Bartram, a Pennsylvania Quaker born in 1699, was self-educated. Before he died in 1777, Linnaeus had called him "the greatest natural botanist in the world." Along with Benjamin Franklin, he was one of the founders of the American Philosophical Society, a member of the Royal Societies of London and Stockholm, and carried on correspondence with the leading scientists of his time. His considerable scientific accomplishments included the introduction into England of such plants as the bush honeysuckle, fiery lilies, mountain laurel, dogtooth violet, wild asters, gentian, hemlock, red and white cedar, and sugar maple.

John Bartram traveled extensively in the American colonies. A trip into the Catskills in 1753 initiated his fourteen-year-old son William into botanical exploration. Long-held ambitions to travel in Virginia and the Carolinas were fulfilled in 1760 and again in 1761. In his writings, John Bartram always referred to the South as a "terrestrial paradise." The longest and most important journey of his career was undertaken in 1765, after he had been appointed "Botanist to the King," at a salary of fifty pounds a year. Taking William with him, he set out to explore eastern Florida and to travel up the St. Johns River. An account of the expedition was published in London in 1766 under the title *A Journal, Kept by John Bartram of Philadelphia, Botanist to His Majesty for the Floridas; Upon a Journey from St. Augustine up the River St. John's, as Far as the Lakes.*

William Bartram was deeply influenced by his father's achievements, and the trip to Florida made a permanent impression upon him. As a youth he had displayed unusual talent for drawing natural objects. His father's friend, the English naturalist John Collinson, had shown examples of the drawings to Dr. John Fothergill, a botanist and a Friend. At Fothergill's expense, William spent almost five years, 1773–77, exploring the southeastern region of the United States. In return, his patron was to receive curious seeds and plant specimens, drawings of birds, reptiles, insects, and plants, and journals. The story of these travels was not published until 1791, when William Bartram issued his famous *Travels through North and South Carolina, Georgia, East and West Florida, the Cherokee Country, the Extensive Territories of the Moscogulges, or Creek Confederacy, and the Country of the Chactaws; Containing an Account of the Soil and Natural Productions of Those Regions, together with Observations on the Manners of the Indians, Embellished with Copper-Plates.*

The route followed by Bartram has been accurately traced, despite the disappearance or changes in names of places mentioned. He sailed from Philadelphia for Charleston, South Carolina, in April of 1773; from there he took ship for Savannah, from which port he traveled by horseback through various parts of Georgia, described as "a level country, well watered by large streams . . . coursing from extensive swamps and marshes," crossing next "an uninhabited wilderness" of "high pine forests" and "dark and grassy savannas." The remainder of this season was spent "in botanical excursions to the low countries, between Carolina and East Florida." Bartram ascended the Altamaha River in a cypress canoe, and recorded his delight in the groves, meadows, forests, domestic herds, and other features of the country.

Part two of the *Travels* covered Bartram's explorations of Florida, after eleven months spent in Georgia. He sailed from Frederica, St. Simon Island, and was put ashore near Amelia Island, Florida, where he bought "a neat little sailboat" and proceeded up the St. Johns River. Along the way, he admired the groves of live oaks, palms, magnolia, and orange trees. Adventures with alligators and a wild tropical storm enlivened the trip. The beauties of the landscape were described in glowing detail. At the conclusion of the expedition, Bartram returned to Charleston to plan future travels.

Part three narrates even more extensive journeys: through the Cherokee territories and Chactaw country, through parts of Georgia and west Florida, into Alabama and Louisiana, along the Mississippi, and finally returning home by way of Charleston, Cape Fear in North Carolina, Alexandria, Virginia, and Maryland to Philadelphia, where he arrived in January 1778.

The fourth and final part of the *Travels* is in the nature of an appendix, entitled *An Account of the Persons, Manners, Customs and Government of Muscogulges or Creeks, Cherokees, Chactaws, etc. Aborigines of the Continent of North America*—evidence of Bartram's avid interest in the southern Indian tribes.

Bartram's descriptive powers are illustrated by his comments on the scenery along the St. Johns River in Florida: "It is very pleasing to observe the banks of the river ornamented with hanging garlands, composed of varieties of climbing vegetables, both shrubs and plants, forming perpendicular green walls, with projecting jambs, pilasters, and deep apartments, twenty or thirty feet high and completely covered . . . it is exceedingly curious to behold the Wild Squash climbing over the lofty limbs of the trees; their yellow fruit somewhat of the size and figure of a large orange, pendant from the extremities of the limbs over the water."

Still more dramatic is Bartram's firsthand account of a tropical hurricane which struck while he was in the same area. The "terrific appearance" of "the approaching tempest . . . confounded me," he wrote, "how purple and fiery appeared the tumultuous clouds! swiftly ascending or darting from the horizon upwards; they seemed to oppose and dash against each other, the skies appeared streaked with blood or purple flame overhead, the flaming lightning streaming and darting about in every direction around, seems to fill the world with fire; whilst the heavy thunder keeps the earth in a constant tremor." When the torrential rain began, it "came down with such rapidity and fell in such quantities, that every object was totally obscured, excepting the continual streams or rivers of lightning, pouring from the clouds; all seemed a frightful chaos." The devastation was tremendous—trees blown down, nearby plantation houses razed to the ground, and valuable crops destroyed.

Other graphically described incidents in Bartram's *Travels* concern his encounters with alligators, which he sometimes refers to as "crocodiles"; ten pages are devoted to "that horrid animal." Early in his Florida stay, while camping one night on a lagoon, he observed "the subtle, greedy alligator" fishing for trout. "Behold him rushing forth from the flags and reeds," Bartram wrote, "his enormous body swells. His plaited tail brandished high, floats upon the lake. The waters like a cataract descend from his open jaws. Clouds of smoke issue from his dilated nostrils. The earth trembles with his thunder. When immediately from the opposite coast of the lagoon, emerges from the deep his rival champion. They suddenly dart upon each other. The boiling surface of the lake marks their rapid course, and a terrific conflict commences." Bartram himself was in imminent peril, on several occasions, from the giant reptiles. While fishing, his canoe was "attacked from all sides. . . . Two very large ones attacked me closely, at the same instant, rushing up with their heads and part of their bodies above the water, roaring terribly and belching floods of water over me. They struck their jaws together so close to my ears, as almost to stun me, and I expected every moment to be dragged out of the boat and instantly devoured." Bartram then remarked that "the alligator when full grown is a very large and terrible creature, and of prodigious strength, activity and swiftness in the water."

Other land and water reptiles also engaged much of Bartram's attention. He called the coach-whip snake "a beautiful creature" and the water moccasin "a large and horrid serpent," the green and riband snakes "beautiful innocent creatures," and the bull snake "large and inoffensive with respect to mankind" uttering "a terrible loud hissing noise, sounding very hollow and like distant thunder." Bartram's philosophy toward wild life was live and let live. He describes with some pride that he saved the life of a "formidable" rattlesnake that had allowed him and his companions "to pass many times by him during the night, without injuring us in the least."

Bartram's descriptions of common wild animals were primarily factual. The bears of the region he explored were "a strong creature, and prey on the fruits of the country, and will likewise devour young calves, swine and sheep," although he heard of no instance of their attacking man. The wolves of Florida were "larger than a dog," but not as large as the Canadian and Pennsylvania wolves; the howls of wolf packs were "terrifying to the wandering bewildered traveler." Of another member of the canine family, he stated that "the foxes of Carolina and Florida are of the smaller red species." Bartram also mentioned the wildcat, or lynx, "a fierce and bold little animal," and reported that "tygers" (actually panthers) were numerous in the region that he explored, a "very strong, mischievous animal" that preyed on calves, young colts, etc. Among other animals appearing in the *Travels* were deer and elk, squirrels, racoons, opossums, rabbits, moles, gophers, the "great land tortoise," rats, mice, weasels, polecats, and bats.

Insects were always present in Bartram's landscape. The swarms of mosquitoes and an "incredible number" of "burning" or biting flies tormented men and animals. Another innumerable insect was the grasshopper, "the favorite delicious food" of rice birds. The rich colors of the multitude of different species of butterflies delighted Bartram. He was most entranced, however, by "the small flying insects, of the genus termed by naturalists Ephemera," and devoted three pages to describing their birth, brief life span, and death. "At evening," he wrote, "they are seen in clouds of innumerable millions, swarming and wantoning in the still air, gradually drawing near the river, descend upon its surface, and there quickly end their day, after committing their eggs to the deep." Bartram was amazed to observe "these beautiful and delicately formed little creatures . . . whose frame and organization is equally wonderful, more delicate, and perhaps as complicated as that of the most perfect human being."

Much of Bartram's travel was by water. It was only natural, therefore, to find his observations frequently concerned with the ocean, numerous rivers, lakes, creeks, lagoons, pools, fountains, springs, and geysers. The bodies of water described swarmed with animal life and were covered with vegetation. In the multiplicity of life forms were the manatee, many species of tortoise or turtle, otters, water snakes, frogs, beavers and, of course, all kinds of fish. Fishes were of special interest to Bartram, and he found that they abounded along the coasts and in sounds and inlets. He noted also that "the bays and lagoons are stored with oysters and varieties of other shell-fish, crabs, shrimp, etc." The immense quantity of fish could be judged by those observed in the St. Johns River, where "from shore to shore, and perhaps near half a mile above and below me, appeared to be one solid bank of fish, of various kinds, pushing through this narrow pass of St. Juans into the little lake, on their return down the river." The fish were met by the "devouring alligators," which were attracted "in such incredible numbers, and so close together from shore to shore, that it would have been easy to have walked across on their heads, had the animals been harmless."

The air and its inhabitants were also important elements in Bartram's biosphere. He was a notable ornithologist, and his list of American birds, included in the *Travels,* is the most complete until publication of Alexander Wilson's *American Ornithologist* (1808–14). The Bartram list contained 215 different species of birds. Among those specifically described were the crying bird, wood pelican, turkey buzzard, wild turkey-cock, savanna crane, snake bird (a cormorant), fishing hawk, jays, butcher bird, rice bird, cedar bird, catbird, and mockingbird. Wild pigeons by the millions were seen, migrating and roosting on low trees, bushes, and in the interior parts of vast swamps. Wagon loads of the pigeons were captured by the natives, using the blaze of pine torches at night to blind the birds.

Primarily a botanist, Bartram found the plant life of the subtropical region of absorbing interest. Among the trees, magnolias fascinated him and he devoted entire pages to describing different varieties. Another favorite was the red or loblolly bay, "Gordonia lasianthus," tall, with "thick foliage, of a dark green colour, flowered over with large, milk-white fragrant blossoms." Special attention was paid to uncommon species of familiar trees and to tropical and semitropical trees. He especially admired cypress, live oak, and palm trees. His biographer, N. B. Fagin, comments that "a complete list of all the trees Bartram describes would fill a fair-sized botanical dictionary."

Even more numerous than trees in Bartram's landscape were shrubs, flowers, and other plants. Here again his emphasis was on tropical plants or uncommon species of semitropical and temperate plants.

Not least interesting of Bartram's observations related to people—the many planters, traders, and aborigines encountered in the course of his travels. Everywhere he met with friendliness and hospitality. Typical of the reception he generally received was a visit to a tribe of Seminole Indians, who were normally hostile to whites. When the chief was informed of the nature of Bartram's work, "he received me with complaisance, giving me unlimited permission to travel over the country for the purpose of collecting flowers, medicinal plants, etc., saluting me by the name of the Flower hunter, recommending me to the friendship and protection of his people." Bartram made his knowledge of medicine freely available to the Indians, and on one occasion won their gratitude by killing a huge rattlesnake that was terrorizing a village.

Bartram's friendly feelings for the Indians was revealed throughout his narrative. He traveled and lived among them, studied their languages and customs, and became acquainted with different tribes and individuals. He was inclined to deplore the effect of civilization on the Indian. The concerns of the aborigine, he noted, closely paralleled those of the white man: to love, reproduce, care for their young, build homes, protect their persons and property, protect the aged, and to worship a Great Spirit. A telling comparison was made by Bartram between Indian "savagery" and white civilization:

> The Indians make war against, kill and destroy their own species, and their motives spring from the same erroneous source as it does in all other nations of mankind; that is, the ambition of exhibiting to their fellows, a superior character of personal and national valour, and thereby immortalize themselves, by transmitting their names with honour and lustre to posterity; or in revenge of their enemy, for public or personal insults; or lastly, to extend the borders and boundaries of their territories; but I cannot find upon the strictest enquiry, that their bloody contests, at this day are marked with deeper stains of inhumanity or savage cruelty, than what may be observed amongst the most civilized nations; they do indeed scalp their slain enemy, but they do not kill the females or children of either sex.

The physical characteristics of the Indians encountered are described in detail by Bartram. He observed that the males of the Cherokees, Creeks, and related tribes were "tall, erect, and moderately robust, their limbs well shaped, so as generally to form a perfect human figure; their features regular, and countenance open, dignified and placid." Their complexion was "reddish brown or copper colour; their hair long, lank, coarse and black as a raven." As for the Cherokee women, they were "tall, slender, erect and of a delicate frame, their features formed with perfect symmetry, their countenance cheerful and friendly, and they move with a becoming grace and dignity." The Muscogulge women were surprisingly small, a majority less than five feet tall. That they were daughters of Eve was revealed by their eyes: "large, black and languishing, expressive of modesty, diffidence, and bashfulness; these charms are their defensive and offensive weapons, and they know very well how to play them off. And under cover of these alluring graces, are concealed the most subtle artifice; they are however loving and affectionate."

The presence of people, especially the whites, inevitably led to a damaged natural environment. Long before the advent of vast cotton and tobacco plantations, Bartram witnessed destruction caused by wasteful agricultural practices. He deplored the devastation of natural beauties that followed the white man's progress. Over two hundred years ago, Bartram expressed an increasingly popular twentieth-century view that man should use his environment wisely and never abuse or destroy it. About fifteen years previously, he and his father had visited "a magnificent Indian mound" overlooking Lake George in Florida. At the time, "there were no settlements of white people, but all appeared wild and savage, yet in that uncultivated state, it possessed an almost inexpressible air of grandeur."

On the occasion of the second visit, all was changed. A large orange grove, live oaks, palms, and magnolias, "a noble Indian highway," and other extraordinarily scenic features had been cleared away to make room for cultivation. Indigo, corn, and cotton had been planted, but the land had then been almost totally abandoned. As described by Bartram, "it appeared like a desert, to a great extent, and terminated, on the land side, by frightful thickets, and open pine forests."

Elsewhere, Bartram wrote, "I have often been affected with extreme regret, at beholding the destruction and devastation which has been committed, or indiscreetly exercised on extensive, fruitful orange groves, on the banks of St. Juan, by the new planters under the British government, some hundred acres of which, at a single plantation, has been entirely destroyed to make room for the Indigo,

William Bartram

Cotton, Corn, Batatas, etc. . . . Some plantations have not a single tree standing, and where any have been left, it is only a small coppice or clump, nakedly exposed and destitute."

The paths of the great early naturalists, such as Bartram, were far from smooth, though the hazards and hardships of travel were not stressed by Bartram in his *Travels*. Settlements were few except along the coast and for a short distance inland along the rivers. Roads connecting the remote settlements were exceedingly primitive, often no more than trails. Camping equipment was limited to what could be carried on horseback, strapped in front of or behind the saddle. Mosquito netting and insect repellants had not yet been invented. Unfriendly Indians and renegades added to the dangers of travel. Diseases such as malaria and yellow fever were always present. Bartram described several periods of severe illness in the course of his journey, and in the light of his subsequent career it appears that his health was to some extent permanently affected.

Within a few years after its Philadelphia publication, Bartram's *Travels* became immensely popular in Europe. Two editions were issued in England (1782 and 1794), one in Ireland (1793), one in Germany (1793), one in Holland (1797), and one in France (1799). The literary influence of the work was extensive. Chateaubriand, Coleridge, Carlyle, Shelley, Tennyson, Southey, and Wordsworth abroad, and Emerson and Thoreau at home, were among numerous writers who came under Bartram's spell. The concept of the "noble savage" was derived, to an important degree, from Bartram's idealistic picture of the American aborigines. A perceptive comment comes from a historian of science, J. M. Edelstein: "In an age of strong scientific curiosity and romantic interest in the far-off and the exotic, it was natural that William Bartram's book should make a deep impression and become an important influence on literature. Nature, landscape, travel, Indians—all the elements of popular interest—are in Bartram."

8
Pursuing the Niger

Mungo Park's Travels in the Interior Districts of Africa,
1795—1797

Nearly two centuries ago and some decades before David Livingstone and Henry Stanley's African adventures, another British explorer, Mungo Park, traveled extensively in the "Dark Continent."

In 1788 Sir Joseph Banks, a wealthy English botanist and explorer, and eleven associates founded the African Association for Promoting the Discovery of the Interior Parts of Africa. Within five years of its establishment, the association had sent three explorers into Africa to determine the source and direction of the Niger River. The first, an American marine named Ledyard, approached the undertaking from Libya, but died in Cairo before his mission had scarcely begun. The second choice, Lucas, a former slave in Morocco, proposed to travel to the Niger country across the Sahara; at the end of five days he turned back when he encountered hostile Arabs. The next selection was Major Daniel Houghton, fort-major at Goree. After proceeding through several Negro "kingdoms," Houghton arrived in Ludamar, an area populated by half-breed Arabs, or "Moors." There he apparently was robbed, crawled on his hands and knees to a Moorish village, was refused food, and either starved to death or was killed.

The remarkable individual chosen for the fourth attempt to reach the Niger, Mungo Park, was a young Scotsman who had recently completed training for the medical profession. He was bored with the life of a Scottish general practitioner and yearned for travel and adventure. On a trip to London, he met Sir Joseph Banks and was offered a position as ship's surgeon on the *Worcester,* a Sumatra-bound East India Company vessel. After a year's absence he returned to London, heard the news of Houghton's death, and applied to Banks for a chance to continue the search for the Niger. The association approved. Park was then about twenty-four years of age.

When Park began his eventful journey, the Niger's course and terminal point had remained an unfathomed secret for more than two thousand years. Among the unresolved questions were: Did it flow east or west? Was it a branch of another major river, perhaps the Congo or the Nile? Did it empty into the Atlantic, into a salt lake in the center of Africa, or into the Mediterranean? Nearly insurmountable difficulties confronted any explorer looking for answers: the climate was deadly, especially to white men; the Sahara Desert and a rain forest presented formidable physical barriers; and the whole area was populated by Christian-hating Moslems and rapacious, often hostile blacks.

None of these fearsome factors deterred Mungo Park from accepting the challenging assignment he was now offered. The fact that not one of his three predecessors had returned failed to dismay the confident young Scot. In May of 1795 he sailed from Portsmouth and, after a month's voyage, landed at Jillifree on the river Gambia. As he himself noted:

> My instructions were very plain and concise. I was directed, on my arrival in Africa, to pass on to the river Niger, either by the way of Bambouk, or by such other route as should be most convenient. That I should ascertain the course, and, if possible, the rise and termination of that river, that I should use my utmost exertions to visit the principal towns or cities in its neighbourhood, particularly Tombuctoo and Houssa; and that I should be afterwards at liberty to return to Europe, either by the way of the Gambia, or by such other route, as, under all the then existing circumstances of my situation and prospects, should appear to me to be the most advisable.

Park carried with him a letter of credit for 200 pounds and an introduction to Dr. John Laidley, a fellow Scotsman and trader in slaves, ivory, and gold at Pisania on the Gambia River. Laidley received him hospitably, but before Park could begin his travels, he came down with a type of African fever—the first of several attacks—and consequently did not leave Pisania until December. During the interim, he concentrated on learning the Mandingo tongue, the language in most general use in that part of Africa. He also became familiar with the domestic economy, such as agricultural practices, the chief crops, livestock, methods of preparing food, and wild animals in the area.

Park had hoped to join a caravan leaving Pisania for the interior. The slave traders were suspicious of a white man, however, and were, as Park commented, "unwilling to enter into any positive engagements on my account." He therefore decided to proceed on his own, equipped with an English speaking Mandingo guide named Johnson, a slave called Demba, a horse, two donkeys, a few days' food supply, a sextant, a compass, a thermometer, two fowling pieces, four pistols, and an umbrella.

Before Park had proceeded far, he was stopped by a native who informed him that he must pay duty to the king of Walli; otherwise, he would not be permitted to continue. Four bars of tobacco were presented to the noisy and demanding agents. This was a routine to be repeated over and over again in the course of Park's travels. Native kings were everywhere, and one of their main sources of revenue was the taxes or duties exacted from slave traders and other travelers passing through their territories. At Fatteconda, the capital of Bondou, the king relieved Park of his best coat, a blue garment whose yellow buttons particularly caught his fancy, and his umbrella. The common tribute exacted by this monarch from travelers was a musket and six bottles of gunpowder. The next holdup was at Maana, where ten of the king's horsemen stopped Park, accused him of entering the capital without first paying the duties, and thus, according to the laws of the country, his people, cattle, and baggage were forfeited; they finally released him after robbing him of half his goods. In Teesee, the king of Kasson was equally avaricious; Park's offer of seven bars of amber and five of tobacco was rejected as inadequate for a monarch of his importance. The matter ended with the king's attendants opening all Park's bundles, spreading the contents on the floor, and confiscating whatever they wished, plundering him, as he remarked, of half the remainder of his possessions. On more than one occasion Park was the victim of outright thievery, leaving him in the end destitute of everything except the ragged clothes on his back.

Mungo Park

In partial justification of the thieving propensities of the Mandingo Negroes, Park wrote: "Before we pronounce them a more depraved people than any other, it were well to consider whether the lower order of people in any part of Europe, would have acted, under similar circumstances, with greater honesty toward a stranger, than the Negroes acted towards me. It must not be forgotten, that the laws of the country afforded me no protection; that everyone was at liberty to rob me with impunity; and finally, that some part of my effects were of as great value, in the estimation of the Negroes as pearls and diamonds would have been in the eyes of a European." Justifying such a forgiving attitude, Park added: "It is impossible for me to forget the disinterested charity, and tender solicitude, with which many of these poor heathens sympathized with me in my sufferings, relieved my distresses; and contributed to my safety."

The natives of the countries bordering on the Gambia, Park noted, though scattered among many different local governments, were divided among four principal classes: the Feloops, the Jaloffs, the Foulahs, and the Mandingoes. A majority were superstitious infidels, though the Mohammedan religion was making progress among them. The Feloops were "of a gloomy disposition, and are supposed never to forgive an injury." On the other hand, they were grateful for any benefactions, honest and faithful. The Jaloffs were an active, powerful, and warlike race occupying the area between the Senegal River and the Mandingo states on the Gambia. Their skin was of the deepest black, but their noses were "not so much depressed, nor the lips so protuberant, as among the generality of Africans." The Foulahs were "chiefly of a tawny complexion, with soft silky hair, and pleasing features." They led pastoral lives as herdsmen and husbandmen and were spread among various kingdoms, paying tribute to the reigning sovereigns.

Most numerous among the native peoples were the Mandingoes, constituting a majority of the inhabitants in the districts visited by Park. In each of their considerable towns there was a chief magistrate whose duties were to preserve order, levy taxes on travelers, and administer justice. Without any written laws of their own, Mohammedan civil law was being generally adopted. This fact had given rise to professional advocates or expounders of the law, concerning whom Park rather sardonically remarked, "If I may judge from their harangues, which I frequently attended, I believe that in the forensic qualifications of procrastination and cavil, and the arts of confounding and perplexing a cause, they are not always surpassed by the ablest pleaders in Europe." Generally speaking, Park found the Mandingoes of "a mild, sociable, and obliging disposition."

Superstition was a powerful force in the lives of the natives. Everyone carried charms as "saphies" to ward off evil. Sheep's horns were used for portable sheaths or cases for keeping and protecting such charms or amulets. At one stop, Park was asked to give the chief a lock of his hair, which was believed to give the possessor all the knowledge of white men. On another occasion, Park provided a saphie to protect his landlord against wicked men by filling a writing board; his host, to be certain of having the full force of the charm, washed the writing from the board into a calabash with a little water and, after saying a few prayers, drank it down.

As Park advanced into Islamic Africa, his problems multiplied. When he reached the town of Jarra in the Moorish Kingdom of Ludamar, the Moors hissed, shouted, and even spat in his face, and when they discovered he was a Christian, decided that his property was "lawful plunder." Worse yet, he was seized by Moorish horsemen and taken to a collection of dirty tents on the edge of the desert, the headquarters of Ali, the Ludamar king. There he was kept prisoner for two and a half months and regularly threatened and humiliated. His fingers and toes were counted by the women to find out whether he was human. Since the Moors had never seen buttons, Park was forced time and again to remove and put on his clothes. His bundles were opened and he was robbed of everything the Moors fancied. A council of chief men was held to determine what should be done with the prisoner. One proposal was to put him to death, another to cut off his right hand, but the plan finally agreed upon was to put out his eyes, which the Moors said resembled those of a cat. The sentence was not to be put into execution, however, until Fatima, the queen, who was away, returned and had her curiosity satisfied by seeing him.

The ladies at Ali's court were full of more intimate curiosity. A group of them came to his tent to find out by actual inspection if Park had been circumcised. "I observed," Park wrote, "that it was not customary in my country to give ocular demonstration in such cases before so many beautiful women, but if all of them would retire, except the young lady to whom I pointed (selecting the youngest and handsomest) I would satisfy her curiosity. The ladies enjoyed the jest and went away laughing heartily."

Eventually, Park escaped from the Moors, but he never got over his detestation for them. In his judgment, "they are a subtle and treacherous race of people; and take every opportunity of cheating and plundering the credulous and unsuspecting Negroes. . . . It is impossible for me to describe the behaviour of a people who study mischief as a science, and exult in the miseries and misfortunes of their fellow-creatures." In Park's view, their "rudeness, ferocity, and fanaticism distinguish the Moors from the rest of mankind." The Moors were rigid Mohammedans, "and possess, with the bigotry and superstition, all the intolerance of their sect." Even their faces repelled Park; he "discovered in the features of most of them, a disposition towards cruelty, and low cunning. From the staring wildness of their eyes, a stranger would immediately set them down as a nation of lunatics."

Park found particularly reprehensible the Moors' treatment of the Negroes: "The treachery and malevolence of their character, are manifested in their plundering excursions against the Negro villages. Oftentimes, without the smallest provocation, and sometimes, under the fairest professions of friendship, they will suddenly seize upon the Negroes' cattle, and even on the inhabitants themselves." The blacks were no match for the aggressive, hard-riding, warlike Moors, and seldom tried to retaliate or thought of resistance. The Negro states bordering on the desert were consequently in a continual state of terror while the Moorish tribes were in their vicinity.

Wars were endemic in the region traversed by Park and he was frequently menaced by active or pending warfare among native tribes. The wars were of two kinds, as Park noted. One resembled European contests: "such wars are openly avowed, and previously declared." In Africa, they were commonly terminated at the end of a single campaign. "A battle is fought; the vanquished seldom think of rallying again; the whole inhabitants become panic struck; and the conquerors have only to bind the slaves, and carry off their plunder and their victims." The chief on the losing side was likely to be executed.

The other species of African warfare was primarily for the purpose of plundering or stealing. It could rise from hereditary feuds and have no immediate cause for hostility. No notice of attack was given, and a chief simply turned his warriors loose for predatory excursions. These plundering expeditions always produced speedy retaliation. Negroes who fell into the hands of their enemies during the tribal wars were kept as slaves by the conqueror or traded away into a distant kingdom to prevent their escape and return.

The matter of slavery was one of the dominant themes in Mungo Park's account. The system was universal. Park estimated that not more than a fourth of the total population was free. Slavery was an ancient institution, which "probably had its origin in the remote ages of antiquity." For two hundred years before Park's time it had been maintained and supported by the slave traffic carried on by European nations. Park observed that there were four principal causes of slavery. The first, war, "is certainly the most general, and most productive source of slavery." A second major cause was famine; freemen became slaves to avoid starvation. During a three-year drought in the countries along the Gambia great numbers of people became slaves in this manner. Large families were often exposed to want and it frequently happened in all parts of Africa that parents would sell their children to purchase provisions for the rest of the family.

A third principal route to slavery was insolvency or bankruptcy. A Negro trader might contract debts in some type of mercantile speculation. If payment was not made within a stated time, his person and his services were forfeited to satisfy the demands of his creditors. The fourth and last avenue toward slavery, though less common than the others, was punishment for certain crimes, specifically murder, adultery, and witchcraft.

When a freeman became a slave, Park found, he generally remained so for life and his children were also reared in servitude.

Would the lot of the Negroes have been improved by the abolition of slavery? On that question Park retained an open mind. "If my sentiments should be required concerning the effect which a discontinuance of that commerce would produce on the manners of the natives," he declared, "I should have no hesitation in observing, that in the present unenlightened state of their minds, my opinion is, the effect would neither be so extensive or beneficial, as many wise and worthy persons fondly expect."

Another aspect of society that intrigued Park's interest was the status of women, both among the Moors and the Negroes. The Moors were permitted up to four wives each, while the Negroes were unrestricted, each man marrying as many wives as he could maintain.

The Moors liked their women inordinately fat. Obese wives proved the affluence of their lord and master. Mungo Park thus described the standards of feminine beauty in Islam:

> The Moors have singular ideas of feminine perfection ... with them corpulence and beauty appear to be terms nearly synonymous. A woman, of even moderate pretensions, must be one who cannot walk without a slave under each arm to support her; and a perfect beauty is a load for a camel ... many of the young girls are compelled, by their mothers, to devour a great quantity of kouskous, and drink a large bowl of camels' milk each morning. ... This singular practice soon covers the young lady with that degree of plumpness, which, in the eyes of a Moor, is perfection itself.

The education of the girls, Park found, was neglected altogether. Women were "regarded as an inferior species of animals; and seem to be brought up for no other purpose, than that of administering to the sensual pleasures of their imperious masters." Persons like Queen Fatima and a few others of high rank spent their time conversing with visitors, performing their devotions, or admiring their charms in a mirror.

Park's comments on the Negro women he met were almost invariably appreciative and complimentary; he stated, for example, "I do not recollect a single instance of hardheartedness towards me in the women. In all my wanderings and wretchedness, I found them uniformly kind and compassionate." The practice of polygamy brought children closer to their mothers than to their fathers, and Park witnessed many instances of maternal care and solicitude in the protection and saving of small children.

In other observations on the manners and customs of the native people of Africa, Park exhibited a fine talent for cultural anthropology. In the kingdom of Kasson, visited by Park early in his travels, the inhabitants, high and low, ate rats, moles, squirrels, snakes, locusts, and so on, although they possessed an abundance of cattle and corn. The usual diet of the Negroes varied in different districts. Breakfast usually consisted of a gruel of meal and water. Lunch was a sort of hasty pudding, with a little shea butter; and supper, the principal repast, seldom eaten before midnight, was almost universally of kouskous (a dish prepared from boiled corn) with a small portion of animal food or shea butter. In Kasson, no woman was allowed to eat an egg, though eggs were freely eaten by the men. Non-Moslem Negroes drank beer and mead, "of each of which they frequently drink to excess." In the interior countries the greatest of all luxuries was salt.

The Mandingoes and the Negroes in general had no method of dividing time, calculating the years by the number of rainy seasons. Great attention was paid by them to phases of the moon, but they had no interest in the stars. Their notions of geography were vague and inaccurate. Surprisingly, Park found a belief in one god and of a future state of reward and punishment universal among them.

The Mandingoes seldom attained old age, fifty-five or sixty being the maximum. Few diseases, however, were found among them. Fevers and dysentery were the most common; also noted were yaws, elephantiasis, and leprosy. Goiters were common in some parts of Bambara, and Park saw a few cases of gonorrhea. The Negroes appeared to him successful in the treatment of fractures and dislocations.

Park gathered considerable information on native arts and manufactures. He found that the Mandingo women were diligent in spinning cotton cloth and then dying the cloth a rich blue color by steeping it in a mixture of indigo leaves and wood ashes. Most highly regarded by the Negroes themselves were the manufacturers of leather and iron. The African blacksmiths generally knew how to smelt gold. In Bambara and Kaarta, the natives made beautiful baskets, hats, and other articles from rushes, both for use and ornament.

For trading purposes, the most valuable products of the area of Africa through which Mungo Park traveled were gold and ivory. Gold was found in some quantity throughout Manding, and when harvests were over men and women went panning for gold in nearby streams. A portion of the gold was used to make ornaments for the women, but a great proportion was spent in buying salt and other merchandise from the Moors. Elephants were numerous in the interior of Africa, Park found. The Negroes made no attempt to tame them, since the animals were less docile than the Asiatic species. Instead, the elephants were hunted and killed for their flesh, their hides for making sandals, and their tusks to sell to Europeans. Park concluded that the "exportable commodities" of the Africans were limited to slaves, gold, and ivory, supplemented to a more limited extent by beeswax and honey, hides, gums, and dyewoods.

Following his escape from Ali, Moorish king of Ludamar, Park experienced a series of incredible hardships and adventures. He was captured a second time by some of Ali's horsemen, to be returned to Ali's camp, and again managed an escape. During the first night of his flight he came near dying of thirst, but was saved when a heavy thunderstorm broke and he was able to suck the moisture from the scanty clothing the Moors had left him. At times he was compelled to go for more than a day or two without food. Swarms of mosquitoes in marshy country made life miserable, and there was constant danger of being eaten alive by prides of lions prowling the countryside. The chieftains of some villages were hospitable in providing overnight shelter and small amounts of food; others turned him away empty-handed. His horse, which had been ridden hard by the Moors, finally had to be abandoned and he proceeded on foot. His servants, Johnson and Demba, had long since been kept as slaves by the Moors. Recurring attacks of fever laid him low on several occasions. He waded or swam across miles of flooded savannah, shaky with fever.

The prime object of Park's mission was achieved on July 20, 1796, ten months after leaving England. He had been traveling with a friendly group of Bambaras, headed east, when he first saw the Niger. One of the natives pointed out to him the water ahead, and Park exclaimed, "I saw with infinite pleasure the great object of my mission—the long-sought-for, majestic Niger, glittering in the morning sun, as broad as the Thames at Westminster [actually twice as wide at that point], and flowing slowly *to the eastward*." Park had hoped to explore the river's course as far as Tombouctou, but the precarious state of his health, added to exhaustion from hunger

Pursuing the Niger

and fatigue, as well as being half naked, penniless, and on foot, forced him to realize that he could not go on. He began the return journey.

"The circumstance of the Niger's flowing towards the east, and its collateral points, did not excite my surprise," Park stated, "for, although I had left Europe in great hesitation on this subject, and rather believed that it ran in the contrary direction, I had made such frequent inquiries during my progress concerning this river, and received from Negroes of different nations such clear and decisive assurances that its general course was *towards the rising sun,* as scarce left any doubt in my mind."

On August 25, crossing steep, rocky ground, Park was surrounded by a gang of armed men who stripped him naked and smashed his compass. They finally left him with a shirt, a pair of trousers, and his hat, noticing that there were papers in the crown of the last and fearing magic. At the next town he was received with kindness, and through intercession by the local chief recovered some of his stolen clothes. On September 16 he arrived at Kamalia and a native trader preparing to send slaves to Gambia allowed Park to accompany him. The rainy season caused a delay of several months, but on April 19, 1797, the group began the long trek. Pisania, from where Park had begun his expedition eighteen months earlier, was reached on June 10. Nobody recognized him at first. He had long been given up for lost like all the explorers who had attempted to penetrate the African jungle before him.

By good fortune, Park's wait in Pisania was brief. Five days after his arrival an American slave ship entered the Gambia and loaded 130 slaves, bound for South Carolina. Park went aboard as ship's surgeon on June 17. The vessel was a leaky one and had to change its course to Antigua, which it reached thirty-five days later. From there, Park took the Chesterfield packet and arrived at Falmouth, England, on December 22, 1797. On landing, he immediately set out for London, having, as he wrote, "been absent from England two years and seven months."

Back in London, Park was cordially received by Sir Joseph Banks and other members of the African Association and was lionized by London hostesses. About a year later he had completed writing the tale of his adventures. *Travels in the Interior Districts of Africa,* published in 1799, is reputed to be the first African travel book issued in English; it was an immediate best seller.

Mungo Park's principal achievements in his 1795–97 expedition were to establish the southern limit of the Sahara and to bring more precise information about the Niger to Europe. He found that the Niger flows eastward, though he was unable to proceed far enough to discover that farther on the river makes a great bend to the south, emptying eventually into the Gulf of Guinea, through several tributaries, forming a wide and marshy delta plain.

Africa continued to fascinate Park. Unwilling to rest on his laurels, his imagination was drawn back again and again to its jungles, deserts, and wide plains. Some eight years after returning to England, Park was selected in 1805 to lead a further exploration of the Niger, under the official auspices of the British government. The party was made up of forty-five Europeans and a native Mandingo guide. The effort was a disaster from beginning to end. The men began dying of fever and dysentery. After four months the Niger was reached and the few survivors set sail on it. Theives had stolen most of their supplies. The rest is conjecture and mystery. According to the testimony of the lone survivor, a slave, after traveling down the Niger a thousand miles, Park and his men came to the Bussa rapids. There the party was ambushed and killed by the natives. Mungo Park was age thirty-five at the time of his presumed death.

9

Rediscovery of America

*Alexander von Humboldt's Personal Narrative
of Travels to the Equinoctial Regions
of the New Continent, 1799—1804*

No scientist of his time, or perhaps any other period, has been so widely acclaimed as Alexander von Humboldt, a naturalist, astronomer, geographer, geologist, botanist, linguist, and artist. "Baron Humboldt," Simón Bolivar once remarked, "did more for the Americas than all the conquistadors," and Charles Darwin called him "the greatest scientific traveler who ever lived." In a sense, America was rediscovered by Humboldt. His publications, numbering thirty huge folio volumes, his influence on America's development from the Panama Canal to the exploitation of guano, his encouragement of South American liberators, and his assistance and inspiration to innumerable explorers who followed him, make Humboldt a unique figure.

A huge area of South America is covered by virgin forest, extending from the Atlantic to the Andes, from Mato Grosso in Brazil to the Caribbean. Much of the immense land mass is jungle, but there are also large regions of open woods and great rivers. Vast expanses are partly or entirely unexplored. Most explorers have relied on river transportation, and avoided the hazardous regions inland. The principal reasons why the forests of Brazil and adjoining countries have not been more fully explored are, first, their impenetrable character, making it necessary for the explorer to cut every foot of his way with a machete; second, millions of acres are flooded during the wet season; and third, warlike tribes of Indians, armed with blowguns and poisoned arrows, have repelled invaders.

Other regions of South America have drawn scientists over the

7

past two centuries, notably the wide plains of southern Brazil, Paraguay, and Uruguay, the grasslands of the Argentine, rugged, windswept Patagonia, and the high plateaus of the Andes.

The first Europeans to explore Latin America were interested in only one thing: gold. Their accounts contain scarcely any mention of the fauna and flora of the regions they explored. The first naturalist of distinction to travel in South America was Alexander von Humboldt. His *Personal Narrative* was the first written account describing the animals and plants of the southern continent.

Humboldt was born in Berlin in 1769. From the beginning, he was attracted to a scientific career and to that end studied foreign languages, biology, astronomy, and geology in Germany's best schools. He became interested in northern and tropical botany, physics, chemistry, engraving and drawing and, later, in comparative anatomy and anthropology. His first scientific expeditions were along the Rhine and in Switzerland, Italy, and various parts of Germany to study the flora and the mountains.

From his early youth, Humboldt dreamed of touring distant and exotic lands. South America was the magnet. In 1799, accompanied by a young botanist, Aimé Bonpland, he went to Madrid and was granted an audience by Carlos IV. The two young scientists were authorized by the king to carry on their research in the Spanish lands overseas. After considerable preparation, Humboldt and Bonpland sailed from Corunna on the frigate *Pizarro* in June of 1799. Various adventures were met with in the course of the voyage: a British blockade had to be run (the Napoleanic wars were in progress); the ship was battered by a gale which threatened to wreck it; on the island of Tenerife, Humboldt climbed its highest peak, 12,500 feet (where for the first time he noticed the effects of elevation on plant distribution, the gradual change from subtropical to temperate flora); and a typhoid epidemic on board claimed the life of a young crew member. Because of the epidemic, the captain changed his course, and instead of landing at Havana, the original destination, made for the port of Cumaná on the Venezuelan coast.

At this point, Humboldt and Bonpland entered upon the outstanding event of their lives—the exploration of the equinoctial regions of the New World, from 1799 to 1804. When the port captain at Cumaná found two scientists on board carrying passports from the king, they were given a royal reception and granted the freedom of the country. Humboldt and Bonpland were in a delirium of excitement. "What magnificent vegetation!" Humboldt wrote, as he and Bonpland began avidly to collect the birds, plants, and insects of the region.

As soon as the rainy season was over Humboldt was ready to go on with his primary mission, to ascend the Rio Orinoco to its source and discover exactly where it connected with the Rio Negro. In November, the two men departed for Caracas. For several months after arrival in Caracas they climbed mountains, measured the air, recorded temperatures, and collected plants.

It was in Caracas that Humboldt's lively interest in matters of race was aroused. Venezuela's total population of 1,000,000 was divided among Indians (about one-eighth of the total), 200,000 Negroes (mostly slaves), mestizos (half-Spanish, half-Indian), and Creoles. As a human geographer (a field which he originated), Humboldt observed three stages of society, based on the country's three geographical zones. The marginal jungle was inhabited by the Indian, a hunter and intermittent agriculturist, living along river banks and in the Orinoco's deltas and plateaus in an anarchial, antisocial society. The flat savannas, or the llanos, were peopled mainly by pure-blooded Spanish living a pastoral life, letting their cattle run loose, families isolated from each other; in fact a decadent society. The third group was engaged in agriculture on land suitable for the purpose. The people here were generally white, sometimes touched by colored blood. This class grew coffee and cacao, exported their crops, employed workers, and carried on commerce—to the contempt of the rigidly class-conscious Creoles. The color of the skin was the supreme test. The Creoles, whose "prerogatives were founded on the distinction they enjoyed in the mother country, Spain," filled the major positions and lorded it over the population in general.

In February 1800, the beginning of the dry season, the two explorers began their arduous trek to the Orinoco, still aiming to "determine just where the connection between the Orinoco and Amazon watershed took place." First they had to cross the llanos of Venezuela, called "the most remarkable plains of the world," a flat, treeless area streaching from the Orinoco deltas to the foothills of

Alexander von Humboldt

the Andes, thinly covered with grass and terrifically hot. At the outset, Humboldt passed plantations of sugar cane, coffee, and cotton; after the llanos began, great herds of cattle were seen grazing. The grass was burned, rivers were dried up, and plants dead; even the "alligators and snakes remain buried in the dried mud until awakened by the first showers."

The fact that only indigo and cotton could be grown on the arid llanos was blamed by the natives on large, reddish, sharp-spined ants, with enormous heads and fierce mandibles. Deep down in the earth these creatures grew fungus gardens, fertilized with cut leaves. The area in which the umbrella ants flourished was almost destitute of plant life.

Among the first of the natural wonders to astonish the travelers was the "cow tree" which produced a thick, creamy liquid like milk, agreeable to the taste. Leaves of the *Palo de vaca* were collected and pressed, and the tree described and drawn by Humboldt and Bonpland.

Even more amazing were the electric eels in the Calabozo area, about halfway between Caracas and the Orinoco. These creatures grew to be five feet in length and emitted shocks of electrical current powerful enough to kill men and horses. When a stream inhabited by the eels was reached, the natives drove horses into it. The eels, like angry, venemous water snakes, swam against the animals and began their electrical shocks. Some horses were drowned and others stumbled out of the water and fell to the ground, their legs too weak for them to stand. Humboldt himself received a violent electrical shock when by chance he stepped on a harpooned eel.

By March 1800, Humboldt and Bonpland finally arrived at the turbulent muddy waters of the Orinoco, which they had reached by way of the Apure River in a pirogue, a large Indian canoe. The Apure, a river draining most of the Venezuelan llanos, is the Orinoco's largest tributary. The travelers had come upon a tropical wonderland. A graphic description of nights in the jungle comes from Humboldt:

> Finding no tree on the riverbank, we stuck our oars in the ground and fastened our hammocks to them. Soon such a racket arose in the surrounding forest that it was impossible to sleep the rest of the night. A wild screaming of creatures terrorized the

woods. There came the monotonous wailing of howling monkeys, the soft whistling of the small sapajous, the rasping growl of the striped night monkey, the staccato howling of the jaguar, of the peccary, sloth, the shrill scream of parrots and other birds. At times the cry of a jaguar came straight out of a tree. At such times the monkeys would sound their complaining whistle as they attempted to escape the strange pursuit.

Hardly less dramatic is Humboldt's account of the jungle at midday:

> How vivid is the impression produced by the calm of nature, at noon, in these burning climates! The beasts of the forest retire to the thickets, the birds hide themselves beneath the foliage of the trees, or in the crevices of the rocks. Yet, amidst this apparent silence, when we lend an attentive ear, we hear a dull vibration, a continual murmur, a hum of insects filling all the lower strata of air. Nothing is better fitted to make man feel the extent and power of organic life. Myriads of insects creep upon the soil, and flutter around the plants parched by the heat of the sun. A confused noise issues from every bush, from the decayed trunks of trees, from the clefts of rocks, and from the ground undermined by lizards and millipedes. These are so many voices proclaiming to us that all nature breathes, and that under a thousand different forms life is diffused throughout the cracked and dusty soil, as well as the bosom of the waters, and in the air that circulates around us.

After paddling up the Apure River to its confluence with the Orinoco, the explorers began their major effort, which was to trace the Orinoco to its source, something never yet done, and to find the connection, via the Rio Negro, between the Orinoco and the Amazon. On the Apure, the Orinoco, the Atabapo, the Negro, and Casiquiare rivers Humboldt and Bonpland traveled an estimated 6,443 miles in seventy-five days in open boats or canoes. The area was one of the wildest, least known places on earth. On the Casiquiare River, the connecting link with the Amazon, for example, the current was so strong that their Indian guides could scarcely make any headway, the humidity was smothering, and torrential rains destroyed most of their provisions. For weeks they lived on rice, bananas, and ants or an occasional fried monkey.

Alexander von Humboldt

As the explorers proceeded, animal life became more common. Great flocks of rose-winged flamingos, black-legged spoonbills, and snow-white egrets filled the sky. Humboldt noted that "animals of different nature succeeded one another. Alligators appeared on the banks, motionless, with their mouths open, while by them and near to them capybaras, the large web-footed rodents that swim like dogs and feed on roots, appeared in bewildering herds, even lying among the alligators, seeming to know that these repulsive creatures do not attack on land. Tapirs broke through the tall grass and slipped down to the river to drink." Bonpland went into the forest to collect palms, orchids, grasses, bamboos, and an endless variety of new plants.

In one region of the Orinoco, the travelers were tortured by tiny insects small enough to pass through a needle's eye, but with a sting like a wasp, drawing blood with every puncture of the skin. The insect plague continued with mosquitoes, flies, gnats, chiggers, and ants.

The most frightening passage on the Orinoco was the Maipures Rapids, a turbulent stretch of water where the boat was tossed about violently. Passing other cataracts, the explorers' canoe was pulled through rapids and their equipment carried on the backs of Indians around the river torrents.

In the port of Encaramada, the explorers met some Carib Indians, whose chief was going up the Orinoco to fish for turtle eggs. At the Uruana mission another tribe was encountered, the Otomaco Indians, who in periods of famine were accustomed to eat a special kind of earth. As described by Humboldt, "this earth is a very fine sticky substance of yellow grayish color, which turns red on roasting." The Otomacos ate up to a pound of the earth, shaped into balls, each day for two months during the wet season, while fishing was impossible.

When Humboldt and Bonpland reached the small mission station of San Fernando de Atabapo, near the confluence of the Orinoco, Atabapo, and Guaviare rivers, they left the Orinoco, went up the Atabapo, crossed the watershed between the Orinoco and Amazon, and then descended the Pimichín to the Rio Negro. Shortly afterward they were on the Casiquiare River connecting the Orinoco and the Amazon. The existence of such a stream had long been a matter for debate and Humboldt had now proven its reality. The Casiquiare is a river of considerable size, navigable throughout, and Humbolt was the first naturalist to travel its entire length. He and Bonpland did not tarry long after their discovery, as they were attacked by swarms of voracious mosquitoes. Still, Humbolt could predict the possible economic importance of the region: "A country nine or ten times larger than Spain, and enriched with the most varied products, is navigable in every direction by the natural canal of the Casiquiare and the bifurcation of the rivers."

By now, Humboldt and Bonpland had been weakened by bad food and exhausting boat travel and decided to return to the coast. The journey back was a fatiguing experience, stretched out in their narrow boat by day and sleeping in hammocks along the banks of the Orinoco at night.

A new crisis arose in Angostura, in southeastern Venezuela, on arrival there. Both Humboldt and Bonpland were stricken by typhoid fever. Humboldt cured himself with a tincture of honey and bitter extract from the angostura tree, but Bonpland's condition became steadily worse until he was near the point of death. They had come into Angostura in mid-June and were forced by Bonpland's slow recovery to remain there until July 10. By September 1, 1800, the travelers were back in Cumaná, their original point of departure. Much of their long journey had been through dangerous and hitherto unexplored jungles.

In the course of their expedition, Humboldt and Bonpland had amassed a great quantity of scientific data and collected 12,000 plant specimens, rock samples, fishes, and reptiles, though Humboldt wrote that "we were barely able to collect a tenth of the specimens met with." They were disappointed to discover that a considerable portion of their plant treasures had been destroyed by extreme humidity and insects before their return to civilization. Aside from other achievements, however, Humboldt had mapped the stream connection between the Orinoco and the Amazon and determined by astronomic observation the location of numerous island stations, mountains, and streams.

Humboldt's explorations exploded an old myth created in the imaginations of map makers, the Lake of Guaiana. According to this fable, there was a great lake in a low valley east of the Casiquiare,

Alexander von Humboldt

out of which many rivers, including the Orinoco, rose. The early geographers placed Manoa Lake here, on the shores of which was the city of Manoa, where lived El Dorado, the Golden Inca. Humboldt found no difficulty in determining that these monstrous lakes, the sources of rivers and storehouses of gold, were nonexistent.

Having missed Cuba on the way to South America because of the typhoid epidemic on board, Humboldt was anxious to visit it now that the first portion of his continental travels was completed. On November 24, 1800, he and Bonpland left the Venezuelan coast and took a small sailing vessel that landed them, after a stormy month's voyage, in Havana. They soon left the capital for the interior and began collecting plants and minerals, describing nature, making cartographic and astronomical studies, and visiting sugar mills and tobacco and cotton plantations. Humboldt was appalled by the condition and treatment of Negro slaves. In a work based on his observations, the *Political Essay on the Island of Cuba,* he noted the effect of Negro slavery on colonial life and how much Cuba's prosperity depended on slavery. He was by nature opposed to human slavery everywhere. It is of interest to note that when Humboldt's *Political Essay* was published in the United States, the section dealing with slavery was omitted. The remainder of the monograph was essentially geographic, treating of such physical aspects of Cuba as land forms, geology, and climate in relation to population, commerce, internal communications, and revenues.

Early in 1801, Humboldt and Bonpland sailed back to South America, reaching Cartagena in March, and from there proceeded by way of the Magdalena River to Honda and later to Bogotá. It appears that Humboldt's chief motivation was to explore an entirely different region of the continent, the high Andes, in order to examine climatic influences and altitudes on plant life and native cultures. He could thus round out and compare knowledge gained from travels in the great river basins. In the Andes, with their wide range of vegetations and climates, the traveler could pass from the humid lowlands to the frozen tops of high mountains. As expressed by Helmut De Terra, Humboldt's chief modern biographer, "the Andes were like a huge ladder leading gradually from floor to floor, each disclosing distinct land forms, climatic conditions, and flora in a state of gradual transformation."

In June, on his way to Lima, Humboldt and three companions set out to climb Chimborazo, at nearly 21,000 feet then considered the highest peak in America, and came within 1,700 feet of the summit, approximately 19,285 feet above sea level, the highest altitude ever reached by man up to that time. Most of the climbing had to be done along a narrow ridge bordered by deep crevasses through mist and snowstorms. Humboldt also ascended another Ecuadorian giant, Cotopaxi, the world's highest active volcano, 19,500 feet in altitude. During the Quito-Lima stage of the journey, crossing the Amazon between Jaén and Cajamarca, Humboldt was the first to determine the magnetic line of the equator.

From Bogotá to Quito the explorers' way was filled with horrible experiences, climbing through the Andes, facing icy cold winds during the day, without adequate shelter at night, lacking food, and following twelve-inch-wide paths across deep abysses. On the Andean trail, 10,000 feet up, the travelers spent Christmas of 1801. They reached Quito in January 1802.

Humbold was deeply impressed in Peru by evidences of the ancient Inca civilization. Splendid highways built by the Incas had been destroyed by the Spanish conquerors in quarrying the pavements. Masterly irrigation works, with terraced fields and aqueducts, had been neglected and were in a state of disrepair. In Lima, Humboldt learned of guano, which had been used by the ancient Peruvians for centuries as fertilizer. The substance was found along the coast and nearby islands, the nesting grounds of innumerable bird colonies. Samples were shipped back to Paris, where analysis showed that guano was richer in nitrogen and phosphate than any other known fertilizer. Some years later, due to widespread publicity, farmers in Europe and America were calling for guano in large quantities and it became Peru's most profitable crop, with thousands of tons shipped annually.

The cinchona tree, source of quinine, was described in detail by Humboldt. This remarkable medicinal plant had been known in Europe since the mid-seventeenth century, and was extensively used by the Incas centuries before under the name of quinquina. Young trees were cut down and stripped of their bark for the manufacture of quinine. Because of the heavy demand Humboldt believed that the quinine trade would soon end: "If the governments in America

Alexander von Humboldt

do not attend to the preservation of the quina, either by prohibiting the felling of the trees or by obliging the territorial magistrates to enforce the cutters to guard them from destruction, the highly esteemed product of the New World will be swept from the country"— a prophecy largely fulfilled a half-century later, when plants sent to India and the East Indies became the chief source of supply.

At the beginning of December 1802, Humboldt and Bonpland sailed from the Peruvian port of Callao to Guayaquil, Ecuador, and Acapulco, Mexico. The voyage gave Humboldt the opportunity to survey the coast and offshore islands. He was interested particularly in measuring the velocity and temperature of the cold current—now known as the Humboldt Current—which flows along the Peruvian coast. Though known for centuries to mariners, Humboldt was the first scientist to study the current and point out how it had influenced the climate and native economies of all the lands of the South American coast.

The travelers reached Acapulco, Mexico's center of Spanish trade with the Orient, on March 23, 1803. Humboldt immediately set up his instruments for more astronomical research and a topographic study of the bay, demonstrating that the Pacific port lay many miles farther west than was shown by existing maps. In April, Humboldt and his party left for Mexico City. A stopover at Taxco, then the source of two-thirds of the world's silver, was made, for Humboldt to visit the mines and to study the extraction and refining of the metal. At another way station, Cuernavaca, the night was spent in the ancient palace of Hernán Cortés.

In Mexico City Humboldt was welcomed by the viceroy, who facilitated his work in every way possible. Humboldt took advantage of his stay to study both natural phenomena and the country's economic, social, and political problems. His findings were later published under the title *Political Essay on the Kingdom of New Spain.* Mountains, ancient archeological ruins, volcanoes, canals, and plantations were visited. With the completion of his studies on geography, economics, population, trade, geological formations, botany, climatalogy, astronomy, and native cultures, Humboldt was ready to move on to the United States.

Humboldt had slight respect for the Spanish clergy in Mexico. The higher church officials were extremely wealthy. The archbishopric had annual revenues from services, landholdings, and business transactions amounting to one-fourth of Mexico's total church income. The country swarmed with priests, monks, and nuns, with three priests for every 200 inhabitants. Humboldt was scathing in his criticism of the Spanish padres' soul-hunting expeditions and cruel treatment of aborigines. Seeing the symbol of the cross carried by missionaries armed with guns and whips was doubtless responsible for Humboldt's disdain for organized religion as practiced in the New World.

After eleven months' exploration of Mexico, Humboldt and Bonpland left for Vera Cruz to take ship to Havana and on to Philadelphia, where they arrived at the end of May, 1804. They were invited to Washington by President Jefferson for a historic meeting. Shortly thereafter the explorers sailed for Europe, with five years of constant study and a journey of nearly 30,000 miles through American territory behind them. Humboldt never returned to the New World.

The magnitude of Humboldt's American achievements is overwhelming. He was interested in everything and his energy was limitless. He sketched, made astronomical and magnetic observations, and collected rocks, minerals, fossils, and Indian artifacts. Detailed notes were made on tides, soils, petroleum, chocolate, rubber, on missionaries, on the physique of the Carib Indians, the anatomy of shellfish, on turtle eggs, howling monkeys, alligators, vampire bats, electric eels, an ugly nocturnal bird called the guacharo, jaguars, on Indian tribes and their strange customs and legends. Humboldt investigated the origin of tropical storms and the effect of geographical environment on the distribution of plants. His magnetic surveys established the law of declining magnetic intensity between the poles. He analyzed the physical properties of ocean waters and the chemical constituents of the atmosphere. His observations on contemporary and ancient South American cultures inspired many later anthropological studies.

Twenty-five years after his return from America, Humboldt undertook an extended tour, subsidized by the czar of Russia, into the interior of Russia and Siberia. His scientific labors during the last several decades of his life were chiefly influenced by the impressions and observations gained from his American travels. At the age of

Alexander von Humboldt

seventy-six he undertook one of his most ambitious works, an encyclopedic account and explanation of the physical universe, called *Cosmos*, the purpose of which, he wrote, was "to recognize unity in diversity, to comprehend all the single aspects as revealed by the discoveries of the last epochs, to judge single phenomena separately without surrendering to their bulk, and to grasp Nature's essence under the cover of outer appearances."

Humboldt died in Berlin on May 6, 1859, at the age of ninety.

In retrospect, Humboldt's work gave a strong impetus to scientific exploration throughout the nineteenth century, inspiring, for example, the voyage of the *Beagle,* with Darwin aboard as the ship's naturalist. Most enduring of Humboldt's contributions to scientific progress is his conception of the unity of science, of nature, and mankind.

10
Spanning a Continent

Meriwether Lewis and William Clark's
History of the Expedition, 1804–1806

At the beginning of the nineteenth century most of the vast country west of the Mississippi River was owned by France. When Great Britain formally recognized the United States as an independent nation, in 1784, the new country's boundary was specified as the Mississippi. Three nations—France, Britain, and Spain—were in deadly rivalry for the immense unsettled territory beyond the great river. Spain, in effect, withdrew from the competition by entering into a secret treaty with France by which she ceded the territory, vaguely known as Louisiana.

Napoleon Bonaparte was, as usual, engaged in war and preparation for war, and badly needed money. Thomas Jefferson, in the White House, immediately recognized an opportunity, and sent a commission to Paris to negotiate purchase of the territory. After prolonged discussion between Talleyrand and the American agents, the French agreed to sell the Louisiana territory to the United States for $15,000,000. Jefferson's enemies in Congress were loudly opposed to the transaction, condemning the expenditure of such a sum to acquire what they called the "Great American Desert." Nevertheless, the Senate promptly ratified the treaty on October 19, 1803.

Under the terms of the Louisiana Purchase, the United States was to obtain the entire area drained by the Mississippi and its tributaries or, as Jefferson phrased it, "the boundaries of interior Louisiana are the high lands enclosing all the waters which run into the Mississippi or Missouri directly or indirectly." No one, not even Jefferson, realized the enormous size of the newly acquired territory. Included were all the lands north of Texas and westward to the crest of the Rocky Mountains, an untraveled wilderness now called Arkansas, Missouri, Iowa, Nebraska, North and South Dakota, nearly all of Oklahoma, Kansas, Wyoming, Montana, most of Minnesota, and part of Colorado.

By 1800, almost a half-million Americans lived west of the Alleghenies, chiefly in Pennsylvania, Ohio, and Kentucky. Beyond lay Indian country, parts of which were sparsely settled, but no white man had ever set foot on a large portion.

For at least twenty years before he became president, Thomas Jefferson had dreamed of an overland expedition to the Pacific. He foresaw that any valid claim to this vast area must be supported by discovery and exploration. Proposals from Jefferson to John Ledyard, Andre Michaux, and George Rogers Clark to carry the American flag across the continent came to nothing, for a variety of reasons. Thus, even before the United States had any legal title to the western region, Jefferson had initiated plans for exploring country that was still almost a blank on the maps. An appropriation of $2,500 was asked for and approved by Congress to finance an expedition to the West Coast. British traders were already penetrating south from Canada and Spanish raiders were moving north from Mexico. There were rumors that the British were about to raise the Union Jack at the mouth of the Columbia River. Obviously, there was need for speedy action if America was to retain its new territory.

Jefferson's message to Congress outlined his purpose:

> The River Missouri and the Indians inhabiting it are not as well known as is rendered desirable by their connection with the Mississippi and, consequently, with us. It is, however, understood, that the country on that river is inhabited by numerous tribes, who furnish great supplies of furs and peltry to the trade of another nation, carried on in a high latitude, through an infinite number of portages and lakes shut up by ice through a long season. The commerce on that line could bear no competition with that of the Missouri, traversing a moderate climate, offering, according to the best accounts, a continued navigation from its source and, possibly with a single portage, from the Western Ocean. . . . An intelligent officer with ten or twelve chosen men, fit for the enterprise, and willing to undertake it, taken from our posts, where they may be spared without inconvenience, might explore the whole line, even to the Western

Ocean, have conferences with the natives on the subject of commercial intercourse; get admission among them for our traders, as others are admitted, agree on convenient deposits for an interchange of articles; and return with the information acquired, in the course of two summers.

To head the expedition, Jefferson selected his private secretary, a fellow Virginian, Meriwether Lewis. Then twenty-nine, Lewis was an experienced soldier and diplomat who brought to his new assignment an impressive knowledge of the frontier and of Indians, a lively mind, great physical stamina, and natural qualities of leadership. In preparation for his formidable adventure, Lewis spent several months in Philadelphia and Lancaster buying scientific instruments and learning how to take latitude and longitude, to use astronomical instruments, and to make maps; obtaining medicines from the famous Dr. Benjamin Rush of Philadelphia; and rounding up equipment from the quartermaster depot.

Jefferson suggested that Lewis select an alternate commander, in case of emergencies, and Lewis nominated a close friend, William Clark, a thirty-four-year-old artillery lieutenant, brother of George Rogers Clark. The choice was ideal. Clark was an experienced cartographer, trained as an army intelligence officer, and skillful with pen and pencil in making sketches of birds, animals, and plants. Furthermore, the personalities of the two men complemented each other perfectly—Lewis was a taciturn introvert, and Clark a red-haired, convivial, friendly extrovert. It is significant that the two leaders remained warm friends throughout the expedition. The authority of the two was equal. As Lewis wrote to Clark, "your situation if joined with me in this mission will in all respects be precisely such as my own." Actually, Lewis ranked as captain, Clark as lieutenant; yet rank or status was of no consequence and for more than two years they worked together without friction.

Jefferson's written instructions, handed to Lewis prior to his departure, were most specific and placed heavy responsibilities on the captains and their men. "The object of your mission," stated Jefferson, "is to explore the Missouri River, and such principal streams of it, as, by its course and communication with the waters of the Pacific Ocean, whether the Columbia, Oregon, Colorado, or any other river, may offer the most direct and practicable water-communication across the continent, for the purposes of commerce."

The president continued with orders to take observations of latitudes and longitudes, beginning at the mouth of the Missouri, at
all "remarkable" points, such as the mouth of tributaries, rapids,
and islands. The explorers were to become acquainted with the
Indian nations, including their names and numbers and the extent
of their possessions; their relations with other tribes or nations; their
languages, traditions, and occupations; their food, clothing, and
living arrangements; their laws, customs, and dispositions; and the
articles of commerce they possessed or desired. In all relations with
the aborigines, they were to be treated in a "friendly and conciliatory
manner," and bloodshed was to be avoided.

As if these charges were not enough completely to occupy the
explorers' time, Jefferson asked his agents to observe "the soil and
face of the country, its growth and vegetable productions, especially
those not of the United States; the animals of the country generally,
and especially those not known in the United States, the mineral
productions of every kind, volcanic appearances; climate, as charac-
terized by the thermometer, by the proportion of rainy, cloudy, and
clear days; by lightning, hail, snow, ice; by the access and recess of
frost; by the winds prevailing at different seasons; the dates at which
particular plants put forth, or lose, their flower or leaf; times of
appearance of particular birds, reptiles, or insects."

Twenty-eight months later, Lewis and Clark had substantially
accomplished the seemingly impossible mission for which Jefferson
had appointed them.

Lewis proceeded by way of Pittsburgh, a principal gateway to the
West, Cincinnati, and Louisville, and the expedition mustered in
Illinois, near the mouth of the Missouri. While Lewis was busy in St.
Louis collecting all available information on the Missouri River
and the Indian nations inhabiting its borders, Clark was enlisting
and drilling men for the westward trek. The winter of 1803–4 was
spent in such preparations. The military members were enrolled in
the army at $10 a month for privates, $15 for three sergeants, and
$80 each for Lewis and Clark. Twenty-nine men were trained in
the rudiments of woodcraft, nine of them recruits from Kentucky;
also in the party were hunters from Virginia, farmers from Vermont,
and carpenters from Pennsylvania. America had already become a
melting pot; included were Irishmen, Scots, Dutch, French, and
Clark's Negro servant, York, destined to become an important figure

among the Crow Indians. To guard against the dangerous Indians of the plains, the captains decided to take an extra corporal and six soldiers, all to be sent back after the Mandan villages were reached. Nine rivermen were added to help row the heavy boats upstream, thus constituting a total company of forty-five men.

Equipment selected for the expedition appeared to provide for every possible contingency. When the party left its river camp on May 14, 1804, to enter the Missouri's mainstream, it traveled on a keelboat and two pirogues (canoe-like boats), standard river transportation. On the keelboat deck was mounted a swivel and a little mill for grinding corn. Under the decks were stowed boxes and barrels of supplies, casks of whiskey, sacks of grain, kegs of powder, bars of lead, flints, spools of rope, a large American flag, wheels and axles to move the boats overland around rapids and waterfalls, and a sectional iron boat to be put together in the mountains (it turned out later that the boat would not float and leaked in all its seams). Dress uniforms, swords, sashes and plumes were packed in lockers. There was also a great quantity of "trade goods" for the Indians: laced coats, ruffled calico skirts, striped silk ribbons, scarlet cloth, gaudy handkerchiefs, medals and beads, small bells, mirrors, tomahawks, knives, rings, brooches, brass kettles, fishhooks, steel traps, burning glasses, and theatrical paint. The iron-framed keelboat, the largest craft that had ever attempted to navigate the Missouri, was fifty-five feet long and equipped with both sails and oars.

Almost immediately, the expedition discovered how treacherous and dangerous the great river, the "Big Muddy," could be. A spring storm stirred up the water. Large trees rolled down the fast current, with bare limbs and ugly roots waving in the air. Mudbanks along the shore undermined by the current, broke off and thundered down into the river with loud explosions. The second day out, "we found that our boat was too heavily laden in the stern, in consequence of which she ran on logs three times to-day. It became necessary to throw the greatest weight on the bow of the boat, a precaution very necessary in ascending both the Missouri and Mississippi rivers, in the beds of which there lie great quantities of concealed timber." Against the main current of the Missouri, oars and poles were useless, and yet the cave-ins along the banks made it highly perilous to approach too near the shore. The swift current frequently turned the boat around, broke the towline, and drove it onto sandbars.

104   Lewis and Clark learned that it would take them all summer to reach their first destination, an extensive Indian settlement called the Mandan villages some 1,500 miles up the Missouri. The country beyond this outpost of civilization, a fur-trading center, was unknown; here the real explorations would begin. Despite navigation problems, the journey up the Missouri was, in many respects, idyllic. There were comfortable camps at night and the party was traversing beautiful country. The two leaders spent the evenings working by firelight on their journals, recording in meticulous detail the events and observations of each day. In one entry, Lewis noted: "In addition to the common deer, which were in great abundance, we saw goats, elk, buffalo, antelope, the black-tailed deer and the large wolves." Fifty-two herds of bison were counted in one day.

Settlers along the river were poor, not far removed from the Indians. The party met only old men, women, and children; all the young men were up the river trading with the Indians for furs and tallow, as much as a thousand miles away and gone for a year at a time.

Throughout the first phase of their travels—the long haul from May 14 to October 24, 1804—the explorers passed through the almost limitless prairies. Farther up the Missouri, few trees except willow and dwarf cottonwood were found. Hardwood ash trees disappeared beyond the Platte River, a misfortune for the boatmen, who needed new poles, oars, masts, or ax helves. For hundreds of miles the Missouri flowed between high bluffs, constantly undermining them, especially in flood seasons, causing huge trees and tracts of land to collapse into the river and be carried downstream.

Gradually the prairies gave way to the great plains. Three months after leaving St. Louis, the voyagers had covered 850 miles and were in the vicinity of what is now Sioux City, Iowa. From here on the going became harder. Sandbars caught the pirogues, one man had a sunstroke, Sergeant Charles Floyd died of colic (the only man lost during the entire expedition), and insects almost drove the men insane. Mosquitoes bit them until they were "covered with blood and swellings," and horseflies, known as "green-heads," tormented both men and horses.

Beyond the Platte, which the party reached on July 21, was Indian country. Most of the Indian tribes encountered were friendly, pleased with the trinkets and drinks of whiskey dealt out to them.

One of the first powwows was held with a group of Oto and Missouri Indians on August 3 at a site which Clark named Council Bluffs, now a thriving Iowa city. Greater apprehensions were felt about the Sioux, farther up the Missouri, the most warlike of the tribes, who claimed a monopoly of the river trade. Placated by presents and doubtless intimidated by the well-armed explorers, the Sioux let them pass, though threatening attacks on several occasions. The Arikara Indians, on the other hand, were too friendly. Their squaws were "handsomer than the Sioux" and "disposed to be amorous." They were so "fond of caressing our men" that they invaded the camp to "persist in their civilities." The big black man York particularly attracted them.

By October, signs of winter were coming fast in the high plains country. The Mandan villages, terminus of the boat trade from St. Louis, were reached on October 26 in cold and snow. The men set to work at once to build winter quarters. Constructed a short distance above the present city of Bismarck, North Dakota, Fort Mandan, as it was called, was triangular shaped, the buildings consisting of wooden huts which joined and formed two sides, while the third side was made of pickets. Six months were spent waiting for the ice in the river to break up. The men were kept busy finding enough food and providing shelter warm enough to keep out the frigid winds (Clark recorded the temperature at forty degrees below zero on January 10). Game was scarce, but hunting parties brought in sufficient meat to keep the fort well supplied. The carefully fortified camp was guarded night and day, so that, despite threats from the Sioux, the company was never attacked.

The boredom of a long winter for Lewis, Clark, and their men was relieved by the easy virtue of the Mandan women—as a consequence of which a number of the party had to be treated for venereal diseases. Health problems occurred throughout the course of the expedition, in fact, including snakebite, sunstroke, frostbite, appendicitis, dysentery, constipation, skin infections—boils, tumors, and abscesses—and gunshot wounds. For treatment, Lewis, who served as a doctor, prescribed pills, poultices, bloodletting, and other remedies learned from Dr. Rush, and also drew upon a wide knowledge of herbs acquired from his mother, a well-known Virginia herb doctor. Mercury ointment was considered a specific for venereal disease, though it could hardly have done more than to relieve the symptoms. In any event, the men generally recovered from their various ailments despite the treatments.

Two misfortunes struck the Indians camped near the post during the winter. A late autumnal fire swept the prairies. Hundreds of men, women, and children were widely scattered across the grasslands, hunting buffalo, roots, and berries. Eventually all were accounted for except one man and one woman, who had burned to death. A trader's half-breed son was saved by lying flat on the ground under a green buffalo hide. On another occasion, one Mandan was killed and two wounded during an attack by the Sioux.

A fortunate occurrence for the expedition, while it was camped at Fort Mandan, was the appearance of Sacajawea, wife of Toussaint Charbonneau, one of the half-breed French interpreters, whom the captains "hope may be useful as an interpreter among the Snake Indians." Sacajawea, the Bird-woman, a member of the Snake or Shoshone tribe, had been captured in her childhood from her people in the mountains by the Minnetarees and sold as a slave to Charbonneau. Now nineteen years of age, slender, with long braids of dark hair, Sacajawea was carrying a young papoose on her back as the expedition resumed its travels. Her presence proved to be the difference between disaster and success for Lewis and Clark.

In February, work was begun on small boats for the ascent of the Missouri. Early in April 1805, Lewis wrote: "The ice in the Missouri has now nearly disappeared. I shall set out on my voyage in the course of a few days. I can see no material obstruction to our progress and feel the most perfect confidence that we shall reach the Pacific Ocean this summer. For myself, individually, I enjoy better health than I have since I commenced my voyage. The party are now in fine health and excellent spirits, are attached to the enterprise and anxious to proceed. Not a whisper of discontent or murmur is to be heard among them. With such men I feel every confidence necessary to insure success." Captain Lewis was perhaps overly optimistic, for tremendous hardships and dangers faced the party before its goal was to be attained.

On April 7, when the expeditionary force embarked from Fort Mandan, it numbered thirty-one men, plus Sacajawea and her infant son. The heavy longboat was left behind, and the party with all its baggage was towed in six small canoes and two large pirogues. "At the same time that we took our departure," wrote Lewis, "our barge, manned with seven soldiers, two Frenchmen, and Mr. Gravelines as pilot, sailed for the United States loaded with our presents and dispatches." From here Lewis and Clark were plunging into unknown territory, "a country on which the foot of civilized man has never yet trodden." At the start snow was in the air and the skies were overcast and cold. The voyagers passed the Little Missouri, the Yellowstone, and Musselshell rivers. Animal life was plentiful—bear, buffalo, wolves, deer, elk, antelope, beaver, and prairie hens.

The explorers were now getting into the country of the grizzly bears, *Urus horribilis*. The Indians had been telling them hair-raising tails about their ferocity, but no white man then knew much about the creatures, and Lewis and Clark were skeptical. Several actual encounters with the huge brutes, from which the explorers barely escaped with their lives, soon persuaded them of the truth of the folklore. The bears were almost unkillable with the muzzle-loading rifles of the early nineteenth century, and one was capable of running a quarter of a mile with a bullet in its heart. On one occasion, pursued by a large grizzly, Lewis saved himself only by plunging from a high bank into the nearby river.

Not until May 26 did Lewis record that he saw the Rocky Mountains. The party was nearing the head of "the heretofore conceived boundless Missouri." In mid-June the Great Falls of the Missouri was reached, revealing scenery so inspiring that Lewis "wished for the pencil of Salvator Rosa or the pen of Thompson, that I might be enabled to give to the enlightened world some just idea of this truely magnificent and sublimely grand object, which has from the commencement of time been concealed from the view of civilized man."

Harsh realities accompanied the great panorama. Ticks, mosquitoes, and rattlesnakes made life miserable. River banks caving in suddenly nearly swamped the canoes. High head winds made navigation dangerous. A violent hailstorm bombarded the men, and it required three weeks to portage the boats and equipment around the falls. On July 4, the supply of whiskey ran out.

Finally, on August 12, the Missouri came to an end in a stream so narrow that it could be straddled by one of the men. The explorers' feeling of triumph was subdued, however, by, as Lewis wrote,

Lewis and Clark

"the immense ranges of high mountains still in the west of us with their tops partially covered with snow" remaining to be crossed.

Strangely, despite the abundance of game surrounding them, the men saw no Indians. On several months of travel from Fort Mandan to the foothills of the Rockies, the expedition failed to meet a single human being, though occasional Indian signs were found. At the western edge of Montana, great smokes began to be sighted on the prairies, signals of a Shoshone band, but the Indians remained elusive. These were Sacajawea's people, who evidently feared the invaders and remained out of sight.

Lewis and Clark knew that they must have guides to find a passable route over the mountains. At last Lewis and several picked men proceeded ahead of the main party and a few days later managed to make contact with the wary Indians. After much persuasion, including generous gifts, the Shoshones were induced to return with Lewis to rejoin the rest of his company. In an amazing coincidence, one of the Shoshones was discovered to be Sacajawea's brother. Lewis bartered ornaments, coats, blankets, and knives for thirty-eight horses.

After the departure of the fickle Shoshones, who shortly deserted them, the explorers wandered on through the Bitter Root Range. Snow began to block the passes, provisions ran low, and wild game vanished. Some of the horses had to be killed for meat. By October the company was reduced to a diet of dog, but the last divide had been crossed. Finally open country was reached and the party emerged into the beautiful Clearwater Valley in Idaho. There the Nez Percé Indians befriended them, fed and nursed the exhausted men, and guided them to the Clearwater River to begin the last stage of their journey to the Pacific. Six crude canoes were constructed for the wild passage down the turbulent streams ahead. Entering the Clearwater, they paddled down to the Snake, and in the middle of October reached the mighty Columbia, which surged out of the north and turned westward. At the Shore Narrows on the Columbia, the tremendous stream was compressed between rock precipices only forty-five yards apart, but the expedition shot the narrows with its canoes, to the astonishment of the watching Indians, "notwithstanding the horrid appearance of this agitated gut swelling, boiling and whorling in every direction."

The great day came on November 7, 1805, when the explorers caught their first glimpse of the Pacific Ocean. With another winter at hand, seven huts were erected on the south bank of the Columbia, near present-day Astoria. According to Clark, the men endured "dreadful weather." The winds were violent and rains were constant. Christmas dinner "consisted of poor elk boiled, spoiled fish, and some roots." For the most part the men subsisted on elk, 131 of which were killed. Fish and berries became available with the advent of spring, and blubber was obtained from a stranded whale.

After the dreary fogbound winter in Oregon, during which most of the men were ill from excessive damp and near starvation, the expedition began its long trek homeward. Fort Clatsop was abandoned on March 23, 1806. Then came the weary retracing of the rivers back to the horses, which had been left with a friendly tribe of Indians, for the passage over the mountains. Heavy snows blocked an immediate crossing, described by Lewis as "that icy barrier which separates me from my friends and country." But by June it was safe to proceed. The return trip required only one third as long as was consumed in traveling west. The explorers now had landmarks to guide them and Sacajawea to serve as guide. Near present-day Missoula, Montana, the captains separated, Lewis leading a party to explore the north across the mountains to the Marias River, and Clark riding south with another group to the headwaters of the Yellowstone. Lewis experienced the only serious mishaps. He and one of his men had to kill two Blackfeet Indians to prevent them from stealing their horses and rifles—and then were forced to ride for their lives to escape vengeance. Two weeks later Lewis was shot in the hip by a nearsighted member of his party, who mistook him for an elk; for three weeks thereafter the captain was unable to walk. The last entry in Lewis' journal is August 12, when he was reunited with Clark. Swiftly the party moved downstream and on September 23, 1806, Lewis and Clark were back in St. Louis.

The nation had long since given the explorers up for dead. They had been gone two years and four months and the last communication received from them was a letter forwarded from Fort Mandan. Thomas Jefferson sent his congratulations and cheering crowds greeted them in St. Louis. Their travels through the wilderness had covered 8,000 miles. The *New York Gazette* had gazed into a clouded crystal ball and predicted that the region would never be traveled again, but the more farsighted Jefferson envisioned "a great, free and independent empire on the Columbia River."

Lewis and Clark

110   The Lewis and Clark expedition stands as a major event in American history, solidly establishing the nation's title to the vast Louisiana territory and later to the Oregon country. The explorations revealed a strange and unknown world, full of exciting wonders, and pointed the way to its potentialities for future development. Lewis was an eloquent writer and Clark's maps and drawings of wildlife were invaluable. Many of the animals and birds that they discovered were new to science, among them the Rocky Mountain rat, the mountain goat, the American antelope, two new species of grouse, the Lewis woodpecker, and the Clark nutcracker. Theirs were the first adequate descriptions, too, of the prairie dog, the coyote, and the grizzly bear. Specimens of plants were preserved and the language of some of the Indians was recorded. The success of the expedition was due in large part to the perfect accord between the two leaders. Each had qualities complementing the other's.

No expedition in history was ever more carefully documented than that of Lewis and Clark. A conscientious journal of daily incidents was kept by Captain Lewis or Captain Clark, and sometimes by both. Jefferson had ordered the journals to be kept "with great pains and accuracy and to be entered distinctly and intelligibly." Other men in the company were also encouraged to record events, observations, and impressions, and seven did so, four of whose accounts have survived. None was comparable in literary quality, however, to those of Lewis and Clark. Even the leaders' diaries have a certain misleading quality. As Jeanette Mirsky pointed out in her *The Westward Crossings*: "They drone on and on, occupied with each pinprick of time in the making; there is a repetition, almost tedious quality in the entries; there is a matter-of-factness, a preoccupation with soil and game, with humdrum minutiae, that obscures the continuity and the heroic mission." Yet the cumulative effect on the reader is of firsthand participation in a great journey filled with infinite variety.

The story of the publication of the several journals that came out of the Lewis and Clark expedition is complex and involved. A series of misfortunes delayed publication, climaxed by the mysterious and violent death of Lewis in a wayside inn near Nashville, Tennessee, in 1809. The journals were not issued in complete form until 1904–5, a century after the great events they recorded.

11
Exploring the American Frontier

Henry Schoolcraft's Narrative Journal of
Travels through the Northwestern Regions
of the United States, 1820

In the decade or two following Lewis and Clark's epoch-making expedition to the Pacific coast, the Great Lakes region drew increasing attention from explorers, fur traders, prospective settlers, and government officials. Last in a series of expeditions was one arranged by Lewis Cass, governor of Michigan Territory, and John C. Calhoun, secretary of war, in 1820.

Cass, who had been appointed by President Madison in 1813, was anxious to promote development of the Michigan Territory, comprising the present-day states of Michigan, Wisconsin, and part of Minnesota; that is, all the old Northwest Territory north of Illinois and west of Lake Michigan. As part of an overall plan proposed to and approved by Calhoun, Cass organized a scientific expedition into the Lake Superior-upper Mississippi region. A young geologist and mineralogist, Henry Rowe Schoolcraft, was invited to join the party. This was the beginning of Schoolcraft's subsequent fame as an explorer, Indian agent, and ethnologist.

Schoolcraft was born in 1793 in a small village near Albany, New York. A public school education was supplemented by studies at home, especially in languages. Unable to afford college, he went to work in his father's glass factory in Geneva, New York, and later was similarly employed in New Hampshire and Vermont. When British glassware flooded the market after the War of 1812, the American industry went bankrupt. Schoolcraft had heard by now of the exceptional opportunities offered in the West and in 1817, at the age of twenty-four, he left home for the Mississippi region, hoping that his knowledge of mineralogy would win a place for him. His travels took him into the rich lead-mining area of Missouri, around Potosi, where he spent the winter visiting mining operations.

Schoolcraft kept a detailed record of his observations in Missouri, and following his return to New York published an account entitled *A View of the Lead Mines of Missouri.* The book attracted favorable attention from scientists, and gave Schoolcraft some national reputation as a mineral expert. Several specific recommendations were offered by the author: more efficient use of the nation's lead resources; a number of mechanical improvements, such as steam-driven pumps and modern furnaces; and establishment of a federal agency to supervise the lead mining industry. The report came into the hands of John C. Calhoun, who was concerned about the exploitation of the nation's resources, and he invited Schoolcraft to Washington to present his ideas to President Monroe, Secretary of the Treasury Crawford, and Calhoun himself. It is clear that the meeting led, a year later, to Schoolcraft's appointment as mineralogist with the Cass expedition—a turning point in his career.

As an introduction to his *Narrative Journal of Travels,* a day-by-day chronicle of the Cass party's explorations, Schoolcraft described the efforts of previous travelers in the Great Lakes region. He gave credit to Father Marquette, a Jesuit missionary, for discovering the Mississippi River, in 1673; for exploring the northwestern area of New France (Canada) ; and for founding Mackinac. Five years later LaSalle, starting from Quebec, went up the St. Lawrence River, passed Niagara River and visited the falls; proceeded through lakes Erie, St. Clair, and Huron to Mackinac; and continued his voyage down the Mississippi. A member of LaSalle's party, Father Hennepin, a Franciscan missionary, led an exploring party into the upper Mississippi River in 1680. "The account which Hennepin published of his travels and discoveries," Schoolcraft commented, "served to throw some new light upon the topography, and the Indian tribes of the Canadas; and modern geography is indebted to him for the names which he bestowed upon the falls of St. Anthony and the river St. Francis." A less reliable reporter was Baron Lahontan, who in 1703 published an account of a voyage to North America and, in particular, his six years' residence in Canada as an officer in the French army. While stationed at Fort St. Joseph above Detroit, he traveled farther west in 1688, reaching the upper Mississippi. His report of having discovered a "River Long" is now regarded as fictitious, but his descriptions of New France are excellent and generally accurate.

Less famous explorers mentioned by Schoolcraft were Pierre Charlevoix, who, commissioned by the French government to find a new route from Acadia westward, in 1721 traveled up the St. Lawrence River, through the Great Lakes, and down the Illinois and Mississippi rivers to New Orleans; Alexander Henry, the first English traveler in the region who, beginning in 1760, spent sixteen years as a fur trader, traveling through Canada and the United States, and whose journal *Travels and Adventures in Canada and the Indian Territories* is a valuable record; Jonathan Carver, American explorer of Lake Superior and much of Minnesota in the 1760s, who published his reminscences under the title *Travels in Interior Parts of America*; Samuel Hearne, an English explorer, who explored northwestern America for the Hudson's Bay Company in 1768-70; Alexander Mackenzie, a Scotsman, who explored the northwest and discovered the Mackenzie River in 1789; and Zebulon Pike, who led exploring parties up the Mississippi in 1805-6.

These were the chief sources of information used by Schoolcraft concerning earlier explorations and discoveries in the northwestern regions of the United States. He found that they revealed much about "the interesting history of our Indian tribes, their numbers, manners, customs, trade, religion, condition, and other particulars connected with the regions they inhabit," but "amidst much sound and useful information, there has been mingled no inconsiderable proportion, that is deceptive, hypothetical, or false."

This was a justification for the Cass expedition: to explore the great chain of lakes in the northwest region and the sources of the Mississippi River; to clear up matters "of dispute between geographical writers"; and to learn everything possible about the region's potentialities for trade and agriculture, its indigenous plants, geology, zoology, mineralogy, and so on. Other specific objects of the journey, as listed by Schoolcraft, were to gather facts on the names, numbers, customs, history, condition, manner of subsistence, and dispositions of Indian tribes; to survey the topography of the country for the purpose of preparing an accurate map; to investigate copper and lead mines and gypsum quarries; and to negotiate with the Indians for the purchase of certain tracts of land.

Schoolcraft began his travels from New York City at the end of the severe winter of 1820; the Hudson River had been frozen solid as far north as West Point and, in February, four feet of snow fell in the streets of New York. By early March, however, Schoolcraft was able to leave in the "citizens' post coach" for Albany. The distance of 160 miles between the two cities was covered in forty hours of actual travel, excluding stops at post offices and taverns, an average of four miles per hour.

The journey was continued by coach on March 10 through the Mohawk Valley, where Schoolcraft recalled the history of the Mohawk Indians, the once powerful and warlike tribe who formerly inhabited the area. Together with other members of the Iroquois Confederacy—the Oneidas, the Onondagas, the Cayugas, the Senecas, and the Tuscaroras—they dominated a large region long before the coming of Europeans. After their defeat by General Sullivan's army in 1779, Schoolcraft noted that "a great proportion of the tribes fled to Canada, and of two entire tribes, the Cayugas and the Mohawks, there is not an individual left."

Late in April, Schoolcraft arrived in Buffalo, New York, a town of about 200 houses, and from there paid a visit to Niagara Falls, which he described in detail. He pointed out that several previous observers, such as Lahontan and LaSalle, had vastly overestimated the height of the falls. Instead of their 600 to 800 feet, he guessed that the falls were approximately 150 feet high. (The actual heights are 158 feet on the Canadian and 167 feet on the American side.)

Detroit was the point of rendezvous with Governor Cass and his exploring party. Schoolcraft noted the "picturesque view" in approaching the town. According to his description, "Detroit occupies an eligible situation on the west banks of the strait that connects Lake Erie with Lake St. Clair. The town consists of about two hundred and fifty houses, including public buildings, and has a population of fourteen hundred and fifteen inhabitants, exclusive of the garrison." The public buildings included Catholic and Protestant churches, an academy, a penitentiary, council house, bank, market, government storehouse, military arsenal, and Fort Shelby. The town's elevation, forty feet above the river, "commands the finest views." Schoolcraft expressed "a high expectation of Detroit's future destination and importance," due to its strategic location.

On May 24, 1820, a three-canoe flotilla manned by soldiers, Canadian voyageurs, and Indians, commanded by Governor Cass, got under way. The explorers were prepared to travel into uncharted regions, possibly overrun with Indians more friendly to the British than to Americans. The Indian canoe turned out to be exactly the kind of boat required by the forty men and all their gear, and Schoolcraft devoted several pages to its construction and advantages. He quoted Gouverneur Morris's statement that "its slender and elegant form, its rapid movement, its capacity to bear burdens, and to resist the rage of billows and torrents, excited no small degree of admiration for the skill by which it was constructed." The largest size canoes, commonly used in the northern fur trade, were thirty-five feet long and six feet wide at their widest point, tapering at both ends. Such a canoe could carry 5,400 pounds of skins and 1,000 pounds of provisions, plus the weight of eight men and their bags or knapsacks. This was an aggregate, Schoolcraft estimated, of four tons. Each vessel was paddled by eight men at the rate of four miles per hour in calm water. Every night the canoes were unloaded and, with the baggage, carried ashore. This was the vessel which Europeans, learning from the Indians, used for exploring the great chain of American lakes and with which the Mississippi and other rivers were discovered. It was, in fact, employed by every pioneer in the northwest region from the time of Father Marquette to Alexander Mackenzie and beyond.

Traveling with the Cass expedition, Schoolcraft began his famous studies of Indian culture. Discussing the state of religion among the northern Indians, for example, he observed that they had no religion in any true sense, though they believed in the existence of a great invisible spirit and in "manitoes." Manitoes were good and bad spirits, one for every cave, waterfall, or other prominent geographical feature in nature. Schoolcraft found all the Indians more or less superstitious, believing in miraculous transformations, ghosts, and witchcraft. They had jugglers and prophets who predicted events, interpreted dreams, and performed incantations. In a ceremony called the medicine dance, all sorts of bodily

Henry Schoolcraft

ailments were treated, and sometimes apparently cured. Attempts to introduce Christianity among the Indians met with indifferent success, except for the moderately effective French Catholic missionaries, who worked with the Hurons.

One of the bad habits quickly acquired by the Indians from white men was an addiction to alcohol. Schoolcraft commented that "nothing appeared to give them so much satisfaction as the whiskey they received. We have since observed, that the passion for drinking spirits is as common to the tribes of this region, as it is to the remnants of the Iroquois, inhabiting the western parts of New York. To procure it they will part with anything at their disposal, and if they have no furs or dried venison to exchange, they will sell their silver ornaments, their guns, and even parts of their dress."

As the Cass party continued to travel west, Schoolcraft made frequent references to problems of weather, especially the high winds and storms over the lakes, causing long delays waiting on shore until it was safe to proceed. About two weeks after leaving Detroit, the expedition reached Mackinac Island, a distance of 360 miles as the canoes traveled, following shore indentations.

The island, the center of the northern fur trade, was called by the Indians Michilimackinac, "Great Turtle," for its shape. The United States had held the island since 1796, and it was one of four settlements when the Michigan Territory was created in 1805. Each summer thousands of Indians brought furs to the headquarters of the American Fur Company founded by John Jacob Astor in 1808. The extent of the trade is shown by figures for one year, cited by Schoolcraft: 106,000 beavers; 2,100 bears; 1,500 foxes, 4,000 kit foxes; 4,600 otters; 16,000 muskrats; 32,000 martins; 1,800 minks; 6,000 lynxes; 600 wolverines; 1,650 fishers; 100 raccoons; 3,800 wolves; 70 elks; 1,950 deer; and 500 buffaloes. Whether the fur trade could continue on such a scale, Schoolcraft remarked, was one of "the secrets of a business of which we are ignorant."

During the stopover at Mackinac, Schoolcraft was sent by Governor Cass to visit St. Martin's Islands, about ten miles to the northeast, to investigate gypsum deposits. He reported back that "we found large detached masses of gypsum, of a very fine quality."

Six days were spent by Governor Cass and his men at Mackinac, preparing the expedition for its plunge into the wilderness. They departed from Mackinac in four canoes on June 14, accompanied by an additional force of soldiers. The next day the Straits of St. Mary's was reached. Here was scheduled a great conclave between Cass and hostile Chippewa Indians. The Sault Sainte Marie, between Lake Huron and Lake Superior, presented the expedition with several formidable rapids to navigate, during which canoes were damaged and time out had to be taken for repairs.

In the small village of Sault Sainte Marie, Schoolcraft met the remarkable John Johnston family, who were destined to play a key role in his later life. Johnston, a highly successful fur trader, had settled there shortly after the close of the American Revolution and married the daughter of a Chippewa chief. He outfitted scores of independent fur traders and did a thriving business directly with the Indians along the St. Mary's River and the southern shore of Lake Superior.

When negotiations with the Indians began, Governor Cass's courage and firmness, assisted by Mrs. John Johnston, saved what appeared to be a dangerous situation. A treaty was agreed upon by which land for a military post (Fort Brady, begun in 1822) was ceded to the United States government.

The abundance of fish in the river between the two lakes was commented on by Schoolcraft. The Indians in the area subsisted almost entirely on whitefish, which the natives caught in large quantities, dried in the sun, and stored for the winter. Schoolcraft noted that "the fish are often crowded together in the water in great numbers, and a skillful fisherman, in autumn, will take five hundred in two hours."

The governor's entourage embarked upon Lake Superior on June 18, to be met with "the most enchanting views in every direction," but true to the lake's reputation for treacherous weather, a storm suddenly arose, compelling the canoes to make a quick landing. For five or six hours the rain fell in torrents, accompanied by "frequent peals of the most severe and appalling thunder." As travel resumed, the lake spread out like an inland sea. To the north could be seen the distant highlands bordering the Canadian shore and on the south the mountain chain extending from the head of the St. Mary's River westward. The explorers kept within a mile or less of the shore. At White Fish Point another storm, approaching

Henry Schoolcraft

from the west, drove them to land. After an early morning start on June 20, noteworthy landmarks observed were an extensive marsh, the Grande Marráis, and the Grand Sable, a lofty sand ridge extending nine miles along the shore. The general impression, according to Schoolcraft, was one of bleakness and desolation. Birds of prey, such as bald eagles and falcons, soared overhead and noisy ravens were common.

While encamped on a sand beach near the Grand Sable, a violent storm struck and raged during the night. High waves on the lake drove over the governor's tent, pitched fifty yards from the edge of the water. When the gale subsided, a heavy rain drenched everything in the camp. A few miles farther, when it was possible to continue the voyage, the "Pictured Rocks" were passed, strung for twelve miles along the shore and described by Schoolcraft as "a series of lofty bluffs which present some of the most sublime and commanding views in nature. We were wholly unprepared to encounter the surprising groups of overhanging precipices, towering walls, caverns, water falls, and prostrate ruins, which are here mingled in the most wonderful disorder."

On Grand Island, where the expedition encamped, the men were welcomed by a tribe of Chippewa Indians who showed their skill in dancing, accompanied by "a kind of tambourine, and a hollow gourd, filled with pebbles, while one of the number beat time upon a stick, and all joined in the Indian chant." In Schoolcraft's opinion, the chorus had "an air of melancholy, but certainly nothing can be more monotonous, or farther removed from our ideas of music." The Indians were poor in clothing and provisions, but the explorers "were struck with their manly figures and beautiful proportions." Another tribe of Chippewas was met on the Ontonagon River, a large tributary to Lake Superior on the southern shore. These aborigines had developed an amazing skill in catching sturgeon and subsisted almost entirely on this fish, eaten fresh, dried, or smoked. Still more Chippewas were seen in a village near the mouth of the St. Louis River, among whom was a Negro, employed by a fur company, who had married an Indian squaw. Schoolcraft was surprised to see that the couple's four children were "as black as the father, and have the curled hair and glossy skin of the native African," from which he concluded that color is "independent of the influence of climate."

A prime object of the Cass expedition was to explore for mineral deposits, and Schoolcraft made frequent reference to his discoveries, including finding "one of the largest and most remarkable bodies of native copper upon the globe." The area was, however, almost wholly destitute of game. A large black bear was trapped by the Indians, a rare occurrence and an occasion for celebration. "The Indians hold this animal in the highest estimation," commented Schoolcraft, "not only on account of their great fondness of its flesh, but because there is no part of it which is useless."

In observations on Superior's violent and unpredictable weather, Schoolcraft quoted and agreed with an earlier explorer, Charlevoix: "When a storm is about to rise on Lake Superior, you are advertised of it, two or three days previous. At first, you perceive a gentle murmuring on the surface of the water, which lasts the whole day without increasing in any sensible manner; the day after the lake is covered with pretty large waves, but without breaking all that day, so that you may proceed without fear; but on the third day when you are least thinking of it, the lake becomes all on fire, the ocean in its greatest rage is not more tossed, in which case you must take care to be near shelter, to save yourself." Schoolcraft found the southern coast difficult to navigate, because of the storms, sudden changes in temperature, fogs, and mists.

The endemic war going on between the Chippewa and Sioux Indians was dwelt upon at length by Schoolcraft. The Chippewas, despite being considerably smaller in number, managed to hold their own during the constant hostilities by keeping their war parties small and "relying upon their cunning and dexterity." Disease was almost unknown among the Chippewas, due to their rugged outdoor life. Schoolcraft notes that "like all savages they possess a great fondness for grotesque ornaments of feathers, skins, bones, and claws of animals. They have also an unconquerable passion for silver bands, beads, rings, and all light, showy, and fantastic articles of European manufacture." Their only domestic animals were dogs, which Schoolcraft concludes were in reality tamed wolves. The lot of Indian women, "doomed to drudgery and hardship from infancy," was truly hard. Chastity was not considered a virtue and the temporary interchange of wives was fairly common.

On July 17 the expedition entered the Mississippi by way of one of the tributary rivers. The Mississippi's current was strong and a number of snags and drifts were encountered. One rapid after another had to be passed. Bird life became more usual, including ducks, plovers, robins, brown thrushes, blackbirds, crows, loons, geese, herons, turkey-buzzards, ravens, eagles, kingfishers, pelicans, pigeons, jays, and cormorants. A flying creature which often drove the explorers almost beyond the point of endurance was the mosquito, which attacked them in "voracious hordes." Concerning this ravenous insect, Schoolcraft remarked: "The traveler who is prepared to withstand the savage scalping knife, and the enraged bear, has nothing to oppose to the attacks of an enemy, which is too minute to be dreaded and too numerous to be destroyed."

Other varieties of wildlife were seen by the Cass party as it proceeded down the Mississippi. Several species of the red barking squirrel were common. A landing was made near the Elk River to hunt buffaloes; several herds were spotted and three of the animals killed. On the night of July 29 a pack of wolves was heard. Schoolcraft commented upon the doleful, frightening howl of the wolf, but declared that it was little to be dreaded: "I have never heard of an instance of its making an attack upon man in the wilderness." Another sound which frequently disturbed the nightly rest of the travelers along the Mississippi was the "half-human cry" of the great white owl, which "utters its most hideous cry a few moments before the first glimpse of day light."

Other points on the Mississippi, well known in modern times and described by Schoolcraft, were the Crow River, Falls of St. Anthony, Prairie du Chien, St. Croix River, Minnesota River, Fox River, and Green Bay. Tribes of Sioux, Fox, Winnebago, Potowatomi, Sac, and Kickapoo Indians were met in various areas near the river. Schoolcraft made an effort to understand and interpret Indian psychology, as he observed it:

> Satisfied with present competence, he thinks not of the long, and dreary winter, which shall soon deform his native sky—of the pinching hunger, which shall await his improvidence—of the

precariousness, of the chase—of the rapid diminution of his tribes, before the resistless march of European population—of the evils, they have introduced into it, and of its slow, certain, and total annihilation; but dreaming of the beauty of his native mountains, envies not eastern monarchs their possessions, while all his bliss—all his hopes—and all his ambition, are centered in the unrestrained enjoyment of liberty, and the land of his forefathers.

Wild rice flourished along the valleys of the Fox River. Waterfowl and Indians competed for the harvest. The birds were killed in such numbers that, while the season lasted, the savages did not need to hunt for any other meat. Schoolcraft noted that the region was also highly favorable to fresh water crustaceans, reptiles, otters, minks, and muskrats, though beavers and martin, once numerous, were becoming rare.

On August 29 the explorers reached Chicago, which Schoolcraft described as a "village of ten or twelve dwelling houses, with an aggregate population, of probably sixty souls." A nearby garrison, with stockade, barracks, and other facilities was occupied by 160 men. "The country around Chicago is the most fertile and beautiful that can be imagined," commented Schoolcraft, who foresaw a great agricultural future for the region.

The Cass party broke up after Chicago, some members, including the governor, traveling overland and others by water. Schoolcraft continued on around Lake Michigan to Mackinac, where he landed on September 9. On September 23, the entire group reassembled at Detroit, having traveled some 4,000 miles in 122 days. The expedition's scientists had examined fauna, flora, and minerals, collected specimens, compiled extensive data, had mapped or charted shorelines and river courses, and had recorded the locations of more than one hundred points en route. No lives had been lost and there were no serious injuries. With an eye to future settlement of the land the weather had been tested, the quality of the soil investigated, and the elevation of prairies and river bottoms estimated. Almost limitless quantities of fish from the upper lakes could supplement the nation's food supply, and the land was rich in such minerals as iron, lead, copper, and silver.

Schoolcraft's later career was distinguished. He took part in a

Henry Schoolcraft

number of other important and often dangerous expeditions. In 1832 he discovered Lake Itasca, the true source of the Mississippi, in the heart of the northern forests. In his account of the 1820 explorations, he was obviously already becoming deeply interested in the Indian race. For nineteen years, 1822 to 1841, he served as Indian agent, with headquarters at the frontier posts of Sault Sainte Marie and Mackinac Island. In that capacity, he served the tribes of northern Michigan, Wisconsin, and Minnesota. He visited all the major tribes in his territory and met thousands of Indians.

Fortunately for the science of anthropology, Schoolcraft took advantage of his position to collect information on all features of Indian life and customs. In this undertaking, he was tremendously aided by the John Johnston family; in fact, he married one of the daughters, a quarter-breed Chippewa girl. Schoolcraft recorded in detail his observations on such aspects of Indian culture as ceremonies, religion, superstitions, hunting and fishing techniques, dress, language, village life, lodge stories, and tribal legends.

Following the *Narrative Journals,* issued in Albany by E. and E. Hosford in 1821, many publications flowed from Schoolcraft's prolific pen. He wrote hundreds of articles for popular and scholarly journals and newspapers and more than twenty volumes describing his explorations and Indian observations. One of the well-known authors who drew upon his Indian lore was Henry W. Longfellow, whose long poem *Hiawatha* is based on legends from Schoolcraft's *Algic Researches.* Schoolcraft's most celebrated work on the Indians was his monumental *Historical and Statistical Information Respecting the History, Conditions and Prospects of the Indian Tribes of the United States.* Published by authority of Congress, 1851–57, in six folio volumes, this work is a repository of much valuable material on Indians, especially since the original sources have subsequently vanished.

12
Untamed Indians

Francis Parkman's The Oregon Trail, 1846

Forty-two years after the Lewis and Clark expedition and twenty-six years after Henry Schoolcraft's explorations in the Great Lakes region, two more intrepid young travelers set out on a memorable trek along the western frontier. Francis Parkman and Quincy Adams Shaw, adventurous Bostonians, retraced, in part, the route followed by Lewis and Clark.

During the intervening four decades vast changes had taken place. Where Lewis and Clark had found unexplored wilderness, America's march westward was well advanced when Parkman undertook his "Oregon Trail" trip in the spring and summer of 1846. The old frontier of the Mississippi had disappeared, and a swelling stream of hunters, traders, missionaries, immigrants, and settlers were pushing steadily toward the West Coast. It was a period marked by the annexation of Texas, war with Mexico, the conquest of California and the Spanish Southwest, and the settlement of the Oregon boundary dispute with England.

In 1840, six years before Parkman's travels, it was estimated that there were only 100 Americans in Oregon, including men, women, and children, less than 100 in California, and even fewer in the Southwest. But by 1846 these regions had become part of the United States and their American population had increased more than fortyfold.

Francis Parkman was a descendant of an old New England family, six generations of whom had lived and labored as scholars, merchants, and clergymen in the Boston area. A comfortable fortune bequeathed to him by his grandfather, a wealthy merchant, relieved him of financial worries. From an early date, Parkman had an absorbing interest in history and nature. His vacations were spent in the woods and mountains of northwestern New England and adjacent Canada. While wandering in the wilderness he looked at trees, rocks, and animals with a naturalist's eye, recording his observations in a series of notebooks.

As a student at Harvard, Parkman spent many hours reading American history. Of most vital concern to him was the period of the French and Indian Wars. To further his understanding of the events of that turbulent era, he explored the wild country where the wars had been fought, paddling and portaging along early trails, visiting Indian camps, old ruined forts, overgrown battlefields, and one-time military roads. Historic spots—anything and everything that related to the struggle between France and England in America—were examined carefully and methodically.

Because of illness, Parkman withdrew from Harvard in the autumn of 1843 and sailed for an extended tour of Italy, France, and England. In Italy he lived for a time in a Capuchin monastery, with the object of gaining a better understanding of Roman Catholicism, a force that had played so important a part in the colonization of the New World.

Every activity in which Parkman was engaged was preparation for one prime purpose. "Before the end of my Sophomore year," he wrote, "my various schemes had crystallized into a plan of writing the story of what was then known as the 'Old French War,' that is, the war that ended in the conquest of Canada." By the time the western expedition began, Parkman had enlarged his scheme to cover a history of the American forest and of the American Indian. He believed that the colonial war had decided the fate of a continent and deserved to be fully chronicled.

It was clear to Parkman that such a history as he envisaged, dealing as it must with the forest and the Indians, could only be written by someone well acquainted with both. "Moreover," as Van Wyck Brooks comments, "he knew that he had a chance, the last and only chance, to picture, in the Indians, who were disappearing—at least in their primitive form—authentic American men of the Stone Age, the forebears of civilization." The first essential was to gain an intimate knowledge of the primitive savage, touched as little as possible by white civilization. The foray into the high plains country was seen, by Parkman, as providing him with the opportunity to "familiarize himself with the habits, customs and character of the Red Man in his still approximately savage state." It was in the West alone that firsthand knowledge could be gained. The Indians of the East had become extinct, tamed, or had been transferred to western reservations. On the plains and in the Rockies, the Indians' primeval way of life had been little changed by their limited contact with mountain men and traders.

Parkman claimed to have read "everything that had been written about the Indians." His imagination was stirred particularly by James Fenimore Cooper's romantic tales. But reading was not enough. As Parkman wrote to a friend, "the Indians' character will always remain more or less a mystery to one who does not add practical observations to his studies." True to his belief, he observed at first hand, at one time or another, the Indian tribes, or what remained of them, from Maine to the Rockies.

The great adventure narrated by Parkman in *The Oregon Trail* was undertaken in company with a cousin, Quincy Adams Shaw. Parkman explained his aim in these words: "I wished to satisfy myself with regard to the position of the Indians among the races of men; the vices and virtues that have sprung from their innate character and from their modes of life, their government, their superstitions and their domestic situation. To accomplish my purpose it was necessary to live in the midst of a village, and to make myself an inmate of one of their lodges."

When Parkman began his western safari he was twenty-three, an excellent rider, an indefatigable hiker and mountain climber, a good shot, and a natural outdoors man. For reasons which are not clear, however, his health was precarious and remained so until his death forty-seven years later.

Parkman proceeded by train, stage, flatboat, and steamboat to St. Louis, where Shaw was to meet him. At Paducah, three flatboats full of West Virginia emigrants came on board for the last lap of the voyage down the Ohio and the Mississippi. Later Parkman was critical of emigrant groups met on the trail west, but of these he wrote: "The men of the emigrant party are manly, open, and agreeable in their manners—with none of the contracted, reserved manner that is common in New Englanders. Neither have the women, who are remarkably goodlooking, any of that detestable starched lackadaisical expression common in vulgar Yankee women."

As Lewis and Clark had done earlier, Parkman and Shaw started their expedition at St. Louis, then the metropolis of the West, home of the great American fur trade, and the outfitting center for emigrants bound for Oregon, California, and New Mexico. Here Parkman and Shaw procured their outfits for travel, including a cart, horses and mules, and a variety of presents for Indians. They also employed two French guides who were to remain with them throughout their journey and whose assistance proved invaluable. One was Henry Chatillon, guide and hunter, described by Parkman as "a fine athletic figure, mounted on a hardy gray Wyandot pony. He wore a white blanket-coat, a broad hat of felt, moccasins and trousers of deer-skin, ornamented along the seams with rows of long fringes. His knife was stuck in his belt, his bullet-pouch and powder-horn hung at his side, and his rifle lay before him, resting against the high pommel of his saddle." The second guide, Deslauriers, a French-Canadian muleteer, had "all the characteristics of a true Jean Baptiste. Neither fatigue, exposure, nor hard labor could ever impair his cheerfulness and gayety, or his politeness."

On April 28, Parkman and his party of four men and eight animals boarded the *Radnor* for their voyage up the Missouri River. In the ship's cabin were Santa Fé traders, gamblers, speculators, and adventurers, while the steerage was crowded with Oregon emigrants, "mountain men," Negroes, and a group of Kansas Indians. For days the heavily loaded vessel struggled upward against the Missouri's rapid currents, grating upon snags and hung up on sandbars for two or three hours at a time. The constantly shifting scene along the riger's banks fascinated Parkman—cottonwoods and elms, limestone bluffs, forests, and ragged islands created by the Missouri's ever-changing channel.

The takeoff point for the Oregon and Santa Fé trails was Independence, a few miles east of present-day Kansas City. On May 5, the *Radnor* anchored nearby. Signs of the great western movement were everywhere, including parties of emigrants with their tents and wagons encamped, surrounded by saddles, harness, guns, pistols, telescopes, knives, and other equipment for prairie travel. A thousand or more emigrants were gathered at Westport, waiting to be joined by other parties from Independence. As Parkman saw them, "they were in great confusion, holding meetings, passing resolutions, and drawing up regulations, but unable to unite in their choice of leaders to conduct them across the prairie." Parkman was curious about the emigrants' psychology, and remarked: "Among them are some of the vilest outcasts in the country. I have often perplexed myself to divine the various motives that give rise to this migration; but whatever they may be, whether an insane hope of a better condition in life, or a desire of shaking off restraints of law and society, or mere restlessness, certain it is, that multitudes bitterly repent the journey, and after they have reached the land of promise, are happy enough to escape from it."

Early in May, Parkman and his men embarked on the prairies, "a great green ocean, a great level expanse." This was Indian territory and many of the eastern tribes were settled here by the federal government—Kansas, Shawnee, Delaware, and Wyandot. At the beginning of the long journey to Fort Laramie, the main destination more than 500 miles away, Parkman and Shaw decided to join forces with a British hunting party. The Britishers were impressively outfitted:

> They had a wagon drawn by six mules and crammed with provisions for six months, besides ammunition enough for a regiment, spare rifles and fowling pieces, ropes and harness, personal baggage, and a miscellaneous assortment of articles, which produced infinite embarrassment. They had also decorated their persons with telescopes and portable compasses, and carried English double-barreled rifles of sixteen to the pound caliber, slung to their saddles in dragoon fashion.

Friction between Parkman's group and the British party arose from the beginning because of differences in temperament and personalties, slow progress caused by the Englishmen's heavy wagon, and disputes over the route, until eventually Parkman made up his mind to proceed without them.

Francis Parkman

Near the junction of the St. Joseph route with the old Oregon Trail, Parkman and his men caught up with a train of "great lumbering ox-drawn wagons" and cattle belonging to an emigrant party. "It was easy to see," Parkman noted, "that fear and dissention prevailed among them. The women were divided between regrets for the homes they had left and fear of the deserts and savages before them."

Late one afternoon, in a stretch of gloomy, barren prairie, Parkman and his companions came suddenly upon the great trail of the Pawnee Indians, leading from their villages on the Platte River to their war and hunting grounds to the south. Each summer passed a "motley concourse: thousands of savages, men, women, and children, horses and mules, laden with their weapons and implements, and an innumerable multitude of unruly wolfish dogs, who have not acquired the civilized accomplishment of barking, but howl like their wild cousins of the prairie."

The hazards to which emigrants were constantly exposed were shown by the misfortunes that met one party described by Parkman. They had lost 123 of their best cattle, driven off by wolves; a swarm of Dakota Indian warriors, some 600 in number, had swooped down upon their camp and driven away all their best horses; and one man had been killed by the Pawnees. It was at the peril of their lives that emigrants ventured to pass through the hunting grounds of the fierce savages. The destruction of animals also was frightful. Bands of warriors, bristling with feathers, and hideous with streaks of black and vermilion, armed with lances, bows and arrows, roamed the wide spaces, sheltered at night in lodges made of poles and buffalo skins that could be set up or removed in an hour. The savages were always ready to form marauding parties when there were scalps or plunder in view.

Under the pressure of primitive travel conditions, treasured family possessions had to be discarded by the emigrants. Parkman observed along the trail "the shattered wrecks of ancient claw-footed tables, well waxed and rubbed, or massive bureaus of carved oak. These, some of them no doubt the relics of ancestral prosperity in the colonial time, must have encountered strange vicissitudes. Brought, perhaps, originally from England; then with the declining fortunes of their owners, borne across the Alleghenies to the wilderness of Ohio or Kentucky; then to Illinois or Missouri; and now at last fondly stowed away in the family wagon for the interminable journey to Oregon. But the stern privations of the way are little anticipated. The cherished relic is soon flung out to scorch and crack upon the hot prairie."

On June 14, Parkman had his first close contact with the plains Indians. His party met a Dakota Sioux village on the march. Its chief was Old Snake, a friend of Henry Chatillon, and therefore Parkman began his Indian studies under favorable conditions. He fed the Indians on sweetened tea, buffalo meat, and biscuit and passed the pipe. The squaws put up temporary sunshades and scattered the packs and utensils about, the boys splashed in the river, and the horses were picketed around.

A tribe of Kansas Indians was also described by Parkman in picturesque terms. The chief's "head was shaved and painted red, and from the tufts of hair remaining on the crown dangled several eagle's feathers, and the tails of two or three rattlesnakes. His cheeks, too, were daubed with vermilion; his ears were adorned with green glass pendants; a collar of grizzly bears' claws surrounded his neck, and several large necklaces of wampum hung on his breast." As Parkman talked with the chief, a procession passed by of old squaws mounted on ponies, tall lank young men armed with bows and arrows, "girls whose native ugliness not all the charms of glass beads and scarlet cloth could disguise," and children—all alike "squalid and wretched."

On June 15, the travelers caught a glimpse of Laramie Peak. Difficulties were encountered attempting to ford the swift current of Laramie Creek to reach the fort on the opposite side, and Parkman's party narrowly escaped having their cart, mules and other possessions swept downstream. Finally, a safe crossing was made and they rode up to Fort Laramie, after thirteen hundred miles of arduous travel over a period of two months. They had crossed the states of Missouri, Kansas, and Nebraska, and penetrated well into Wyoming. The course followed by the explorers had taken them northwest to the Big Blue River and then up the Little Blue; turning north, they struck the North Platte, which was followed all the way to Fort Laramie. Subsequently, a circular tour was made through the Medicine Bow Mountains.

Francis Parkman

The exotic atmosphere of Fort Laramie made a strong impression on Parkman, according to his later account:

> Looking back, after the expiration of a year, upon Fort Laramie and its inmates, they seem less like a reality than some fanciful picture of the olden time; so different was the scene from any which this tamer side of the world can present. Tall Indians, enveloped in their white buffalo-robes, were riding across the area or reclining at full length on the low roofs of the buildings which enclosed it. Numerous squaws, gaily bedizened, sat grouped in front of the apartments they occupied; their mongrel offspring, restless and vociferous, rambled in every direction through the fort; and the trappers, traders and *engagés* of the establishment were busy at their labors or their amusements.

Parkman's main objective was achieved when he fell in with a band of Sioux Indians, with whom he lived for some weeks, observing their habits, customs, and ways of thought. He became intimately acquainted with the inhabitants of the lodges and tepees, remained with them in their moving villages, tramped, rode, and hunted buffalo with them; shared their feasts of dog meat; watched the tribes gather for a war of retaliation; and sat around the campfires listening to accounts of the braves' exploits and folklore.

One of the most memorable characters sketched by Parkman is a formidable young brave, Mahto-Tatonka:

> He never arrayed himself in gaudy blanket and glittering necklaces, but left his statue-like form, limbed like an Apollo of bronze, to win its way to favor. His voice was singularly deep and strong, and sounded from his chest like the deep notes of an organ. See him now in his hour of glory when at sunset the whole village empties itself to behold him, for tomorrow their favorite young partisan goes out against the enemy. His headdress is adorned with a crest of the war-eagle's feathers, rising in a waving ridge above his brow and sweeping far behind him. His round white shield hangs at his breast, with feathers radiating from the centre like a star. His quiver is at his back; his tall lance in his hand, the iron point flashing against the declining sun, while the long scalp-locks of his enemies flutter from the shaft. Thus, gorgeous as a champion in panoply, he rides round and round within the great circle of lodges, balancing with a

Untamed Indians

Tribal government and organization were matters of keen interest to Parkman. He noted that the Sioux, with their many sub-tribes, ranged over a vast territory. They were divided into several independent bands, without a central government or common head. Language, customs, and superstitions were the chief bond between them. They did not unite even in their wars, which made easier their conquest by the white race. The bands of the east fought the Ojibwas on the upper lakes, while those of the west made incessant war upon the Snake Indians in the Rocky Mountains. Each band was divided into villages. Sometimes a village was made up principally of the relatives and descendants of one chief, in which case the wandering community had a patriarchal character.

The buffalo supplied the Indians with the necessities of life: habitation, food, clothing, beds, fuel, strings for their bows, glue, thread, cordage, trail ropes for their horses, coverings for their saddles, vessels to hold water, boats to cross streams, and the means of purchasing what they wanted from the traders.

"War is the breath of their nostrils," Parkman wrote of the Indians. "Against most of the neighboring tribes they cherish a rancorous hatred, transmitted from father to son, and inflamed by constant aggression and retaliation."

After his weeks of observation, Parkman concluded that the Sioux Indians were "thorough savages. Neither their manners nor their ideas were in the slightest degree modified by contact with civilization. They knew nothing of the power and real character of the white men. Their religion, superstitions, and prejudices were the same handed down to them from immemorial time. They fought with the weapons their fathers fought with, and wore the same garments of skin. They were living representatives of the 'stone age.'"

The lot of Indian women was hard. Parkman noted that "the squaws of each lazy warrior made him a shelter from the sun, by stretching a few buffalo-robes, or the corner of a lodge-covering upon poles; and here he sat in the shade, with a favorite young squaw, perhaps, at his side, glittering with all imaginable trinkets."

Francis Parkman

The heaviest labors of the camp fell upon the old women, "ugly as Macbeth's witches," who must harness the horses, pitch the lodges, dress the buffalo robes, and bring in meat for the hunters. Occasionally a white trapper would buy a squaw for a wife, available for the established price of one horse. She was no bargain, however, for as Parkman pointed out, "it involves not only the payment of the price, but the burden of feeding and supporting a rapacious horde of the bride's relatives. They gather about him like leeches, and drain him of all he has."

Parkman had a strong desire to accompany and to observe an Indian war party in action. It appeared that he would gain his wish when he found some tribal trouble brewing among the Sioux. A young brave had been treacherously killed by some Snake Indians. The murdered man was the son of an Ogillalah chief called Whirlwind, and all the Dakota or Sioux tribes within a radius of 300 miles were stirred up for a revenge war against the Snakes. After a prolonged wait, the war finally came to nothing but a buffalo hunt, though Parkman did have a chance to see the warriors in his tribe prepare for the conflict. According to his colorful description, "they circled round the area at full gallop, each warrior singing his war-song as he rode. Some of their dresses were superb. They wore crests of feathers, and close tunics of antelope skins, fringed with the scalp-locks of their enemies; many of their shields, too, fluttered with the war-eagle's feathers. All had bows and arrows at their backs; some carried long lances, and a few were armed with guns. The White Shield, their partisan, rode in gorgeous attire at their head, mounted on a black-and-white horse."

Even though Parkman did not have an opportunity to witness an Indian war, he did take part in another type of adventure: a buffalo hunt. Like other early observers before destruction of the great buffalo herds, Parkman was astounded by the immense numbers of the animals. In one instance, he noted that "from the river-bank on the right, away over the swelling prairie on the left, and in front as far as the eye could reach, was one vast host of buffalo. In many parts they were crowded so densely together that in the distance their rounded backs presented a surface of uniform blackness."

Untamed Indians

The slaughter of the buffalo by white and Indian hunters was appalling. Many bulls, in particular, were killed for sport, and left for wolves and carrion-eating birds to devour.

Two methods of hunting buffalo were found by Parkman to be practiced: "running" and "approaching." The chase on horseback, known as "running," was "the more violent and dashing mode of the two," and a skillful, experienced hunter could sometimes kill five or six cows in a single chase, loading his gun again and again as his horse rushed among the herd. The second technique, "approaching," was done on foot, for which the chief requirements, Parkman discovered, were a hunter who "must be cool, collected, and watchful; must understand the buffalo, observe the features of the country and the course of the wind, and be well skilled in using the rifle."

There was no lack of other wildlife in the western country. Along with his study of the ways of the Indian tribes, Parkman included descriptions of animals, reptiles, birds, insects, trees, herbs, and blossoming plants spread over the prairies and forests. Even where desirable game was scarce, "the wolves will entertain the traveler with a concert at night, and skulk around him by day; his horse will step into badger-holes; from every marsh and mud-puddle will arise the bellowing, croaking, and trilling of legions of frogs, infinitely varied in color, shape, and dimensions. A profusion of snakes will glide away under his horse's feet; while the pertinacious humming of unnumbered mosquitoes will banish sleep from his eyelids." Rattlesnakes "as large as a man's arm, and more than four feet long" rattled and hissed at travelers. A host of little prairie dogs barked at them from the mouths of their burrows. Herds of elk were seen along river banks, "their antlers clattering as they walked forward in a dense throng." The wolves were incredibly numerous and hundreds of them howled in concert around the camp sites. From an island in the Platte River, "a horrible discord of low mournful wailings, mingled with ferocious howls arose for several hours after sunset."

Turning eastward, Parkman and Shaw began their long trek home. They traveled towards the Missouri River again, finding plenty of buffalo on the way. The borders of civilized life were reached with worn-out equipment and broken-down horses. The

Francis Parkman

passage to St. Louis on the Missouri took eight days, about a third of which time was spent stuck on sandbars. Parkman and Shaw had been absent for five months. Two weeks after bidding their guides an affectionate farewell in St. Louis they were back home.

Only an indomitable spirit carried Parkman through the ordeal of his travels to the West. The hardships experienced almost wrecked his weak constitution. The glare of the sun and the harsh alkali dust of the plains left him nearly blind; his digestion was ruined by the rough fare supplied by Indians and trappers; he became a lifelong victim of insomnia and was crippled by arthritis.

Because of Parkman's partial blindness after his return home, *The Oregon Trail* had to be dictated. The original version was written with the help of his trail companion, Quincy Adams Shaw, and Sara Barlow Shaw, who read aloud Parkman's journal to him and then recorded the sentences that he dictated. Another cousin, Charles Eliot Norton, proofread the book and made editorial revisions.

The Oregon Trail is a misnomer. The original title was *The California and Oregon Trail.* The closest that Parkman ever got to Fort Hall, in present-day Idaho, where the trail branched off for Oregon, was 500 miles. More accurate was the title used for one early edition, *Sketches of Prairie and Rocky Mountain Life,* which is precisely the subject matter of the book.

Though obviously fascinated by what he saw of actual Indian life on the plains, Parkman was repelled by the Indians' sanitary habits, their unreliability, cruelty, and utter savagery, and their promiscuous sexual behavior. The romantic illusions about the "noble red man" gained from reading Cooper's novels were quickly dispelled. Instead, Parkman concluded that the Indian was a hopelessly barbaric savage. "Ambition, revenge, jealousy, are his ruling passions," he asserted, "a wild love of liberty, an utter intolerance of control, lie at the base of his character." It seemed to Parkman, along with a great majority of white Americans of his time, that the Indians were inherently incapable of being absorbed into the white civilization and were therefore doomed to vanish from the earth. Even while writing *The Oregon Trail,* Parkman foresaw that "a time would come when those Plains would be a grazing country, the buffalo give place to tame cattle, farm houses be scattered along the watercourses, and wolves, bears and Indians be numbered among the things that were."

Parkman was fortunate in choosing the year 1846 for his travels into Nebraska, Colorado, and Wyoming. A few more years and he would have been too late. *The Oregon Trail* is a record of a West that was still wild and an unforgettable picture of the original Americans on their own hunting grounds.

Francis Parkman

13
Origin of Species

Charles Darwin's The Voyage of the Beagle, 1831–1836

When Charles Darwin sailed from England on his five-year voyage as naturalist on H.M.S. *Beagle,* he had no doubt about the literal truth of every word in the Bible. He was a firm believer in the Mosaic account of creation; in addition, he accepted Archbishop James Ussher's dictum that the earth dated from 4004 B.C., and that every species of life had come into existence at the same instant on that date, and had since remained unchanged.

But on the *Beagle*'s long voyage Darwin was to observe many phenomena new to him which he could not reconcile with his accepted beliefs. The great natural laboratories of South America and the Galápagos Islands sowed the seeds of his theory of evolution. Bishop Ussher's date of creation, based on the number of generations since Adam and Eve, was soon rejected. As Paul Sears comments in his biography of Darwin, the young scientist "was about to set a stage . . . for a magnificent reconstruction of the pageant of terrestrial life. It was a great moment in the history of human thought."

As a youth, Darwin showed little promise of becoming a world-famed scientist. He was descended from a family of distinguished scholars and professional men, but even his father expressed grave doubts that he would ever amount to anything. In grammar school, young Charles was bored by the study of dead languages and by the rigid classical curriculum. He was rebuked by the headmaster for wasting time on chemical experiments and in collecting insects and minerals. Following in his father's footsteps, he was sent to the

University of Edinburgh at sixteen to study medicine; after two years, he and his father agreed that the medical profession was not for him. Whereupon he was transferred to Cambridge to train for the ministry. From the point of formal study, Darwin considered his three years at Cambridge wasted. But he did have the good fortune to form close friendships with two influential teachers, John Stevens Henslow, professor of botany, and Adam Sedgwick, professor of geology. With them he spent a great deal of time in field excursions, collecting beetles, and in natural history observations—useful preparation for his future career.

It was through Sedgwick's influence that Darwin received an offer to sail as naturalist on board the naval ship *Beagle,* starting out on an extensive surveying expedition in the southern hemisphere. Darwin was twenty-two. Looking back on this voyage in later years, he rated it "by far the most important event in my life." It determined his whole career. The idea of becoming a clergyman "died a natural death" on the *Beagle.*

During the next five years, from 1831 to 1836, the *Beagle* touched on nearly every continent and every major island as she circled the world. Darwin was called upon to serve as geologist, botanist, zoologist, and general man of science—superb training for his subsequent life of research and writing. Everywhere he went, he made extensive collections of plants and animals, fossil and living, earth-dwelling and marine forms. He investigated, with the eye of a naturalist, the flora and fauna of land and sea—the pampas of Argentina, the dry slopes of the Andes, the salt lakes and deserts of Chile and Australia, the dense forests of Brazil, Tierra del Fuego, and Tahiti, the deforested Cape Verde Islands, geological formations of the South American coast and mountains, active and dead volcanoes on islands and the mainland, coral reefs, fossil mammals of Patagonia, extinct races of man in Peru, and the aborigines of Tierra del Fuego and Patagonia. The great rivers and recently elevated layers of sedimentary rocks, often full of fossils, together with the mountains, lava beds, islands, and coral formations in tropical waters constituted an open book of nature's secrets.

The *Beagle* was one of a small, lightly armed class of ships common in the British Navy at the time, 242 tons and 90 feet in length. The crew of seventy-four included, besides officers and seamen,

A native of Tierra del Fuego, from a nineteenth-century engraving

three natives of Tierra del Fuego, picked up on a previous voyage and now being returned to their homes to spread Christianity and civilization among their primitive tribal members, an experiment that failed. During the long voyage, disease and accidents took their toll. The ship's clerk was drowned and the purser died at sea. A corporal of marines was drowned and buried on Christmas Day, 1833. Three of the crew died of malarial fever contracted near Rio.

En route to the mainland, the *Beagle* made several island stops. On January 16, 1832, she anchored in the Cape Verde Islands. This was the first time that Darwin had seen volcanic islands. He was intrigued with the sea slug and the cuttlefish, or octopus, with its powers of change of color and inky effluent. A month later, the *Beagle* hove to at the cluster of rocky islands known as St. Paul, about 600 miles from the South American coast. Everyone was astonished at the vast number of seafowl which covered the rocks and rose in great circles, almost blacking out the sky. For fishermen, groupers of enormous size were plentiful, but a shoal of sharks appeared and often seized the fish off the lines before they could be pulled in.

Two months after departing from England, the *Beagle* came into port at San Salvador and landed at the beautiful ancient town of Bahía. Darwin recorded his delight in for the first time being able to walk through a tropical Brazilian forest. He writes of "the elegance of the grasses, the novelty of the parasitical plants, the beauty of the flowers, the glossy green of the foliage. . . . A most paradoxical mixture of sound and silence pervades the shady parts of the wood. The noise from the insects is so loud that it may be heard even in a vessel anchored several hundred yards from the shore; yet within the recesses of the forest a universal silence appears to reign. . . . The land is one great wild, untidy, luxuriant hothouse, made by nature for herself." Darwin collected numerous spiders, beetles, and large butterflies.

As she proceeded along the coast, the next stop for the *Beagle* was Rio. There Darwin arranged to join an Irishman named Patrick Lennon who was planning a visit to his coffee plantation 150 miles north of the capital. This gave Darwin further opportunities to observe the wonders of a tropical forest. He was especially impressed by the flowering parasitic plants, conical ant hills twelve feet high,

Charles Darwin

flocks of egrets and cranes, and the deep wounds inflicted on the party's horses by vampire bats gorging themselves at night. In walks around Rio, his olfactory senses were keenly aroused by the strong aroma of the camphor tree, the pepper, cinnamon, and clove. He continued to collect Brazilian insects—butterflies, moths, beetles, spiders, and ants and also bees, wasps, and cockroaches. In a single day, sixty-eight species of beetles were caught.

As the *Beagle* rode out of the Rio harbor on July 5, Darwin noted the busy sea life around them, the hundreds of porpoises, seals, and penguins. The ship arrived at Montevideo on July 26 and began its primary mission: the surveying of the extreme southern and eastern coasts of South America, south of La Plata. Here they would explore the largely unknown lands of Patagonia and Tierra del Fuego. After a brief stop at Buenos Aires, the *Beagle* proceeded on about 400 miles south to the little town of Bahía Blanca. Darwin spent almost six months ashore. He was fascinated by the Argentine pampas, which he found a gold mine of huge fossil bones of enormous, long-extinct animals. He dug them from the clay or pried them loose from riverside cliffs. Bones of the mastodon, the giant armadillo, toxodon, mylodon (an extinct elephant), a giant sloth, megatherian, and macrauchenia, animals gone from the earth for thousands, perhaps millions, of years were excavated. Darwin brought on board the enormous fossil head of a toxodon, a beast as large as a hippopotamus, and the oddly shaped macrauchenia, which had the neck of a camel and the trunk of an elephant. Remembering Noah's Flood, Darwin considered these animals too large to have been carried on the Ark. Wandering in Argentina, he found fossils of a horse millions of years old, but there were no horses existing in North or South America until brought in by Europeans.

As he unearthed extinct monsters, Darwin noted the similarity of the fossils to much smaller living animals. Any lingering belief that he may have had about the immutability of species vanished. Until his time little research had been done in South American paleontology, and the fossilized creatures that Darwin was discovering were virtually unknown to contemporary zoologists. To Darwin the proof seemed positive that different species were constantly changing and developing. Any that failed to adapt themselves to their environment disappeared.

Throughout the five-year voyage on the *Beagle,* Darwin had two crosses to bear. Invariably he became seasick when aboard ship, to the point that he was nearly or completely incapacitated. The second problem was the violent temper of Captain Robert FitzRoy, commander of the *Beagle.* The two men quarreled on a number of occasions about slavery and the literal interpretation of the Bible. Slavery was not completely abolished in Brazil until 1888, and as he observed its workings, Darwin found it an abhorrent institution. FitzRoy, on the other hand, maintained that the slaves were happy and did not wish to be free. Even fiercer arguments flared up over any doubts that Darwin raised about the Bible's complete authenticity, since FitzRoy was fanatical in his orthodoxy. In fact, at the outset the captain had seen the voyage as a great opportunity to substantiate the Bible, especially the Book of Genesis. He anticipated that as a naturalist Darwin would find evidences of the Flood and of the first appearance of all species of creatures on the earth.

When the *Beagle* landed in Tierra del Fuego, Darwin turned his attention to the study of a different kind of animal—man. He marveled that the Fuegian Indians had chosen to live in what he considered "one of the most inhospitable countries within the limits of the globe." How could human beings accept such an existence, or even survive in such a place, with a diet composed mainly of shellfish, seabird eggs, seal meat, and whale blubber? They were little removed from animals. These reflections on Darwin's part matured years later in his *Descent of Man,* which ends with this statement: "The main conclusion . . . namely that man is descended from some lowly organized form, will, I regret to think, be highly distasteful to many. But there can hardly be a doubt that we are descended from barbarians. The astonishment which I felt on first seeing a party of Fuegians on a wild and broken shore will never be forgotten by me, for the reflection at once rushed into my mind— such were our ancestors. These men were absolutely naked and bedaubed with paint, their long hair was tangled, their mouths frothed with excitement, and their expression was wild, startled, and distrustful."

Charles Darwin

One of the ways in which the Fuegians survived was by becoming cannibals. "It is certainly true," wrote Darwin, "that when pressed in winter by hunger, they kill and devour their old women before they kill their dogs; the boy being asked by Mr. Low why they did this, answered, 'Doggie catch otters, old women no.' " Cannibalism was also practiced upon enemies defeated in battle.

There is no question that Tierra del Fuego has an appalling climate, one of the worst in the world. Yet the Fuegians went about practically unclothed in the foulest of weather. Darwin was amazed to see a native woman suckling a newborn child while the sleet fell on her naked body and on the skin of the child.

The rough seas around Tierra del Fuego posed serious hazards for the *Beagle*. She arrived there during the summer and had to battle mountainous waves for a month trying to round the Horn. On one occasion a giant wave engulfed her, carried away one of the boats, and came near capsizing her. Safe anchorage was found at last, but even there glaciers reached down to the sea and frequently broke off to cause tremendous waves. Inland were dense beech forests, and in the distance, through fog and drizzle, could be seen snow-covered mountains more than 7,000 feet in altitude.

From the inhospitable land at the tip of the southern continent, the *Beagle* paid a brief visit to the equally disagreeable Falkland Islands, and then proceeded up the west coast. Darwin noted that "tremendous and astonishing glaciers" stood at the head of almost every arm of the sea for 650 miles northward of Tierra del Fuego. The sound of masses of ice breaking off from them was "like the broadside of a man-of-war." Valparaiso, Chile's chief seaport, was one of the first stops, on July 23, 1834. From here Darwin set out for a geological tour into the lower Andes.

In Chile, at Valdivia, Darwin experienced his first earthquake. At Concepción, farther up the coast, the quake had been especially devastating—"the most awful yet interesting spectacle I ever beheld," Darwin remarked when he reached there. The Andes were crossed from Santiago, Chile, to Mendoza, Argentina. His observations convinced Darwin that the Andes had "been slowly upheaved in mass" by earthquakes, for he saw fossil seashells even at 14,000 feet and petrified coastal trees high on the Argentine side of the mountains. He realized that immense natural forces had been operating in the Andes since time immemorial, and concluded that "nothing, not even the wind that blows, is so unstable as the level of the crust of this earth."

Darwin was highly pleased with his excursions into the high Andes, but he paid a price for the experience. He was infected from the bites of "the great black bug of the pampas," which he called "Benchuca, a species of Reduvius," a loathsome bloodsucker about an inch long. The "attack of the Benchuca," as Darwin decribed it, left him an invalid for the rest of his life; the bug is the principal carrier of Chagas' disease, a lasting, debilitating ailment akin to African sleeping sickness.

Darwin was struck by the aridity of northern Chile. Rain occurred no more often than once in several years. The *Beagle* anchored at Iquique, the most northern town of any size in Chile. Its 1,000 inhabitants had to depend on every necessity, such as water, food, and firewood, being brought by boat. On a trip to the saltpeter works about forty miles away, he saw no life except a vulture that preyed on the carcasses of beasts of burden left to die of fatigue. Otherwise no bird, beast, reptile, or insect was to be seen. The entire landscape was covered with a crust of common salt.

As Darwin and the *Beagle* prepared to leave South America and head west on the Pacific, he meditated on what he had observed and experienced—the dense forests of Brazil, primitive man in Tierra del Fuego, earthquakes and their effects, seashells 14,000 feet high in the Andes, the differences and similarities among birds, beasts, and creeping things, insects, fishes, and plants, and the eons-old fossils. Though still groping for logical explanations, it was evident that the theory of evolution and the origin of species was beginning to take shape in his mind.

Further confirmation came with the *Beagle*'s next stop, the Galápagos, that strange group of volcanic islands and rocks 600 miles west of Ecuador. Of all the regions visited by the *Beagle*, none impressed Darwin as forcibly as the Galápagos.

On these isolated, uninhabited, and rather barren islands he saw giant tortoises, elsewhere found only as fossils; huge lizards long since extinct in other parts of the world; enormous crabs; and sea lions. He was particularly struck by the fact that the birds

Charles Darwin

were similar to those in South America, but not identical. Furthermore, there were variations among the different species of birds from island to island. Marine lizards, numbering in the thousands and several feet in length, turned out to be miniature dragons. A similiar phenomenon was the land iguana, which grew to four feet or more. On one island, Darwin counted twenty-six species of land birds, all unique.

After a month's stay in the Galápagos, the *Beagle* was ready to depart. Back on board, with many specimens of plants, seashells, insects, lizards, and snakes, Darwin had time to think about what he had seen. The strange phenomena of the Galápagos Islands, added to certain facts previously noted in South America, lent further credibility to the concept of evolution. According to Darwin's own account:

> I had been deeply impressed by discovering in the Pampean formation great fossil animals covered with armour like that on the existing armadillos; secondly, by the manner in which closely allied animals replace one another in proceeding southwards over the Continent; and thirdly, by the South American character of most of the productions of the Galápagos archipelago, and more especially by the manner in which they differ slightly on each island of the group; none of the islands appearing to be very ancient in a geological sense.

To Darwin, the important fact was that a majority of the species discovered on Galápagos were unique, found nowhere else. This was true of plants, birds, reptiles, fish, shells, and insects. They resembled South American species, but were different. As Darwin commented, "It was most striking to be surrounded by new birds, new reptiles, new shells, new insects, new plants, and yet by innumerable trifling details of structure, and even by the tones of voice and plumage of the birds to have the temperate plains of Patagonia, or the hot, dry deserts of northern Chile, vividly brought before my eyes." Never again could Darwin accept as credible the teachings of Genesis, that every species had been created whole and had come down through the ages unchanged.

With the majority of her mission accomplished, the *Beagle* headed home by way of Tahiti, New Zealand, and Australia. The

3,200-mile voyage to Tahiti from Galápagos took twenty-six days. En route, the ship passed the Lagoon Islands, curious rings of coral land rising above the water, posing a mystery that was to intrigue Darwin for years to come. He found little to challenge his scientific interests in Tahiti, but here too, while canoeing among the island's coral reefs, he began to question how they were formed. "It is my opinion," he wrote, "that besides the avowed ignorance concerning the tiny architects of each individual species, little yet is known, in spite of the much that has been written, of the structure and origin of the Coral Islands and reefs."

Another twenty-three days of sailing brought the *Beagle* to New Zealand on December 19, 1835, completing the crossing of the Pacific. Darwin was astonished to find that despite its mild climate and fertile soil, New Zealand possessed only one indigenous animal, a small rat, and even that single species was being destroyed by an imported animal, the Norway rat. Similarily, native plants were being crowded out by weeds introduced from abroad. Darwin's comments on the aborigines, the Maori, were derogatory; he judged them distinctly inferior to a related race, the Tahitians. The excessive tattooing of faces and the filthy condition of their homes, bodies, and clothing he found repulsive.

From New Zealand the *Beagle* set all sail, and in fourteen days made Sydney, Australia. The Australian aborigines met by Darwin "appeared far from being such utterly degraded beings as they have usually been represented." In his opinion, however, they had no future, for "wherever the European has trod, death seems to pursue the aboriginal," which brought him to the conclusion that "varieties of man seem to act on each other in the same way as different species of animals."

A biological question puzzling Darwin concerned the curious differences between the animals of Australia and those of the rest of the world. He noted that most of the Australian mammals were marsupials, such as kangaroos. Most extraordinary to him were the egg-laying mammals, such as the duckbill or platypus and spiny anteater; they alone of all mammals lay eggs instead of bearing their young alive.

By now, all the men on the *Beagle* were homesick for England. In the spring of 1836 the ship sailed for home, still several months away. The route was through the Indian Ocean to the Cocos, or Keeling Islands. Marvels of nature to be seen there were numerous: a huge, coconut-eating land crab, a coral-eating fish, dogs which caught fish, clams that were large and powerful enough to grab a man's leg and hold him until he drowned, and rats making their nests at the top of high palm trees.

A brief stop was made on the island of Mauritius, after which two months were spend rounding the Cape of Good Hope. Captain FitzRoy decided that in order to complete his circle of chronological measurements of the world he must return home by way of South America. A few days in Bahía and Pernambuco delayed the voyagers somewhat, but they began the final leg of their world circumnavigation on August 19, were favored by the winds, and six weeks later sailed up the English Channel to end their five-year odyssey.

In retracing and recapituation of Darwin's famous travels, Captain Alan Villiers concludes: "Because young Darwin was on board the *Beagle*, the journey became far more than the hydrographic survey that was its official mission. To some it ranks as one of the epochal voyages of all time, perhaps equal in its impact to the feats of Columbus and Magellan." The voyage on the *Beagle* gave Darwin the germ of his theory of natural selection and a vast amount of firsthand data to support it. It also provided the material for the early books and papers that established his reputation and created an audience for his evolutionary hypothesis.

14
Iberian Vagabond

George Borrow's The Bible in Spain, 1835—1840

George Borrow liked to think of himself as a wanderer. "I have been a rover the greater part of my life," he stated, adding, "indeed, I only remember two periods, and those by no means lengthy, when I was strictly speaking stationary."

Borrow came by his wanderlust quite naturally. His father, Captain Thomas Borrow, joined the Coldstream Guards and took his family along as the regiment was transferred from place to place in the British Isles. The father was an expert boxer, and took pride in the fact that he had fought and nearly beaten "Big Ben" Bryan, British boxing champion. Captain Borrow taught his son that he should read the Bible often and be handy with his fists when the occasion demanded. George's education was unsystematic, and he was far more influenced by being constantly on the move and associating with soldiers than by anything learned in the classroom. He seems to have become fascinated early by gypsies met on the road, and formed an affinity for their wild, free ways and strange language. Doubtless this was one of the factors that stimulated his lifelong interest in, and astonishing aptitude in the learning of, various languages. He early acquired a score of languages, learning Welsh, for example, by reading twice through a Welsh translation of *Paradise Lost*.

Beginning at about age twenty, Borrow spent several years in a solicitor's office and in literary hack work around London. He then took to the open road and wandered through southern Europe, as well as England. Meanwhile, he was exploring all possible channels to obtain an appointment from the British government or other agency for a foreign assignment, offering his linguistic ability as a chief asset. The break came in 1831, when the British Bible Society commissioned him to translate the New Testament into Manchu, the diplomatic language of China. After a year and a half studying the Manchu language in London, Borrow was sent by the Society to St. Petersburg, the Russian capital, to complete the work. He was in residence there for two years, enjoying the opportunity to learn odd dialects and to travel in new lands. His intention was to continue on eastward towards Canton, Peking, or the court of the Grand Lama, but the Russian government rejected his request for a missionary's passport, and he was forced to return to England in 1835.

Borrow's keen desire for further travel adventures was again satisfied by the Bible Society, which next sent him to an area which he had long desired to visit. In the preface to his *The Bible in Spain*, he wrote:

> In the day-dreams of my boyhood, Spain always bore a considerable share, and I took a particular interest in her, without any presentiment that I should, at a future time, be called upon to take a part, however humble, in her strange dramas; which interest, at a very early period, led me to acquire her noble language, and to make myself acquainted with the literature, her history and traditions; so that when I entered Spain for the first time I felt more at home than I should otherwise have done.

Originally the Bible Society planned to send Borrow to Portugal, following his return from Russia. He had previously visited several cities and towns of that nation and used its language with facility. The assignment was to be flexible, however, for it was noted that "our correspondence about Spain is at this moment singularly interesting, and if it continues so, and the way seems to open, Mr. Borrow will cross the frontier and go and enquire what can be done there." The official resolution adopted by the society, authorizing the Borrow mission, reads: "Resolved that Mr. Borrow be requested to proceed forthwith to Lisbon and Oporto for the purpose of visiting the Society's correspondents there and of making further enquiries respecting the means and channels which may offer for promoting the circulation of the Holy Scriptures in Portugal." The society's aim in sending Borrow to Spain and Portugal was clear. He was to spy out the land to determine in what directions it would be most useful to proceed. In particular, he was to direct his attention to schools and was "authorized to be liberal in *giving* New Testaments."

On November 6, 1835, Borrow sailed from the Thames to Lisbon on the *London Merchant*. The voyage was uneventful, except for the tragic death of a sailor who fell overboard, after having predicted his own fate a few minutes earlier.

The conditions confronting Borrow as he undertook his assignment in the Iberian Peninsula is well described in Seton Dearden's biography, *The Gypsy Gentleman*: "Here he was to have no position, few friends, and little more security and amenities than might have been among the tribes of Central Africa ... he would have to consort with thieves, bandits and peasants. In Russia, he had but to produce the Scriptures, in despite of a disapproving government; here he had to dispense them through a nation torn with civil war." Everywhere he would be faced with bigotry and superstition.

The first rude shock came when Borrow's ship anchored in Lisbon. He was irritated by the customs officers, who were excessively slow and insistent upon a minute examination of every article that he possessed. His lodgings, found with difficulty, were "dark, dirty and exceedingly expensive without attendance." Neither was he impressed by the capital city of Lisbon, finding it a "huge ruinous city, still exhibiting in almost every direction the vestiges of that terrible visitation of God, the earthquake, which shattered it some eighty years ago." Borrow's prejudices show through in such comments; basically, he did not like the Portuguese people. At the time of his arrival, Portugal was just ending eight years of civil war. The government of the young Queen Maria II had been trying to rule constitutionally with the aid of Portugal's ancient ally, England. The queen's right to the throne had been contested by her uncle, Dom Miguel, who was finally forced to give up, leaving the country in shambles.

A skeptical view of foreign aid programs was taken by Borrow in commenting on the Portuguese situation. After meeting with discourtesy from various officials, he remarked:

> This is one of the beneficial results of protecting a nation, and squandering blood and treasure in its defence. The English, who have never been at war with Portugal, who have fought for its independence on land and sea, and always with success, who have forced themselves, by a treaty of commerce, to drink its coarse and filthy wines, which no other nation cares to taste, are the most unpopular people who visit Portugal. The French have ravaged the country with fire and sword, and shed the blood of its sons like water; the French buy not its fruits, and loathe its wines, yet there is no bad spirit in Portugal towards the French. The reason of this is no mystery; it is the nature not of the Portuguese only, but of corrupt and unregenerate man, to dislike his benefactors, who, by conferring benefits upon him, mortify in the most generous manner his miserable vanity.

Borrow was discouraged by the general attitude of the Portuguese with whom he talked. He found the people indifferent to religion—most particularly the lower classes, none of whom appeared to have read the Scriptures or to be aware of their contents. Nevertheless, he did not propose to accept defeat easily. Upon inquiry, he was told that the most ignorant and benighted province of Portugal was the Alemtejo, a region of "heaths, broken by knolls and gloomy dingles [small wooded valleys], swamps and forests of stunted pine," infested with bandits. Robberies and horrible murders were common occurrences in the area. Here, Borrow decided, was a proper field for his labors. Accompanied by a servant, he headed for the principal town, Evora, formerly a seat of the dreaded Inquisition, about sixty miles east of Lisbon. After many adventures, including a dangerous crossing of the Tagus, Borrow arrived at his destination. The following days were spent exploring the neighborhood and talking to hundreds of the natives, while distributing quantities of religious tracts, Bibles and Testaments. According to one account, the inn where Borrow was staying "became rapidly transformed into a sort of wild Sunday school." Muleteers, peddlers, gypsies all had tracts thrust into their hands. Even a party of smugglers listened to a reading from the Scriptures and "expressed their approbation of what they had heard."

After remaining at Evora for a week, Borrow returned to Lisbon with his stock of religious literature exhausted and well pleased with the results of his journey. Two weeks over Christmas were spent in Lisbon to become better acquainted with the city, in getting to know the Jewish community there, and making preparations to proceed to Spain. He had concluded that Portugal was not a fertile field for religious propaganda because of the generally irreligious state of the people. Perhaps Spain would be more receptive to his message.

On January 1, 1836, Borrow set out by muleback for Badajoz, one hundred miles south of Lisbon, where he intended to take the stagecoach for Madrid. The route followed again took him into the dangerous and desolate Alemtejo, on a four-day journey "over the most savage and ill-noted track in the whole kingdom," accompanied only by a half-witted guide. One adventure en route came near to ending in tragedy. Borrow overtook a string of carts transporting ammunition to Spain. One of the Portuguese soldiers began to curse all foreigners and Borrow in particular, whom he mistook for a Frenchman. When Borrow laughed at him, two well-aimed bullets sang past his ears. Borrow, recognizing that discretion was the better part of valor, put spurs to his mule, and soon left the soldiers behind. On January 6, after fording the stream separating Portugal and Spain, he entered Badajoz. He had reached Spain, "in the humble hope of being able to cleanse some of the foul stains of Popery from the minds of its children."

Borrow's stay of nearly five years in Spain was vastly complicated by the country's turmoil, far worse even than Portugal's. After being ravished by Napoleon's armies, the nation was now in the throes of civil war. King Ferdinand VII had twice been restored to the throne by foreign aid—mainly English—against the wishes of the people. Despite his pledge to govern constitutionally, the king dissolved the Cortés and became an absolute monarch. The people suffered the king's tyranny for six years and then revolted. Ferdinand again accepted the constitution, but in 1823 a French army occupied Madrid in his support and he promptly reverted to absolutism. In 1830, the king married for the fourth time, and on the birth of a daughter, Isabella, declared her heir-apparent to the throne. His brother Carlos protested against his exclusion from the succession, and when Ferdinand died in 1833 Carlos provoked civil war to support his claim. Isabella II was proclaimed queen and her mother Christina regent. The two factions were soon engaged in bloody strife. Not until 1841 was peace restored. This was the situation when Borrow crossed the Portuguese frontier early in 1836 "to undertake the adventure of Spain."

Immediately after his entry into Spain, Borrow renewed his acquaintance with gypsies. He had already begun a translation of the Gospel of St. Luke into Caló, the language of the Spanish gypsies. This work was printed at Badajoz in 1837. Many gypsies were wandering in the Badajoz area and Borrow, with his knowledge of their language, was quickly accepted as he went among them. Though deeply intrigued by these people and their vagabond way of life, a style with which he was empathetic, Borrow found much to appall him. "The result of my observations," he wrote, "was a firm belief that the Spanish Gitanos are the most vile, degraded and wretched people upon the earth; but the worst of all was the evil expression of their countenances, denoting that they were familiar with every species of crime." Borrow concluded that "the great wickedness of these outcasts may, perhaps, be attributed to their having abandoned their wandering life and become inmates of the towns, where, to the original bad traits of their character, they have superadded the evil and vicious habits of the rabble."

The Gitanos were spread throughout Spain, depending for their livelihood on dealing in horse and mule flesh, fortune-telling, occasional smuggling, and stealing. Borrow spent a fortnight or more among the Badajoz gypsies, for further study of their language, to translate the Lord's Prayer, attend a gypsy wedding, and to collect "Speciments of the Horrid Curses in Use amongst the Spanish Gypsies," a copy of which was transmitted to the Bible Society. His opinion of the race at the end of his stay among them was contained in a letter to the society: "The Gypsy of Spain is a cheat in the marketplace, a brigand and murderer on the highroad, and a drunkard in the wine-shop, and his wife is a harlot and thief on all times and occasions." Nevertheless, Borrow always felt at home in gypsy company, and accepted an invitation from one of the leaders to accompany him part of the way to Madrid.

Early in February Borrow reached Madrid. He found lodging on "a dark, dirty street" which was, however, in the most central part of the city, where four or five principal streets met and which was "the great place of assemblage for the idlers of the capital, poor or rich."

Borrow's main reason for going directly to Madrid was to obtain permission to print the New Testament in the Castilian language for circulation in Spain. The times were not propitious for such a venture in a nation torn with bitterness, barbarism, and civil war. The capital itself did not impress Borrow. In a letter to his mother, he reported that the city was "crammed with people, like a hive with bees. . . . Everything in Madrid is excessively dear to foreigners, for they are made to pay six times more than natives. I manage to get on tolerably well, for I make a point of paying just one quarter of what I am asked." Borrow suffered considerably from the frost and cold. Living conditions were nearly intolerable. "There is more comfort in an English barn," he remarked, "than in one of the Spanish palaces." He never went out at night, for the streets were crowded with rival factions, intent on "cutting and murdering one another."

Later, Borrow seems to have revised his opinion of Madrid and its inhabitants. Indicative is a statement from *The Bible in Spain*: "Within a mud wall scarcely one league and a half in circuit, are contained two hundred thousand human beings, certainly forming the most extraordinary vital mass to be found in the entire world." He had little interest in the upper classes, but he was attracted by Spaniards of the lower orders, whom he regarded as "extraordinary men." Their spirit of proud independence he thought particularly admirable.

When Borrow arrived in Madrid, he was a stranger, friendless, and without letters of introduction to influential persons. His first step, therefore, was to call upon the British ambassador, Sir George Villiers, later the earl of Clarendon, for advice and help. The ambassador received him cordially and time and again over the next several years endeavored to facilitate his mission. A key person in obtaining the permission that Borrow desired for printing a

Spanish version of the New Testament was the premier, Juan Alvarez y Mendizábal, a Christianized Jew. Overcoming many difficulties, Borrow was granted an interview with him, but no progress was made. In fact, there seemed little prospect that any responsible head of state would approve the application of a foreigner to print an unauthorized translation of the Scriptures. To have done so would have aroused bitter opposition from the priesthood. Mendizábal was forced to resign as premier about a month after Borrow's interview with him, and meetings with his successors were no more productive.

Intervention by Ambassador Villiers eventually won the day. The Spanish government ministers agreed to evade the law, rather than try to change it. Borrow was authorized to proceed with the printing, with the recommendation that the government's confidential printer be employed in order to keep the matter secret. That permission was granted at all was a tribute to the influence of the British ambassador on the Spanish Cabinet, and evidence of Borrow's close relations with the ambassador.

With the hard-earned battle over the New Testament printing won, Borrow returned to London, in October, for a month to confer with officers of the Bible Society. The voyage back to Spain, by way of Lisbon and Cádiz on the steamer *Manchester,* nearly ended in shipwreck in stormy seas. But by November 21, Borrow was back in Spain.

After a short stopover in Cádiz, Borrow went on to Seville, where the condition of affairs was truly dreadful. Famine, plunder, and murder prevailed. There was virtually no communication with the capital. Bandits robbed, tortured, and slew in the name of Don Carlos. The peasantry was stripped of all it possessed. Borrow was extremely cautious about taking sides in political disputes; his philosophy in maintaining good relations with all sorts of factions was explained as follows: "I am invariably of the politics of the people at whose table I sit, or beneath whose roof I sleep; at least I never say anything which can lead them to suspect the contrary; by pursuing such system I have more than once escaped a bloody pillow, and having the wine I drank spiced with sublimate"—an expedient but wise policy under the circumstances.

Borrow was anxious to get back to Madrid to complete the printing of the Spanish New Testament. Braving roving bands of banditti, wandering Carlists, and other dangers, he moved on to Carmona, Moncloa, and Córdoba, reaching Madrid in late December. The Bible Society reported to Borrow's mother that "his journey was exceedingly perilous, more perilous that we should have allowed him to take had we sooner known the extent of the danger."

On arrival in Madrid, Borrow proceeded at once to make final the arrangements for producing the Spanish version of the New Testament. The translation used was one which had been made in 1790 from the Latin Vulgate by Padre Felipe Scio, confessor of Ferdinand VII. The notes and commentaries had been removed and the text carefully edited by Borrow and an associate, a Spanish scholar, Don Luis Usoz. Early in April of 1837 the first Testaments ever printed in Madrid came from the press, in an edition of 5,000 copies.

Next to be considered was the question of systematic distribution. After much thought, Borrow came to the conclusion that the only satisfactory method was for him to "ride forth from Madrid into the wildest parts of Spain," where he thought that the Gospel message was most needed and wanted. He proposed to do what he was convinced "no other individual will undertake to do; namely, to scatter the Word upon the mountains, amongst the valleys and the inmost recesses of the worst and most dangerous parts of Spain, where the people are more fierce, fanatic and, in a word, Carlist." The plan was to distribute about 1,200 copies in this manner and to dispose of the remainder of the stock through established book shops. Ambassador Villiers announced his intention to purchase a large number of the Testaments and to send them to the various British consuls in Spain.

In preparation for his forthcoming strenuous travels, Borrow acquired "a black Andalusian stallion of great size and strength, and capable of performing a journey of a hundred leagues in a week's time." He created a sensation by riding the magnificent beast around Madrid "with a Russian skin for a saddle, and without stirrups."

On arriving in Salamanca, his first objective, Borrow inserted an advertisement in the local newspaper and had bills printed for posting in various parts of the town. Similar bills were distributed as he progressed through the villages. The next stops were in Valladolid and León. By this time the antagonism of the Catholic clergy was beginning to build up against him. They threatened dire consequences to any who read or purchased "the accursed books" brought in by Borrow. A further complication was a severe fever which prostrated him for a week while in León.

Undaunted, Borrow went on to a succession of towns and villages, "through the wildest mountains and wildernesses" to Lugo. Because of the perils of the roads, travelers generally attached themselves to the Grand Post, which was always guarded by an escort. As a rule, however, Borrow was too independent, too much in a hurry, and too indifferent to danger to wait for such protection against the robber-infested highways. At Cape Finisterre, he and his guide were arrested as Carlist spies, and would have been shot if he had not been able to convince the local *alcalde* that he was an Englishman, not Don Carlos in disguise.

Months of travel followed, by way of Santiago, Corunna, Ferrol, Oviedo, and Santander. Miraculously, Borrow escaped unharmed though, as he stated, "robberies, murders, and all kinds of atrocity were perpetrated before, behind, and on both sides of us." Back in Madrid after an absence of five months, he decided to concentrate his missionary efforts on the capital city. A book shop was set up, from which his Testaments could be advertised and sold. Also available for sale were copies of the recently printed St. Luke in Romany and Basque. Three thousand copies of an advertisement on yellow, crimson, and blue paper were struck off "with which I almost covered the sides of the streets," and a sandwich board man was hired to walk the streets with a placard.

Clerical opposition was immediate and violent. A furious attack upon the Bible Society was made in a letter addressed to the editors of *El Español*, describing it as "an infernal society." Borrow replied to the assault in a long letter which apparently silenced the critic. At the same time, the spiritual governor of Valencia issued a circular forbidding the purchase or reading of Father Scio's Bible. The crisis came on January 12, 1838, when Borrow received a peremptory order from the civil governor of Madrid to sell no more of his version of the New Testament in Spanish. All efforts to get the prohibition rescinded were futile. Publication of the gypsy St. Luke aroused a fresh campaign againt Borrow, with the result that all copies of both the Basque and Gitano versions were siezed by the authorities.

The next episode in the series of Borrow's trials and tribulations was his arrest and imprisonment on the charge that he was continuing in secret to dispose of the "evil books." On May 1 he was clapped into the main prison of Madrid without charge or explanation. He remained there for twelve days, while the British ambassador's office was bombarding the Spanish officials with protests against "an unjustifiable outrage that had been committed upon a British Subject." Borrow was able to pay for a separate room; otherwise he would have been herded with the common prisoners, who existed in a state of foulness and misery. A typhus epidemic was raging among the prisoners at the time; the disease was contracted by Borrow's faithful Basque servant, Francisco, who died within a few days.

The Spanish official responsible for Borrow's arrest soon perceived his mistake and offered him his freedom. The latter refused to leave the prison, on the advice of Ambassador Villiers, until there was a public apology and the police officer responsible for his arrest was dismissed, conditions which the Spanish prime minister reluctantly accepted.

Borrow was now freed from prison, but his operations in Spain were thoroughly hamstrung. The government banned the publication of all evangelical religious matter; it had seized and confiscated stores of Borrow's books deposited in storehouses in the provinces, and had prohibited sales from his Madrid shop. At this point he decided to make a short, final expedition with his Testaments, during the second half of 1838, going into regions where he was unknown. Two journeys were made, one to villages lying north of the Tagus and the other to Segovia and the villages west of Valladolid. The adventures experienced and the perils encountered were similar to those he had met earlier. At Seville, he was imprisoned for thirty hours on November 24–25 because of a dispute over his passport.

When Borrow returned to Madrid, he found a message from the Bible Society recalling him to England. After eight weeks at home, the society authorized him to return to Spain for the third time, "in order to dispose of the copies of Scriptures remaining on hand in Madrid, and in the other depôts established in various parts of that country."

On December 21, 1838, Borrow left London and traveled to Seville, arriving on January 2. Avoiding Madrid, he proceeded to sell Testaments among the inhabitants of outlying villages. The clergy again brought pressure on the government and an order was sent out to all village heads to seize any Testaments found in their districts. Borrow's final effort was to employ salesmen to sell the books secretly in Madrid, but his own mission in Spain was effectually finished. After his return to London on April 11, 1840, he terminated his relations with the Bible Society, married a wealthy widow, and settled on her estate in Suffolk.

The Bible in Spain, the chronicle of Borrow's years in Spain, was an immediate success. It was published in three volumes in 1842 and made the author famous overnight. Its combination of thrilling adventure and religious zeal appealed to a large audience in England and America. The pages were crowded with assassins, thieves, eccentric guides, romantic gypsies, and dangerous revolutionaries, all of which made exciting reading for the armchair traveler.

Borrow's view of Spain and the Spanish people was ambivalent. The literary critic H. W. Boynton comments that "Spain was not a land of romantic glamor to Borrow. It was a land of gross ignorance and superstition, of duplicity, of kind hearts, of pleasantly various dialects, of engrossing wayside encounters." Elsewhere, Borrow wrote that "the Spaniards are a stupid, ungrateful set of ruffians, and are utterly incapable of appreciating generosity and forbearance." Spain, he added, was "the chosen land of the two fiends—assassination and murder," and the nation's chief passions were avarice and envy.

On the other hand, as Borrow wrote in the preface to *The Bible in Spain,* "in Spain I passed five years, which, if not the most eventful, were, I have no hesitation in saying, the most happy years of my existence." He had "the warmest admiration" for

Spain as a country. Of her people, he observed much that was "lamentable and reprehensible," but also "much that is noble and to be admired." Despite the mistreatment to which he had been subjected, Borrow was convinced that the Spanish were "still, to a certain extent, a high-minded and great people."

15
View from the Forecastle

Richard Henry Dana's Two Years before the Mast, 1840

The most popular marine travel book before the Civil War, and one which has remained high in public demand since, was written by the son of Boston blue bloods, a youth who shipped as a common seaman on a voyage around Cape Horn. One critic, Lawrence Clark Powell, maintains that *"Two Years before the Mast* was the first, and it remains the greatest book of maritime California."

Accounts of sea voyages are a common variety of travel literature from ancient to modern times, from *Sinbad the Sailor* and the *Odyssey* to *Mutiny on the Bounty* and *Kon-Tiki.* Of the two-dozen works treated in the present volume, adventures at sea constitute a good proportion—the chapters on Amerigo Vespucci, Magellan, Captain James Cook, Darwin, Dana, Joshua Slocum, and Thor Heyerdahl—and such adventures are frequently important elements in other narratives. Invariably, however, the story is told from the point of view of the captain or a passenger; seldom, if ever, is it based on the experiences of ordinary seamen, who would normally be incapable of writing literate prose. Thus, Richard Henry Dana's *Two Years before the Mast* is almost unique in the literature of travel.

Dana could hardly be called a common sailor. His descent was from a long line of prominent Bostonians. His father, Richard Henry Dana, Sr., was an editor and author, and he himself was a Harvard undergraduate. Two events interrupted his collegiate career. Near the end of his freshman year, he was "rusticated" for six months, along with many of his classmates, for refusing to inform on a fellow student who had broken the rules. The second break occurred at the beginning of his junior year, when poor health and weak eyesight, brought on by an attack of measles, forced him to drop out of his class. At that point, he decided to go to sea before the mast, hoping that hard work, plain diet, and an open-air life would restore his health. Young Richard enlisted in the crew of the brig *Pilgrim* in 1834 on her voyage from Boston to San Francisco. The ship sailed two weeks after Dana's nineteenth birthday, and he was away from home for more than two years.

Dana's opening paragraph set the stage: "The fourteenth of August was the day fixed upon for the sailing of the brig *Pilgrim*, on her voyage from Boston, round Cape Horn to the western coast of North America. As she was to get under way early in the afternoon, I made my appearance on board at twelve o'clock, in full sea-rig, with my chest, containing an outfit for a two or three years' voyage." Though dressed as a sailor, Dana realized that he was "known as a landsman by every one on board as soon as I hove in sight . . . my complexion and hands were quite enough to distinguish me from the regular salt, who with a sunburnt cheek, wide step, and rolling gait, swings his bronzed and toughened hands athwart-ships, half opened, as though just ready to grasp a rope." Two years at sea changed all that for Dana and converted him into a seasoned tar. From here on, his story was crowded with action, with man against the sea, often with man against man, with arduous labors and perilous situations. The ship's assignment was to peddle merchandise in California and to bring back a heavily loaded cargo of hides for the Boston tanneries.

Dana enjoyed the solitude of night watches and the opportunity they furnished for reflection. "I felt for the first time," he remarked, "the perfect silence of the sea. . . . However much I was affected by the beauty of the sea, the bright stars, and the clouds driven over them, I could not but remember that I was separating myself from all the social and intellectual enjoyments of life."

Captain Thompson lost no time in letting the crew know where it stood. In a short characteristic speech, walking the quarterdeck with a cigar in his mouth and dropping the words out between puffs, he harangued the men: "Now, my men, we have begun

Richard Henry Dana

a long voyage. If we get along well together, we shall have a comfortable time; if we don't we shall have hell afloat. All you have got to do is to obey your orders, and do your duty like men—then you will fare well enough; if you don't, you will fare hard enough—I can tell you. If we pull together, you will find me a clever fellow; if we don't you will find me a bloody rascal. That's all I've got to say."

The first division of Dana's book described the five-month voyage from Boston to Santa Barbara. The routine of life on board a merchant vessel is pictured in minute detail, together with the author's impressions of sea life and skillful characterizations of his shipmates, from the brutal Captain Thompson down to his fellow common sailors and the cook.

Soon after getting under sail, Dana suffered a violent attack of seasickness, laying him low for several days. On the way to recovery, the cook, "a simple-hearted African," advised him: "My lad you are well cleaned out. You must begin on a new tack—pitch all your sweetmeats overboard, and turn to upon good hearty salt beef and ship bread, and I'll promise you, you'll have your ribs well sheathed, and be as hearty as any of 'em, afore you are up to the Horn"—a remedy that proved completely efficacious in Dana's case.

The supreme power of a captain aboard ship was described by Dana: "The captain is lord paramount. He stands no watch, comes and goes when he pleases, is accountable to no one, and must be obeyed in everything, without a question, even from his chief officer. He has the power to turn his officers off duty, and even to break them and make them do duty as sailors in the forecastle." The only officer with comparable power was the chief mate, who was "the prime minister, the official organ, and the active and superintending officer, the first lieutenant, boatswain, sailor-master, and quarter-master."

A bit of excitement was furnished the *Pilgrim* and her crew when the watch reported a small clipper-built brig with a black hull bearing down upon them. Evidently a pirate ship, armed, full of men, and showing no colors, the vessel pursued them for hours. As night came on, the *Pilgrim's* light was removed from the binnacle, steering was done by the stars, perfect silence was maintained, and at daybreak the horizon was clear.

The sighting of sea animals and birds broke the monotony of long days of sailing. Passing between the Falkland Islands and Staten Island, far to the south, the ship was surrounded by shoals of sluggish whales and grampuses, "heaving out those lazy, deep, and long-drawn breathings which gives such an impression of supineness and strength." Dana was also greatly intrigued by the albatross, noting that "one of the finest sights that I have ever seen was an albatross asleep upon the water, during a calm, off Cape Horn, when a heavy sea was running. There being no breeze, the surface of the water was unbroken, but a long, heavy swell was rolling, and we saw the fellow, all white, directly ahead of us, asleep upon the waves, with his head under his wing; now rising on the top of one of the big billows, and then falling slowly until he was lost in the hollow between."

Dana gives a graphic account of the stormy passage around Cape Horn. By then, from a frock-coated, kid-gloved weakling, he had become a sunburned, vigorous, healthy sailor, able to reef or furl a sail as well as any able-bodied seaman. He recalled with pride his first turn at the wheel: "Inexperienced as I was, I made out to steer to the satisfaction of the officer, and neither Stinson [a young Bostonian also on his first voyage] nor I gave up our tricks, all the time that we were off the Cape. This was something to boast of, for it required a good deal of skill and watchfulness to steer a vessel close hauled, in a gale of wind, against a heavy head sea . . . a little carelessness in letting her ship a heavy sea might sweep the decks, or take a mast out of her."

Danger was a constant companion as the sailors scrambled aloft in high seas while gales raged, heavy rains descended, or fog and snow covered the rigging. A slight slip could mean instant death. One such tragic incident was recounted by Dana. A young English sailor, George Ballmer, lost his footing and fell into the sea. Dana offers a poignant comment upon the catastrophe:

Death is at all times solemn, but never so much as at sea. A man dies on shore, his body remains with his friends, and "the mourners go about the streets," but when a man falls overboard at sea and is lost, there is a suddenness in the event, and a difficulty in realizing it, which give to it an air of awful mystery . . . at sea, the man is near you—at your side—you hear his voice, and in an instant he is gone, and nothing but a vacancy shows his loss. Then, too, at sea—to use a homely but expressive phrase—you *miss* a man so much.

The *Pilgrim's* first landfall before reaching California was a visit to Robinson Crusoe's island of San Fernandez, 103 days after leaving Boston. "I shall never forget," Dana wrote, "the peculiar sensation which I experienced on finding myself once more surrounded by land, feeling the night breeze coming from off shore, and hearing the frogs and crickets. The mountains seemed almost to hang over us."

Forty-seven days of sailing still lay ahead of the ship before she would anchor at Santa Barbara, on January 14, 1835. The crew was becoming increasingly irritable and restless after the long voyage. Fresh provisions were gone and the captain had stopped the ration of rice, leaving the men with nothing but salt beef and salt pork throughout the week, except for a small plum pudding on Sunday. When the bread ration was reduced, the crew went in a body to present their grievances to the captain. The captain's response was to clinch his fist, stamp his feet, swear, and order everyone forward, threatening to make the ship a hell on earth for the men.

The *Pilgrim* docked in the beautiful bay of Santa Barbara 150 days from Boston. A major portion of *Two Years before the Mast* deals with the sixteen months that Dana and his shipmates spent along the California coast. Cargo brought from Boston was being sold at retail to the natives while the crew was in process of collecting 40,000 hides for the homeward voyage. The business was dull, dreary, and back-breaking, but Dana avoided tediousness in the narrative through his descriptions of California in the days of the Spanish rancheros and the Mexican hidalgos and of such colorful events as Mexican weddings and dances.

From the headland now known as Dana Point, hides were thrown to the beach below. Here was the routine, as described by Dana:

View from the Forecastle

Down this height we pitched the hides, throwing them as far out into the air as we could; and as they were all large, stiff, and doubled, like the cover of a book, the wind took them, and they swayed and eddied about, plunging and rising in the air, like a kite when it has broken its string. As it was now low tide, there was no danger of their falling into the water; and as fast as they came to ground, the men below picked them up, and, taking them on their heads, walked off with them to the boat. It was really a picturesque sight; the great height, the sailing of the hides, and the continual walking to and fro of the men, who looked like mites on the beach. This was the romance of hide-droghing!

Along with the traffic in hides came trading. Boat loads of men, women, and children were shuttled back and forth between shore and ship to inspect and buy the merchandise with which the ship was loaded. The cargo was designed to meet almost every conceivable demand: spirits of all kinds (sold by the cask), teas, coffee, sugar, spices, raisins, molasses, hardware, crockery, tinware, cutlery, clothing of all kinds, boots and shoes, calicos and cottons, crapes, silks, shawls, scarfs, necklaces, jewelry, combs, furniture, and even Chinese fireworks and English cart-wheels.

Dana had little respect for the West Coast inhabitants, who at the time were, of course, predominantly Mexican and Spanish. He termed laziness "the California disease," and concluded: "The Californians are an idle, thriftless people, and can make nothing for themselves. The country abounds in grapes, yet they buy, at a great price, bad wine made in Boston . . . and buy shoes, as like as not made of their own hides, which have been carried twice around Cape Horn." A Dana editor, Charles Warren Stoddard, was inclined to believe that this judgment was too harsh, pointing out that in Dana's day the California missions were wealthy in flocks, crops, and herds, and the natives possessed ample means to purchase foreign delicacies and other imported goods.

The spectacular nature of the California coast fascinated Dana and many passages in his book give eloquent testimony to his feelings. He foresaw the rise of San Francisco and observed that Monterey was "decidedly the pleasantest and most civilized-looking place in California."

Richard Henry Dana

Other beautiful scenes were not lost on Dana. Partly, no doubt, because he did not want to risk offending the Victorian prudery of the era and in part due to a natural reticence, he omitted material that would have made his book even livelier reading. Native girls were free and easy with their favors along the California coast. A shipmate, B. G. Stinson, wrote to Dana in 1841, asking why he failed to mention "the beautiful Indian lassies, who so often frequented your humble abode in the hide house, and rambled through those splendid groves attached thereto or the happy hours experienced rambling over those romantic hills, and sitting at twilight on those majestic rocks, with a lovely Indian girl resting on your knee."

Soon after the arrival of the *Pilgrim* on the coast there occurred an incident destined to have important repercussions. Captain Thompson was an evil-tempered bully who ruled the ship with a tyrannical hand. Absolutely no back talk from subordinates was tolerated. For apparently no good reason he took a violent dislike to a sailor named Sam, "a large, heavy-moulded fellow from the Middle States." By the captain's order, the mate placed Sam "against the shrouds, with his wrists made fast to them, his jacket off, and his back exposed." The captain then proceeded to administer a merciless flogging with a thick, strong rope. When another sailor, John the Swede, asked the reason for the beating, the captain ordered him put into irons and subjected him to the same treatment.

These violent proceedings made young Dana "feel sick and almost faint, angry and excited as I was. A man—a human being, made in God's likeness—fastened up and flogged like a beast." But to resist, as he knew, was mutiny, and to seize the ship was piracy. So, "disgusted, sick, I turned away," wrote Dana, "and leaned over the rail, and looked down into the water." It was after this shameful and debasing episode that Dana "vowed that, if God should ever give me the means, I would do something to redress the grievances and relieve the sufferings of that class of beings with whom my lot had so long been cast."

While stationed on land for several months during hide-curing operations, Dana had an opportunity to observe the region's wildlife. Coyotes, rabbits, and hares were plentiful and rattlesnakes far too abundant. During the winter months the waters were cov-

View from the Forecastle

ered with wild ducks and geese. Crows, too, abounded and often lighted in great numbers upon the hides, to pick at pieces of dried meat and fat. Bears and wolves were numerous in the upper parts of the coast.

Dana was highly critical of the Spanish government of California. Originally the Jesuit and Franciscan missions had great wealth and power, employing Indians as serfs. Later, laws were passed stripping the missions of all their possessions and confining priests to spiritual duties. According to Dana, the wealth of the country was now "given over to be preyed upon by the harpies of the civil power, who are sent there in the capacity of administradores, to settle up the concerns; and who usually end, in a few years, by making themselves fortunes, and leaving their stewardships worse than they found them."

For months on end, the *Pilgrim*'s crew continued the arduous task of assembling cattle hides for shipment to New England. Then word came through that all the hides collected were to be transferred to a larger ship, the *Alert,* and the *Pilgrim* was to remain two more years in California. Dana had previously obtained permission to return home on the *Alert,* and despite Captain Thompson's threats to force him to stay with the *Pilgrim,* he sailed from San Diego on the *Alert*'s homeward voyage.

As the *Alert* prepared to leave California, on May 8, 1836, she was unbelievably crowded. Dana wrote: "Our forty thousand hides and thirty thousand horns, besides several barrels of otter and beaver skins, were all stowed below, and the hatches calked down. All our spare spars were taken on board and lashed, our water-casks secured, and our livestock [bullocks, pigs, sheep, and poultry] were all stowed away in their different quarters." The unusually large cargo, together with the stores for a five-months' voyage, brought the ship's channels down into the water.

The return voyage was made in winter weather and was therefore a much rougher, more hazardous adventure than the outward trip had been. Dana's memorable account of the storms at sea, rounding Cape Horn, is unsurpassed in maritime literature:

> Rain, sleet, snow, and wind enough to take our breath from us, and make the toughest turn his back to windward. The ship lay

Richard Henry Dana

nearly over upon her beam ends; the spars and rigging snapped and cracked; and her top-gallant masts bent like whip-sticks. . . . The decks were standing nearly at an angle of forty-five degrees, and the ship going like a mad steer through the water, the whole forward part of her in a smother of foam. . . . The violence of the wind, and the hail and sleet, driving nearly horizontally across the ocean, seemed actually to pin us down to the rigging.

The ship was further imperiled by giant icebergs; a collision with one would have ended the voyage. Dana described the first one encountered:

And there lay, floating in the ocean, several miles off, an immense, irregular mass, its top and points covered with snow, and its centre of a deep indigo color. This was an iceberg and of the largest size. As far as the eye could reach, the sea in every direction was of a deep blue color, the waves running high and fresh, and sparkling in the light, and in the midst lay this immense mountain-island, its cavities and valleys thrown into deep shade, and its points and pinnacles glittering in the sun. . . . But no description can give any idea of the strangeness, splendour, and, really, the sublimity, of the sight. Its great size—for it must have been from two to three miles in circumference, and several hundred feet in height—its slow motion, as its base rose and sank in the water, and its high points nodded against the sky; the dashing of the waves upon it, which, breaking high with foam, lined its base with a white crust; and the thundering sound of the cracking of the mass, and the breaking and tumbling down of huge pieces; together with its nearness and approach, which added a slight element of fear—all combined to give it the character of true sublimity.

When the *Alert* emerged into the Atlantic Ocean, the first land seen was Staten Island, just east of Cape Horn. "A more desolate-looking spot I never wish to set eyes upon," Dana remarked— with its bare ground, rocks, ice, and broken hillocks—but it was a pleasant sight to him and his shipmates, showing them that they had passed the cape and were in the Atlantic.

The remainder of the *Alert's* passage homeward was comparatively peaceful, with favorable winds and sunny weather. The poetic

streak in Dana's nature emerged in his description of those days,
when he had time to contemplate the beauties of the ocean. Writing of a calm night in tropic waters, he observed: "The sea still as an inland lake; the light tradewind was gently and steadily breathing from astern." A ship with "all her sails is the most glorious moving object in the world." An inspired passage continues:

> So quiet, too, was the sea, and so steady the breeze, that if these sails could have been sculptured marble they could not have been more motionless. Not a ripple upon the surface of the canvas; not even a quivering of the extreme edges of the sail, so perfectly were they distended by the breeze. I was so lost in the sight that I forgot the presence of the man who came out with me, until he said (for he too, rough old man-of-war's-man as he was, had been gazing at the show), half to himself, still looking at the marble sails—"How quietly they do their work."

The *Alert* reached Boston on September 22, 1836. Her voyage had taken 137 days, compared to the *Pilgrim*'s 150. Dana reentered Harvard and graduated from the law school. Nearly four years passed before *Two Years before the Mast* was published. Harper's Brothers paid $250 outright for the manuscript, and despite the fact that the book became and remained a best seller, Dana received nothing more.

The literary influence of *Two Years before the Mast* was felt at once. At least three dozen books with titles resembling Dana's were published in the twenty years following. Realistic tales of the sea, notably Herman Melville's early novels, became the vogue.

An element adding to the book's popularity was the opening up of the gold fields in California in 1848. Dana's work proved to be the best and perhaps the only available full-scale treatment of the region. Book stores were soon sold out.

The direct effect of Dana's book on the lives of common sailors in the merchant marine appears more debatable. Samuel Shapiro, in his *Richard Henry Dana, Jr., 1815–1882,* questions the long-held belief that Dana "did for the common sailor what Mrs. Stowe was to do for the Negro slave," and concludes: "His book had far more effect on prospective immigrants to California and young boys anxious to go to sea than it did on congressmen who might pass legislation benefiting seamen." On the other hand, Dana's contemporary, J. Ross Browne, wrote to congratulate him for "putting down quarter-deck tyranny with might and main," and the noted literary critic Van Wyck Brooks maintained that Dana "battled like an avenging angel for seamen's right." Another critic, John A. Kouwenhoven, asserted: "As propaganda it succeeded; both in England and the United States it led to legislation benefiting seamen."

In any event, *Two Years before the Mast* was a democratic book, invariably taking the side of the crew, not the captain, and arousing the reader's sympathies for the miserable sailors. After Dana began his law practice, he was a frequent advocate for men before the mast who had been abused and unfairly treated. In a second book, *The Seaman's Friend* (1841), Dana compiled a reference volume of terms, customs, and legal rights of common sailors.

Two Years before the Mast reveals, though perhaps unconsciously on Dana's part, the inevitability of American expansion to the shores of the Pacific Ocean. In 1859, en route around the world, he paid a return visit to California, and in a revised edition of his book added a chapter, "Twenty-Four Years After." This time he was a passenger on "the superb steamship *Golden Gate*," landing in San Francisco and occupying "a commodious room in the Oriental Hotel." The state had been transformed since its admission to the Union in 1850. Santa Barbara was revisited, but had changed little. Los Angeles had become "a large and flourishing town of about twenty thousand inhabitants." Everywhere, Dana was greeted as a celebrity and was pleased to find that practically everyone had read his book.

16
Shrines of Islam

*Richard Burton's Personal Narrative of a Pilgrimage
to El-Medinah and Meccah, 1853*

Few "infidel dogs" or unbelievers have ever penetrated the
sacred walls of Mecca, holy city of the Moslem faith. A rare exception was Richard Burton, one of the most remarkable, and at
times flamboyant, individuals to come out of the Victorian era in
England.

In his *Personal Narrative,* Burton summarized the exploits of
several non-Moslems or "temporary converts" who had succeeded
in visiting Mecca before him. As early as 1503, Ludovico de Var-
thema, an Italian traveler, temporarily embraced Islam, came to
Mecca, and corrected the widespread myth that Mohammed's coffin
was suspended in mid-air by giant magnets; that is, held between
heaven and earth. Late in the seventeenth century, in 1680, Joseph
Pitts, an Englishman, was captured at sea by Moslem pirates, forcibly converted, and taken by his master on the pilgrimage. Pitts
ate pork in private, called the Prophet "a bloody imposter," and
finally escaped back to England, where he wrote a lively book describing his adventures.

Three other non-Moslems are known to have seen behind the
curtain of mystery surrounding Mecca before Burton. An Italian,
Giovanni Fanati of Ferrar, a deserter from the Italian army, became a convert in Albania to escape a prison sentence; seduced
the favorite wife of a Turkish general; fled to Egypt; and then
went to Mecca in about 1805. Two years later, a Spanish geologist
and botanist, Domingo Badia y Leblich, traveled to Mecca as a
wealthy Moslem scholar. His knowledge of Arabic enabled him

to pass without detection. The last was a Swiss ethnologist, Johann Ludwig Burckhardt, an explorer of the sources of the Niger River, who traveled up the Nile to Dar Mahass, then crossed the Nubian Desert and the Red Sea to visit Mecca and Medina. Buckhardt wrote a four-volume account of his adventures and observations.

But such undertakings were highly perilous for the nonbeliever. Mecca and Medina were held to be particularly sacred and inviolate by devout Moslems. In 629 A.D. Mohammed had decreed Mecca forbidden to all except true members of the faith. Over the centuries, the ban against unbelievers had been strictly enforced. Christians and Jews attempting to penetrate the shield, if discovered, had been impaled or crucified, two Jews as late as 1845.

Burton's parents were nomadic, wandering all over Europe, never staying more than a few years in any one place. His education was irregular, with scarcely any direction. A childhood spent in France and Italy gave him a love of travel and great fluency in vernacular languages. His Irish father intended for Burton to enter the ministry and sent him to Oxford, where he remained only about a year. While there, however, he began the study of Arabic.

At the beginning of 1842, a cadetship was obtained for Burton in the Indian army. For the next seven years he was in the British military service in India. The chief attraction of this assignment for Burton was the opportunity to study oriental life and languages, for he found military discipline exceedingly irksome. His first station was Baroda, the capital of a native principality in Gujarat. After a year, his regiment was transferred to Sind. This was a formative period in Burton's life. He acquired an amazing proficiency in Gujarati, Sindhi, Punjabi, Sanskrit, Pushtu, Marathi, and Hindustani, as well as Persian and Arabic. His knowledge of Oriental culture increased rapidly while he spent three years wandering about in what was then India's most purely Mohammedan province. He also engaged private teachers and lived for weeks as a native— or, as his brother officers expressed it, as a "white nigger." The intimate familiarity with Mohammedan manners and customs was invaluable to him in his later adventurous journey to Mecca.

Languages were valued by Burton not for their own sake, but as a key to thought. The Koran was opened to him by Arabic and

Richard Burton as Mirza Abdullah

Richard Burton

the mystic philosophy of Sufism by Persian. He practiced the religious exercises of Islam as a means of getting to the heart of Moslem theology. While in India, Burton also made himself adept in, among other things, falconry, horsemanship, Indian religions, gypsy lore, and erotic practices.

Because of a breakdown in health, Burton returned to England. During four years at home, however, he continued to polish his orientalism and to cherish the dream of a pilgrimage to Mecca. His original aim was to cross the Arabian peninsula, from west to east; this is one of the world's most formidable deserts, largely unexplored up to Burton's time, even by the Bedouins. The support of the Royal Geographical Society was obtained for the enterprise. But the directors of the East India Company refused the three-year leave of absence that would have been required; instead, all that they would grant was an additional furlough of twelve months with the stated purpose that Burton "might pursue his Arabic studies in lands where the language is best learned."

In a manuscript by Burton, published in 1899 by the Royal Society of Literature some years after his death, he stated: "I had long wished to make the pilgrimage to Mecca and Medinah, the birth-place and burial-place respectively of the Prophet, and to study the inner life of the Moslem." On April 3, 1853, he embarked at Southampton, disguised as a Persian mirza, or dervish, and entered himself in the ship's books in that way. He was careful not to let anyone know of his intention beforehand, as the slightest publicity would have been fatal to his scheme, which was, of course, to travel as a pilgrim to Mecca.

Burton took great pains with his disguise. For months he allowed his hair to grow long naturally until it fell nearly to his shoulders; he let his beard grow far down on his chest; he browned and stained his face and hands, arms and legs with a thin coating of henna; he wore the oriental dress and turban; and he assumed the name of Mirza Abdullah. The disguise was so perfect that no one discovered it on board ship. On landing at Alexandria, he was blessed as a true Moslem by the native population.

Burton lived in Alexandria for some months disguised as a dervish. Here he perfected his knowledge of the Koran and Moslem prayer and all the ceremonies of the faith. One of his main purposes was to explore the mysteries of Arab family life and for that reason he played the part of combination dervish and doctor. According to Burton, a dervish was "a chartered vagabond," on the order of a monk, who could travel safely without servants or weapons. The additional role of doctor was the best way to "see people face to face, and especially the fair sex." Burton had long been "a dabbler in medical and mystical study," and was familiar with Eastern medicine, which consisted largely of magic nostrums, charms, incantations, simple diets, cathartics, and prescriptions for aphrodisiacs. His equipment consisted of calomel, bread pills dipped in aloes, cinnamon water, and a magic mirror. So successful were his methods, including frequent resort to hypnosis, that the natives concluded he was a holy man, gifted with supernatural powers.

From Alexandria, Burton went to Cairo by boat, still disguised as a dervish and traveling as a deck passenger with the natives. He traveled light; a bag of dates, bedding, pen and inkhorn, a few necessary changes of clothes, and the simplest toilet articles completed his equipment. Passage on the wretched tub called the *Little Asthmatic* was taken for politicial reasons. Three days and nights were spent on the boat, while the burning desert sun beat down on the unfortunate pilgrims squatting on the deck. "To me," Burton wrote, "it seemed to be Sind over again—the same morning mist and noon-tide glare, the same hot wind and heat clouds, and fiery sunsets, and evening glow; the same pillars of dust and 'devils' of sand sweeping like giants over the plain; the same turbid water." During the voyage Burton sat alone, telling the beads of his big rosary continuously; for refreshment he drank the filthy water of the river and munched bread and garlic "with a desperate sanctimoniousness."

At Cairo, Burton changed his character and became an Indian, born of Afghan parents and, of course, a true Moslem. The switch was made on the advice of a benevolent Turkish trader met on the boat, who reminded him that the Sunni Arabs beat and spit upon the Shia heretics of Persia, pilgrims or not. "If you persist in being a Persian," his wise old friend told him, "you will be cursed in Egypt; in Arabia you will be beaten because you are a heretic; you will pay the treble of what other travellers do, and if you fall sick you may die by the roadside." And so Burton, while still remaining a doctor, was speedily transformed and dressed as an effendi, or gentleman.

It was the height of the pilgrim season in Cairo. Large crowds of travelers filled the streets; the equipage of wealthy merchants, with its rich crimson, gold, and silver decorations made a gorgeous show on the way to Mecca; clamorous beggars hung around the doors of every mosque; and Cairo merchants tried to force their goods on the pilgrims at exorbitant prices. Every shade of brown, from the shiny ebony of the Nubians to the dark milk of the Persians, was to be seen among the throngs of pilgrims. All the better-class hotels were jammed full. Burton found two miserable rooms in the Greek section of town: filthy, verminous quarters.

Burton was in Cairo during Ramadan, the Lent-like month of Moslem fasting, when eating and drinking were forbidden during the daylight hours. The time of the pilgrimage grew near and Burton made his preparations for departure. Two servants were hired: Nur, a quiet East Indian lad, and Mohammed, a Meccan youth, fat, jolly, fond of wine and girls, and very clever.

The visit to Mecca by devout Moslems is planned from the seventh to the twelfth of the month of the year prescribed by the Islamic calendar. The truly remarkable phenomenon is repeated annually, drawing pilgrims from the most remote Mohammedan nations, from every race. A vast stream of pilgrims converge upon the arid shores of Arabia, mainly through Alexandria, Damascus, and Bagdad. A medley of nationalities and races, rich men and ragged beggars, brave intense heat, hunger and thirst, and attacks by bloodthirsty tribesmen en route to reach the sacred cities of Mecca and Medina. An informed estimate is that almost a third of the enormous throng perish each year along the way from bullets, thirst, or disease. In fact, each pilgrim was expected to carry a shroud against the not unlikely event he would fall by the wayide and have to be buried in a shallow desert grave.

From Cairo to Suez, a distance of eighty-four miles, Burton traveled by dromedary across a hot, dusty inferno. A flaming wind parched the lips of the men in the caravan, the glare blinded them, and the sand rose and swirled around them. At the end of the long ride, jolting along on a hard wooden saddle, every muscle in Burton's body ached. He found Suez a squalid, filthy town overrun with pilgrims. He described his quarters in the George Inn: "The walls of our rooms were clammy with dirt, the smoke rafters foul with cobwebs, and the floor bestrewed with kit, in terrible confusion, was black with hosts of cockroaches, ants, and flies." Goats and jackasses wandered in and out.

A long delay at Suez followed the ride from Cairo. Endless formalities and red tape consumed many days. Finally, a mass of pilgrims was herded onto an open boat, the *Golden Thread,* to cross the Red Sea to Yambu. The boat's extreme passenger capacity was sixty, but she had nearly one hundred on board. The two-masted, fifty-ton steamer lacked compass, log, chart, or spare ropes. Frequent fights broke out among the pilgrims fighting for space. Burton noted that "the voyage took twelve days, and they were twelve days of horror, for we pilgrims were herded together more like cattle than men and women, and the heat of the sun, and the stench, and the insects, to say nothing of the constant washing of the sea over the open boat, made our days and nights a misery." The pilgrims crouched in a half-stupor under the blazing sun, stung by desert winds. At sunset, they roused up to cook simple meals of rice and onions in square wooden boxes lined with clay and sand, then sang and told stories into the night.

Seton Dearden, author of *Burton of Arabia,* pointed out that "it must be understood that the whole of the transport system of the pilgrim route was one vast piece of blackmail and exploitation run by local Pashas. Unable to help themselves except by bribes, the poorer pilgrims were herded like cattle from point to point, robbed, overcharged, and delayed for as long as suited the pockets of the local officials. Vessels were often held back until they could be crammed to suffocation, and then were pushed off under the care of untrained sailors with their crammed, suffocated, and dying human cargoes." Thus did greedy Moslems treat their devout brethern. And this was the kind of treatment experienced by Burton.

While wading ashore at Marsa Mahar, Burton stepped on a prickly sea urchin, an organism covering the shallow water along the Red Sea. A poisonous spine penetrated his foot, became infected, and was soon so swollen and painful he could hardly walk. The unfor-

Richard Burton

tunate accident continued to cause him difficulties long afterwards.

On landing, Burton dressed as an Arab to avoid the tax on strangers, covering his head with a red kerchief bordered with yellow, his body with a cotton shirt and a camel's hair cloak, while a red sash, a crooked dagger, a matchlock and sword on his back, a camel stick, and a pouch slung around his shoulder holding a Koran completed the outfit. Several camels were hired and Burton and his servants joined a caravan, made up of several hundred men and beasts bound for Medina. While passing through one of the mountain gorges, known as Pilgrimage Pass, the pilgrims were attacked by predatory Bedouins, led by a ferocious chief named Saad. Burton wrote: "They took up comfortable places on the cutthroat eminence and began firing upon us with perfect convenience to themselves." Twelve pilgrims and numerous camels were killed before the caravan escaped from the trap.

After a journey of 130 miles, the eyes of the pilgrims were rejoiced by the tall towers and the great green dome that covered the tomb of Mohammed rising among the palm trees of Medina. A month was spent by Burton in Medina at the home of Sheikh Hamid, whose favor he had gained by the loan of money. His days were filled with visits to the tomb of the Prophet and to the numerous shrines in the town, in ceremonies to be performed, and in the usual prayers, five times daily. The first day after arrival, he and Sheikh Hamid rose at dawn, washed, prayed, and broke their fast upon a stale piece of bread. They then dressed in the spotless white clothes beloved by the Prophet, and picked their way through the narrow streets to approach the Prophet's Tomb. Expecting something splendid and perhaps spectacular, Burton was disappointed in the mosque. "I was astonished," he wrote, "at the mean and tawdry appearance of a place so universally venerated in the Moslem world. The longer I looked at it, the more it suggested the resemblance of a museum of second-rate art, an Old Curiosity Shop, full of ornaments that are not accessories, and decorated with pauper splendour."

When they had completed the performance of various set ceremonies, Burton and his companion moved into the actual Tomb chamber, a large square structure about fifty-five feet across. Here towered the Tomb of the Prophet himself, and the smaller burial places of Fatima, Mohammed's favorite daughter, and the disciples Omar and Abu Bakr. There followed a final short sequence of prayers before departure from the Prophet's Mosque.

Afterward, Burton wrote that "although every Moslem, learned and simple, firmly believes that Mohammed's remains are interred in the Hujrah at Al Madinah, I cannot help suspecting that the place is as doubtful as that of the Holy Sepulchre at Jerusalem." He concluded his religious duties at Medina by visiting the Five Mosques of the Prophet, the Mosques of Kuba, the cemetery of Al Bakia, and the martyr Hamyah's tomb at the foot of Mount Ohod.

To reach Mecca, Burton joined a huge caravan of some 8,000 pilgrims from Damascus, starting on August 31, 1853. An inland, rather than the coastal, route was followed, a road which was largely waterless and thus far untraveled by any European. The route was littered with the carcasses of ponies, camels, and donkeys that had died of heat and exhaustion. Much of the marching was done by night. In another ambush, several dromedaries were killed, but the robbers were driven off.

Burton wrote a picturesque description of the marching pilgrims, whom he classified as of "eight degrees." The lowest walked on heavy staves; "there are the itinerant coffee-makers, sherbet sellers and tobacconists, country folk driving flocks of sheep and goats with infinite clamor and gesticulation, negroes from distant Africa, and crowds of paupers." Among other categories were "humble riders of laden camels, mules and asses" and "respectable men mounting dromedaries or blood-camels." Women, children and invalids of the poorer classes sat upon rugs or carpets spread over the large boxes on the camels' backs. The rich had led horses or litters slung between camels or mules with scarlet and brass trappings. In short, each pilgrim traveled in whatever style he could afford, and Burton noted that the expense "may vary from five pounds to as many thousands."

The country through which the caravan was passing was one to try men's souls. "For the most part it is a haggard land," Burton noted, "a country of wild beasts and wilder men. . . . In other places

180 it is a desert peopled only with echoes, an abode of death for what little there is to die in it. . . . Few animals except vultures and ravens met the eye."

On Friday, September 9, the caravan camped at Zaribah, forty-seven miles or two days' ride from Mecca. The men's heads were shaved; all were bathed, perfumed, and dressed in the official pilgrim costume, a simple cotton garment with red stripes and fringes. The women replaced their beautiful veils with an ugly mask of dried palm leaves. The pilgrims were forbidden to kill any living thing except the "five nuisances": a crow, a kite, a rat, a scorpion, or a biting dog. The caravan wound its way into Mecca after nightfall on September 11. Burton spent the night in the home of his servant Mohammed's mother.

After a few hours of sleep and a ceremonial ablution, Burton donned his pilgrim garb and, after a long traditional prayer, hastened to the House of Allah, as the Great Mosque of Mecca is called, in order to worship at the huge bier-like structure, the Kaaba. The Kaaba, placed in the court of the mosque, contains a sacred black stone; it is the supreme goal of Islamic pilgrimages to Mecca and the point toward which Moslems turn in praying. The shrine was covered with embroidered black brocade, with inscriptions from the Koran in gold. According to tradition, the black stone had been white when given to Abraham by the angel Gabriel, but had become black by the sins of the pilgrims who kissed it. All idols in Mecca had been abolished by Mohammed except this one, believed to be a pagan idol centuries older than Mohammed himself. Burton remarked that "whilst kissing and rubbing hands and forehead upon it I narrowly observed it, and came away persuaded that it is an aerolite," that is, a meteorite.

On his second day in Mecca, Burton journeyed to the sacred Mount of Arafat, competing for standing room with an estimated 50,000 other pilgrims. The third day, mounted on an ass, was devoted by Burton to a trip to Muna, where he took part in the ceremony called Stoning the Devil, again battling with dense mobs of the faithful.

After visiting some fifty-five other wonders of Mecca, Burton sent his servant Nur with heavy boxes to Jeddah, the port of Mecca, and followed soon after with Mohammed. The one sight to be seen in Jeddah, the tomb of Eve, was visited, and then he bade farewell to Mohammed, who returned to his home in Mecca. Burton boarded the English ship *Dwarka* to return home. His six days in Mecca had given him everything he wanted to know—enough in fact to fill his three-volume account entitled *Personal Narrative of a Pilgrimage to El-Medinah and Meccah,* published in London two years later. As he prepared to depart, he wrote, "I now began to long to leave Mecca. I had done everything, and seen everything."

Questions were subsequently raised about the ethics of Burton entering Islam's most holy shrines disguised as a pilgrim, and especially by his performance of all the religious rites of the Moslems. Burton dismissed such doubts by saying "I recognize no man's right to interfere between a human being and his conscience." One commentator, Stanley Lane-Pole, agreed that "he is probably within his rights in maintaining that this is a matter which concerns nobody but himself," and adds "there can be no question that his impersonation multiplied the difficulties of the task. In the new convert much might be excused on the ground of unfamiliarity with the customs, rituals, and language; but the born Moslem has no such refuge."

Burton's colorful career continued long after his return from Mecca. He led two even more hazardous expeditions into East Africa and became the first white man to return from the forbidden city of Harrar in Abyssinia, again disguised as an Arab. In a third expedition he discovered Lake Tanganyika. Later he visited the United States, including the Mormon settlement in Utah, and was given consular appointments in various remote places from Santos in Brazil to Trieste.

Burton was a prolific writer, producing more than seventy books in all. His crowning literary achievement was a monumental translation of *The Arabian Nights, the Thousand Nights and a Night,* in sixteen volumes (1885–88), the language of which was so frank and unexpurgated that it caused a scandal in Victorian England.

Richard Burton

17
Orient Meets Occident

Fukuzawa Yukichi's Autobiography, 1860

For centuries Japan was a closed society. Intercourse with the western world was sporadic and intermittent. About 1543, a storm drove a Portuguese ship to a Japanese island south of Kyushu. The crew was so well received that seven Portuguese expeditions were sent to Japan over the next several years for trading purposes. Among other innovations, the Portuguese were the first to introduce guns into Japan. A short time later, the Spaniards began to arrive, also for commercial dealings. Because these European traders came to Japan by way of the southern seas, they were called the "Southern Foreigners."

Only six years after the first arrival of the Portuguese, in 1549, Francis Xavier came to Japan with two Jesuit priests and began a campaign to convert the Japanese to Christianity. The "Religion of the Heavenly Father," as the Japanese called it, had considerable success at first among the Japanese leaders, though handicapped at times by the opposition of Buddhist priests and by resentment against too aggressive propaganda and the burning of temples.

An important event occurred in 1600, when the Dutch first landed in Japan. A Dutch ship, the *Liefde,* was towed into harbor at Funai in Bungo after a terrible storm. The merchantman belonged to the Netherlands East India Company. Two members of the crew, Jan Joosten, a Hollander, and Will Adams, the English pilot major, were summoned to the shogun's court for an audience. Adams was subsequently made master shipbuilder in the Yedo (Tokyo) government and employed as adviser and diplomatic agent in dealing with foreigners. In 1605 the shogun gave the Dutch a license to trade, and four years later the Dutch East India Company established a factory at Hirado. Similar permission was given the English in 1613. Hirado and Nagasaki were opened as ports where these foreign traders might carry on business. The English built a factory in Hirado, but it was not a commercial success and closed after ten years. The English withdraw, but the Dutch stayed on, despite severe restrictions on their activities and frequently virulent hostility towards foreigners. In 1639, the country was closed against the Portuguese.

The Japanese government finally ordered that no Japanese might go abroad and no foreigner might enter Japan, except for a limited number of Dutch traders operating under special conditions. This state of affairs remained substantially unchanged until ships from the United States Navy, under the command of Commodore Matthew Perry, arrived in 1853. In the long interim the edict against dealing with all foreigners except the Dutch was strictly enforced by the shogun's government. Weather or other causes occasionally forced foreign ships into Japanese ports, but they were generally driven away by gunfire. Because of depredations by the crew of an English vessel near Kagoshima, local authorities were ordered to stop any foreign ships from putting into port and to arrest or execute any foreigners who might land.

The American government, unhappy with the treatment of its ships touching Japanese ports, finally decided to send a formidable force of ten naval vessels and 2,000 men to, in effect, compel the Japanese to conclude a commercial treaty. At first, the Japanese were inclined to fight, but finally decided that effective resistance was impossible. After some weeks of negotiations, a treaty of peace and friendship was signed. Among its stipulations were: (1) the ports of Shimoda in Izu and Hakodate should be opened to United States ships and Americans would be allowed to frequent them within definite limits; (2) United States consuls or agents might reside in Shimoda; and (3) shipwrecked sailors should be relieved and ships might obtain fuel and provisions in Japanese territory. Russia, Holland, and England soon secured similar treaties for themselves. Thus, after a long period of enforced seclusion from the rest of the world, Japan entered the society of nations. Through

Fukuzawa Yukichi

184   the open door western ideas poured in: schools were founded, books were published, and the study of astronomy, geography, medicine, literature, architecture, and painting flourished.

Among the interested spectators of these developments was a young Japanese, Fukuzawa Yukichi, living at Nakatsu on the coast of Kyushu, who was eighteen years old at the time of Commodore Perry's visit to Japan. His father belonged to the samurai class.

Though the Dutch had been active in Japanese commercial affairs for two and a half centuries, no one in young Fukuzawa's town could understand the Dutch language, "the strange letters written sideways." The news of the appearance of the American fleet in Tokyo had made a strong impression on even the most remote towns in Japan. The problem of national defense and the new art of warfare were of foremost interest to the samurai. The study of gunnery could only be undertaken under Dutch instructors, which meant that the Dutch language must be learned. Fukuzawa had no particular concern for armaments; he saw the study of Dutch, however, as a way to get ahead in the world and to escape from the provincial village of Nakatsu, with which he was thoroughly bored. He went to Nagasaki, therefore, to become proficient.in the Dutch language. At the time Nagasaki, with its Dutch compound, was the only port in Japan in touch with the ouside world.

Fukuzawa made fairly rapid progress in the study of Dutch while in Nagasaki. Then a disagreement with the family with whom he was living caused him to go on to Tokyo, several hundred miles away, a distance traveled primarily on foot for lack of money. An intermediate stop was made in Osaka, where the study of Dutch was continued. The student's principal tool was a German-Dutch dictionary that had been translated into Japanese.

The greatest opportunities in government or otherwise were to be found in Tokyo. Here, Fukuzawa noted, "though the country's intercourse with foreign lands was yet at its beginning, there were constant demands for the Western knowledge from the government offices and from the various feudal nobility resident there. Consequently anyone able to read foreign books, or make any translation, secured the reward of this patronage." Osaka, a city of merchants devoted to internal commerce, had placed little practical value in studying a foreign language.

The year after Fukuzawa Yukichi reached Tokyo, in 1859, the so-called Treaty of the Five Nations was signed and the port of Yokohama was formally opened for trade with foreign countries. To his dismay, when Fukuzawa attempted to talk with the merchants showing their wares, they were unable to understand him, or vice versa. Neither could he read the signboards over the shops nor the labels on the bottles for sale. The strange new language used here was English. Fukuzawa was bitterly disappointed to discover that Dutch, which he had been studying so assiduously for years, was a minor language, not widely used or understood, rather than the lingua franca, which would admit him to an understanding of Western civilization.

The day after returning from Yokohama, Fukuzawa resolved to begin the study of English. However, not a single English teacher was to be found in Tokyo. By good fortune, a Dutch-English dictionary and a small English conversation book were procured, and Fukuzawa started forming English sentences from the Dutch dictionary. The knowledge of anyone who knew any pronunciations, such as shipwrecked Japanese fishermen who were brought back on foreign vessels, was drawn upon. Also, his study of Dutch had not been in vain; he found enough similarities between Dutch and English to facilitate his learning of the latter.

The year after Fukuzawa settled in Tokyo, 1859, he received an opportunity for foreign travel. "The government of the Shogun," he wrote, "made a great decision to send a ship-of-war to the United States, an enterprise never before attempted since the foundation of the empire. On this ship I was to have the good fortune of visiting America." The so-called warship was actually a small sailing craft equipped with an auxiliary steam engine of one hundred horsepower, to be used for maneuvering in and out of harbors. In the open sea, the ship had to depend entirely on sail. The Japanese government had purchased her from the Dutch a few years before and named her the *Kanrin-Maru*.

Japanese officers and crews had been preparing for the voyage by studying navigation and the operation of steamships since the opening of ports in 1855. Help had been secured from Dutch residents at Nagasaki, and now the Japanese felt themselves qualified to take a ship across the Pacific to San Francisco, serving as an escort for the American warship carrying Japan's first envoy to Washington. The entire crew totaled ninety-six men, larger than usual for the ship. It was an epoch-making adventure for the Japanese nation. Every member of the crew was determined to make the voyage unassisted by any foreigner, in order to gain full honors for its anticipated success.

Through influential connections, Fukuzawa Yukichi was granted "his greatest wish," to be taken along on the voyage, serving as personal steward to the captain. In February 1860, the *Kanrin-Maru* left Tokyo from the shores of Shinagawa.

After leaving Tokyo bay, the small ship sailed on a far northern route. No sooner did it get into the open sea than it ran into storms; rough weather continued all the way across. To eat sitting down at a table was practically impossible. Fukuzawa piled his rice in a bowl and poured soup and all other food over it, and ate standing up. In winter, on a tempestuous sea, the *Kanrin-Maru* faced the voyage under sail, without aid from the steam engine. Two of four lifeboats were lost overboard. Storms followed each other and waves continually broke over the decks. At times the ship was tilted by as much as thirty-eight degrees. Any sharper list would probably have capsized her and sent her to the bottom, but she kept her course. For a month the crew saw nothing but waves and clouds, except for a single American vessel carrying Chinese workmen to the United States.

Near the end, the ship's supply of water began to run low, and the question of making port in the Hawaiian Islands was considered. It was finally decided to go straight on to San Francisco, and by restricting the use of water to drinking the voyage was completed without a stop. San Francisco was reached after thirty-seven days at sea. Fukuzawa expressed pride in the achievement of his fellow countrymen—the Japanese had never seen a steamship until 1853; two years later they began to learn about navigation from the Dutch at Nagasaki; and five years after that they were proficient enough to sail a ship across the Pacific.

When the *Kanrin-Maru* docked at San Francisco, many important persons came aboard to greet the company, and along the shore thousands of people lined up to see the strange newcomers. A salute fired on shore was returned by the ship's navigator. The Americans seemed to feel a personal pride in the Japanese visit, for it was their Commodore Perry who had opened Japan to the world eight years earlier. All kinds of hospitality was extended to the visitors, including special entertainment, an official residence at the naval station on Mare Island, food prepared Japanese fashion, and the placing of their ship in dry dock for repairs before beginning the return voyage.

The customs and habits of American life were unknown, of course, to the Japanese, and caused some confusion and embarrassing moments. The visitors had never before ridden in horse-drawn vehicles. When the Japanese observed hotel floors covered with valuable carpets and rugs, they were shocked to see the Americans walking on them without removing their shoes. Another shock awaited them when champagne was served with ice cubes floating in the glasses, while warm spring weather prevailed outside; some of the Japanese swallowed the frozen particles, others "expelled them suddenly," and others chewed them up. On another occasion, the visitors were invited to a dancing party, and found it amusing to see "the ladies and gentlemen hopping around the room together." These were some instances of Japanese bewilderment at the strange customs of American society. The greatest shock of all came when they were invited to have dinner at the home of a prominent local physician; the pièce de résistance turned out to be a whole pig, roasted—head, legs, tail, and all—brought in on a dish.

Fukuzawa was inclined to be critical of the Americans for their wastefulness. He noted that there was an enormous waste of iron everywhere, such as old oil tins, empty cans, and broken tools— items that would have been treasured in metal-poor Japan. Perhaps related was the high cost of standard commodities in California, far above prices in Japan.

A naval salute marked the departure of the *Kanrin-Maru* for home. Fukuzawa's last purchase before leaving was a Webster dictionary, the first, he believed, to be imported into Japan. En route, a stop of several days was made in Hawaii to take on a supply of coal. Fukuzawa was little impressed by the Hawaiian natives. To him they appeared to be barbarians and their general state "pretty miserable," while the king and queen showed no earmarks of royalty.

Fukuzawa Yukichi

Following a southern route the sea was calm, and the Japanese ship sailed safely homeward, anchoring first in Uraga after a six months' absence. Back in Japan a strong antiforeign movement had developed while Fukuzawa was away; the pro-Western chancellor to the shogun had been assassinated; and a national slogan, "expel the foreigners," had become popular. Fukuzawa, whose sympathies were distinctly in favor of Western orientation for Japan, resumed teaching English, but he had to exercise considerable caution because of the risk of violence from fanatical anti-Western Japanese.

Two years after Fukuzawa's return from the first American visit, a second chance for foreign travel was offered him. He was sent by the Japanese government as an official interpreter with a group of Japanese envoys being carried by an English war vessel, the *Odin*. The ship sailed in December 1861 by way of Hong Kong, Singapore, and other ports in the Indian Ocean, through the Red Sea to Suez, by rail to Cairo, and then by boat across the Mediterranean to Marseilles. Some twenty days were spent in Paris, following which England, Holland, Berlin, and St. Petersburg in Russia were visited. The party of forty included three ambassadors, various secretaries, doctors, interpreters, cooks, and general servants. Assuming that they would not be able to obtain proper food in Europe, hundreds of cases of polished rice had been placed in the baggage of the Japanese, an unnecessary precaution, it turned out, for the group was suitably fed everywhere it traveled.

Features of European civilization that particularly impressed Fukuzawa were the enormous size of hotels, by Japanese standards; central heating; gas lighting; and railways, which went in all directions. At the time of Fukuzawa's first visit to America, San Francisco was not yet connected by rail to the rest of the country.

Ridiculous incidents, arising out of the Japanese unfamiliarity with Western customs, occurred. Fukuzawa noted, for example: "When one of our lord-envoys had occasion to use the toilet, he was followed to the doorway by one of his personal attendants, who carried the lighted paper lantern, as is the custom in the homeland. The attendant in his most formal dress was to be seen squatting patiently outside the open door, holding his master's removed sword. This happened to be in the bustling corridor of the hotel where people were passing constantly, and the gas was burning as bright as day. But unperturbed sat the faithful guardian." Fukuzawa happened along and shut the door.

The country in Europe which gave the Japanese the most cordial welcome was Holland. This was natural because of the special relationship that had existed between Japan and Holland for several centuries. Also, any members of the party who knew any foreign language had studied Dutch.

During his European stay, Fukuzawa tried to learn as much as possible about foreign culture, even the most commonplace matters. He made inquiries about the operation of hospitals, the postal system, military conscription, and the functioning of representative government. In gathering information, however, he was handicapped by instructions from his superior officers to avoid meeting foreigners or seeing the country any more than was strictly essential. As Fukuzawa commented, "We were under the 'seclusion' theory even while we were traveling in foreign territory on a tour of friendship."

The Japanese mission's return journey was made from France by ship to Portugal, and then retracing the course through the Mediterranean and the Indian Ocean. Japan was reached after nearly a year of traveling.

Fukuzawa's third and last voyage to foreign lands was made in 1867, again to the United States. The purpose of the mission was to complete the purchase of the second of two warships for which the Japanese government had previously contracted. By this time, a regular packet service had been opened between Japan and America, and the Japanese delegation traveled on the *Colorado,* of which Fukuzawa wrote: "It was a fast steamer of four thousand tons, veritably palatial in comparison with the small boat on which I had previously crossed." Only twenty-two, instead of thirty-seven, days were required to reach San Francisco. Another ship was taken to Panama, the isthmus was crossed by train, and a third ship provided transportation to New York, from which the Japanese proceeded at once to Washington. The deal for the warship, plus several thousand rifles, was completed, and the Japanese sailed home in it the following year, in 1868.

Back in Japan, Fukuzawa found the sentiment against foreigners growing in bitterness and intensity. Political assassinations of high officials with pro-Western inclinations were increasingly common. Fukuzawa's outspoken speeches and writings favoring close connections with the West caused him to be subjected to a certain amount of discipline by the government and to run the risk of being killed by extremists. As evidence of the prejudice against aliens, he cited the case of the duke of Edinburgh, who arrived to pay a formal visit to the palace in Tokyo. There was much discussion as to the propriety of conducting a foreign visitor into the imperial presence. The decision was that this could not be done without an elaborate purification ceremony prior to the English prince's crossing the bridge over the moat to the castle—a ritual that was duly performed.

Fukuzawa's later career was distinguished. His Tokyo school eventually became Keio University, one of Japan's most notable centers of higher education, and probably the most Western-oriented of Japanese universities. Feeling the lack of a proper medium for transmitting his ideas and ideals to the general public, Fukuzawa also established, in 1882, an influential newspaper, the *Jiji-Shimpo*. The breadth of view derived from his foreign travels were reflected in both enterprises.

18
Breaker of Stones

Henry M. Stanley's Through the Dark Continent,
1871—1877

In all the tales of travel and exploration, no line is more famous than Henry Stanley's "Dr. Livingstone, I presume?"—a prim and stilted question which gave rise to a whole new school of humor and embarrassed Stanley for the rest of his life. But there was nothing prissy about Stanley himself. In the course of a strenuous career as perhaps Africa's greatest explorer, he richly earned the African natives' nickname for him,"Bula Matari," Breaker of Stones, the all-powerful one who allowed no obstacle to stand in the way of achieving a desired objective.

Few historical celebrities have had a more unpromising start than Stanley. Born John Rowland in 1841 in Wales, he was the illegitimate son of a maidservant who abandoned him and a farmer who was killed in a public house. Until age four he was cared for by his grandfather. After the latter's death, two uncles took him in charge for a couple of years but, unwilling to bear the expense of his upkeep, they consigned him to a fearful place known as St. Asaph Union Workhouse, where he was to remain for the next nine years. The schoolmaster at St. Asaph was a savage misanthrope named James Francis, who had lost a hand in a coal mining accident. Francis terrorized the boys, beating them mercilessly on the slightest provocation. Charles Dickens gives a vivid picture of such an institution in his *Oliver Twist*.

At age fifteen, young Henry refused the master's command to strip and be beaten; the two engaged in a terrific struggle, Henry beat the schoolmaster with his own blackthorn stick until insensi-

A popular depiction of the meeting of Stanley and Livingstone

ble, and then escaped. Following a series of odd jobs, he enlisted as cabin boy on a ship bound for New Orleans, a voyage of fifty-two days. Life aboard ship was as cruel and hard as any Henry had experienced, and in New Orleans he fled from it. One of the first persons he met there was a prosperous merchant named Henry Morton Stanley, who adopted him and gave him his own name.

Next ensued what Stanley later described as "the golden period of my life." He accompanied his adopted father on journeys to the backwoods settlements of the Missouri and Arkansas frontiers, and was employed at good wages by a firm of New Orleans merchants. The situation changed when Mr. Stanley and his wife died and Henry became unemployed. At the outbreak of the Civil War, Henry enlisted in an Arkansas regiment on the Confederate side, and was captured by Union Army troops at the battle of Shiloh. Conditions at Camp Douglas, Illinois, where he was imprisoned, were appalling, and after enduring them for two months he won his freedom by joining the U.S. Artillery Service. Politics meant

Breaker of Stones

little to him. Illness, however, prevented him from taking part in
active service and he was discharged as physically unfit.

In 1862, young Stanley was back in England. He survived a shipwreck off Barcelona and enlisted in the U.S. Navy. When the Civil War was over, he went to Colorado and was soon making a name for himself as a newspaper correspondent, especially in reporting on an expedition against the Indians for the *Missouri Democrat* and other papers. His lively, descriptive writing won him roving assignments overseas. In the autumn of 1866 he traveled in Asia Minor and while there was attacked by brigands, robbed, and imprisoned for a time. By now he had attracted the attention of James Gordon Bennett, Jr., owner of the *New York Herald,* who sent Stanley with the British expedition of 1867–68 against Emperor Theodore of Abyssinia. Later he traveled to Crete, then in rebellion, and from there to Spain, where he witnessed the flight of Queen Isabella from Madrid and the republican rising of 1869.

Now came a momentous event in Stanley's life. He was summoned to Paris to meet Bennett. On his arrival he was told that his next assignment was to go into central Africa and find David Livingstone. Originally, Livingstone had gone to Africa under the sponsorship of missionary societies, but was later financed as an explorer by the British government, the Royal Geographical Society, and one or two wealthy individuals. His expedition had started in 1865 with the objective of studying the watershed between lakes Nyasa and Tanganyika. Rumor held that Livingstone had been killed by Zulus in 1866 and no communications had come through from him for a period of two or three years—due, in fact, to his serious illness and lack of facilities for sending messages. Despite the long period of complete silence, Bennett believed that the great explorer was still alive, and Stanley's mission was to find him and aid him in any way possible.

Oddly, though, despite the supposed urgency of the matter, Bennett gave Stanley several other commissions to complete before beginning an active search for Livingstone. He was instructed to proceed to Egypt to observe the opening of the Suez Canal; from there to Philae, Egypt; to Palestine; Constantinople; the battlefields of the Crimea; across Persia to Bushire; and on to Bombay.

From Bombay he sailed for Africa, reaching Zanzibar on January 6, 1871.

Stanley showed himself at once to be an explorer of outstanding ability. Inquiries at Zanzibar were nonproductive; no one had any news of Livingstone. Some thought him dead, and others that he was lost. In organizing a search expedition, Stanley was a martinet, earning his title of "Breaker of Stones," driving others as he drove himself, and not infrequently resorting to the whip. Two months after his arrival in Africa his safari of 180 men, 27 donkeys, and 2 horses set out for Ujiji, an important caravan station on the eastern shore of Lake Tanganyika, where Livingstone had last been reported.

For weeks, progress was exceedingly slow and full of hardships. Writing an account of the trek, Stanley often spoke of dense forests, swamps, gorges, and mountains, of extortionate demands made by hostile native chiefs, of mutinies, illnesses, and losses. The journey to the interior began on March 21 and ended on November 10, 1871, at Ujiji. Stanley had been told that if Livingstone heard that a rescue mission was on the way, he might disappear. Accordingly he drove his entire force of men and beasts to the limit in order to arrive before Livingstone got word of his coming. In order not to lose time and to avoid the greedy chiefs with their demands for tribute, Stanley forced the expedition to march even during the night across wilderness and uninhabited areas. Actually, Livingstone was in no condition to flee, even if he had been so inclined: his bearers had deserted, taking his medical supplies with them, he was seriously ill of malaria, and had been near death from starvation. Stanley described in his journal how the only two white men in all equatorial Africa from the Zambezi to the Nile finally met:

> The head of the expedition had halted and the Kirangozi [flag bearer] was out of ranks, holding his flag aloft, and Selim said to me, "I see the Doctor, sir, Oh, what an old man. He has got a white beard." My heart beats fast, but I must not let my face betray my emotions, lest it should detract from the dignity of a white man appearing under such extraordinary circumstances. So I did that which I thought was most dignified. I pushed back the crowds, and passing from the rear, walked down a living avenue of people, until I came in front of the semi-circle of

Arabs before which stood the "white man with that beard." I would have run to him, only I was a coward in the presence of such a mob—would have embraced him, only, he being an Englishman, I did not know how he would receive me; so I did what moral cowardice and false pride suggested was the best thing—walked deliberately to him, took off my hat and said: "Dr. Livingston, I presume?" "Yes," said he with a kind smile, lifting his cap slightly. I replace my hat on my head, and he puts on his cap, and we both grasp hands and then I say aloud: "I thank God, Doctor, I have been permitted to see you." He answered, "I feel thankful that I am here to welcome you."

Years later, after Stanley had been honored by Queen Victoria, knighted, and had become an international hero, he was asked by an old friend, "You didn't really say 'Dr. Livingstone, I presume?' did you, Sir Henry?" For a while, Stanley did not answer. Finally, he said abruptly, "Yes, I couldn't think what else to say."

Long before meeting Stanley, Livingstone had become one of the most celebrated of African explorers. Among his exploits were crossing the Kalahari Desert and discovering Lake Ngami, reaching the Zambezi River and tracing its course to the Indian Ocean; discovering Victoria Falls and crossing the continent from west to east; exploring the Zambezi region and discovering Lake Nyasa. It was during the last phase of his career that he was found by Stanley. In 1866, as British consul to Central Africa, Livingstone set out to find the headwaters of the Nile. He explored the Lake Tanganyika region and the headquarters of the Congo River, despite the fact that he was constantly hampered by serious illness and unfaithful, thieving natives.

With the generous stocks of food and medicines brought by Stanley, Livingstone soon gained back much of his strength and health. A close friendship grew up between the young reporter and the former missionary. Stanley urged Livingstone to return with him to England to make a full recovery, but the latter was adamant in insisting that he should remain in Africa until he had finished his exploration of the Nile. Stanley and Livingstone did, however, join in navigating the northern shores of Lake Tanganyika, in order to ascertain if the Rusizi River flowed into or out

Henry M. Stanley

of it. The expedition paddled to the mouth of the river and quickly determined that it flowed into Lake Tanganyika and not toward the Nile.

Following this expedition it was arranged that Livingstone should accompany Stanley back to Tabora, to pick up the stores sent to the former from England and also to have turned over to him any surplus stocks that Stanley would be able to leave for him. The route was planned to avoid the savage, tribute-demanding chiefs and their people. On arrival at their destination, Stanley handed over for Livingstone's use no less than forty loads of cloths and beads, wire, rifles, guns, ammunition, and other equipment needed for further explorations. In return, Livingstone handed to Stanley, to take back to England, his precious journal containing notes on all of his journeys since 1866, revealing in detail the important discoveries and the strenuous experiences of the great traveler.

So they parted—Stanley to return to civilization to inform the world that he had found the missing explorer, and Livingstone to continue his search for the source of the Nile. About a year later, Livingstone became ill and on May 1, 1873, his servant found him dead, kneeling by his bedside. The long-sought mystery of the Nile was still unresolved. Stanley was the last white man ever to see Livingstone alive.

From the time that he left Zanzibar until his return there, Stanley had traveled 2,250 miles in 411 days. Some 1,500 miles were through country never before seen by any white man. The expedition had taken the lives of eighteen of the native carriers and two white members of his force. Stanley himself had lost seventy-six pounds from attacks of malaria and dysentery and his black hair had turned gray—at age thirty-two. But he had accomplished his mission and established his reputation as a leader of men and an able explorer.

The news that Stanley had found Livingstone created immense excitement in Europe and America. But, unfortunately, some suspicion and resentment also greeted him. A charge was made that the story was a hoax and Stanley had not even seen Livingstone. The president of the Royal Geographical Society made the malicious remark that it was Livingstone who had found Stanley, rather than the reverse. Livingstone's journal, letters, diaries, and other papers brought home by Stanley helped to silence the critics. His book *How I Found Livingstone* (1872) was an instant success and widely read. Queen Victoria presented him with a gold snuffbox set with brilliants and thanked him for his services. Nevertheless, the shock of his reception, so completely different from what he had expected, left Stanley bitter and alienated. Years later, he wrote: "All the actions of my life, and I may say all my thoughts, since 1872, have been strongly colored by the storm of abuse and the wholly unjustifiable reports circulated about me then."

Lecture tours in England and America followed Stanley's return from Africa. In 1873 he was sent by the *New York Herald* as a war correspondent to accompany General Wolseley's expedition to Ashanti, British protectorate in Ghana. Stanley described the campaign, together with his Abyssinian experiences, in a book entitled *Coomassie and Magdala: Two British Campaigns* (1873).

David Livingstone's death before his explorations could be completed deeply grieved Stanley. He immediately started dreaming of finishing the work Livingstone had begun, tantalized by the prospect of solving the principal geographical problems of Africa still remaining. "My tale of the discovery of Livingstone has been doubted," he wrote. "What I have already endured in that accursed Africa amounts to nothing, in men's estimation." Now, if given an opportunity, he would show his merit. When a proposal was presented to the *Daily Telegraph* in London and the *Herald* in New York, they agreed to sponsor what became known as the Anglo-American Expedition. Stanley left England on August 15, 1874, headed for his greatest adventures and most significant discoveries.

When plans for the new expedition first appeared in the press, Stanley was swamped with applications from persons eager to accompany him. "I might have led," he said, "5,000 Englishmen, 5,000 Americans, 2,000 Frenchmen, 2,000 Germans, 500 Italians, 250 Swiss, 200 Belgians, 50 Spaniards and 5 Greeks, or 15,005 Europeans to Africa." The list included retired colonial officers, hotel managers, mechanics, seamen, bank clerks, market gardners, and even clairvoyants, mediums, and magnetizers. Stanley rejected them all and chose two fishermen from the county of Kent, already known to him, and a London hotel clerk.

Henry M. Stanley

This, Stanley's second major expedition into interior Africa, began with a landing on the island of Zanzibar; its series of momentous explorations started from there on November 12. The long trek lasted two years, eight months, and twenty days. Its results are recorded in Stanley's *Through the Dark Continent; or, the Sources of the Nile, around the Great Lakes of Equatorial Africa, and down the Livingstone River to the Atlantic Ocean* (1878).

Stanley began his extensive travels into the jungle at the head of 356 men, many of whom had served under Livingstone. Included in the bulky supplies and equipment carried was the *Lady Alice,* a launch built in England, which turned out to be invaluable. The boat was so constructed that it could be rapidly dismantled into a number of sections, each weighing about sixty pounds and capable of being managed by a single porter.

After a journey of 720 miles marked by pestilential fevers, struggles through thorny jungles, and with scanty food and water, Lake Victoria Nyanza was sighted in March 1875. Circumnavigating the lake, Stanley discovered it to be over 4,000 feet above sea level, to be nearly 22,000 square miles in area, and over 500 feet deep in places—the proportions of an inland sea. He was greatly aided by Mtesa, a powerful and able Negro king of Mohammedan faith, who proved friendly and furnished an escort, which enabled Stanley to explore a part of the adjacent mountain region. From Lake Victoria, Stanley turned south to the East African rift valley via Lake Kivu to Lake Tanganyika, to complete the circumnavigation originally begun in company with Livingstone. He wanted to find out whether there was any connection between Lake Tanganyika and Lake Victoria, and whether water from Lake Tanganyika flowed into the Nile. In both cases, the answer was negative. Lake Tanganyika itself he found to be about one-half the size of Victoria, with an elevation of some 2,700 feet. The Lualaba River, which Livingstone had believed to be the source of the Nile, was later discovered by Stanley to be the Upper Congo.

At the end of the first two months, twenty-one of Stanley's force were dead, including one of his white companions, Ted Pocock; eight had been left behind because of illness; and eighty-nine had deserted. Stanley had been warned repeatedly against turning west at Lake Tanganyika and going through the territory of a notorious cannibal tribe, the Manyuema, but he obstinately refused to heed the advice. When his porters learned of his intended route, thirty-eight of them deserted at once. Undeterred, Stanley and his remaining men continued to march along the banks of the Lualaba. Even if this river was an extension of the Congo, he was still 1,250 miles from the nearest Portuguese settlement.

The first battle occurred at the end of January, 1875. A dispute arose with a tribe barring the way about the terms on which the expedition would be allowed to pass. One of Stanley's men was murdered and in the ensuing fight twenty-one other men were lost. When his carriers refused to cross such dangerous country without an armed escort, Stanley made a deal with Tippu Tib, part Arab, part Negro, and the most successful slave trader of Central Africa, to accompany him for sixty days with a private army of 140 riflemen and 70 spearmen. At the end of the contract period, Tippu Tib had enough and would proceed no farther, declaring that never before had he been in such a hellish region.

It is clear that Stanley had underestimated the dangers, rigors, and deprivations of the terrible jungle area now being traversed. After reaching Nyangwe, Livingstone's most distant point, in October 1876, Stanley plunged into the unknown. Viewed from the high banks of the Lualaba, nothing could be seen except a silent, unbroken mass of black-green forest. Inside this green hell the sky was invisible, a gloomy darkness prevailed, and the air was oppressively humid and hot. The Rain Forest, as it was appropriately named, was inhabited by fierce and inhospitable tribes, and swarmed with every kind of beast and insect dangerous to man.

Finally Stanley realized that it was impossible to continue through the jungle and decided that it would be preferable to travel down the Lualaba itself. The *Lady Alice* was unpacked and assembled, twenty-three canoes were bought or confiscated from the natives, and the entire expedition became waterborne. The river journey proved as difficult, however, as had the jungle march. The Lualaba was wide and Stanley and his men kept to its center. Landing on either side was perilous. All along the route could be heard a "dreadful drumming," warning tribes down the river of their approach. Time after time, fleets of canoes came out to intercept them, the largest over eighty feet in length, manned by as many

Henry M. Stanley

as thirty-five paddlers armed with muskets, spears, and bows and arrows. The superior firepower possessed by Stanley's forces drove off the attackers with heavy casualties. The natives, cannibals all, wanted meat.

By February 1877, the last year of the expedition, Stanley had fought twenty-six battles on the river. Showers of arrow fell on the launch and among the canoes, and Stanley's guns would answer, sending bullets into the forest. Another hazard was met when the expedition reached Stanley Falls, a series of seven cataracts; the negotiation of the falls took three weeks of the new year, during which the explorers were under constant attack by tall warriors of the Bakomo tribe.

Discovering that the Lualaba took a sharp turn westward at this point, Stanley calculated that the river had to be the Congo, and that it would eventually flow into the Atlantic. But the expedition's troubles were far from over. Thirty-two cataracts, in rapid succession, were faced next. These were named the Livingstone Falls by Stanley. Canoes were lost and six men were drowned. Then the river slowly widened to an average distance of nearly two-and-a-half miles. High waves required great care to prevent the launch and canoes from capsizing. The natives along the shore became peaceful and friendly, and plentiful food supplies could be obtained by barter.

On one occasion, however, Stanley was confronted by a dangerous situation. The natives observed him writing in his journal and, suspecting black magic, a force of 500 armed warriors demanded that he burn his record of 900 days of traveling, containing his descriptions of places, altitudes, ethnological notes, barometric readings, meteorological and hydrographic data, maps, sketches, and plans. To avoid such a catastrophe, Stanley deceived the natives by handing the chief a volume of Shakespeare. A giant fire was lit and the book thrown into it and reduced to ashes.

As the expedition proceeded, portages became more difficult and perilous. At one point the boats had to be dragged over a 1,500-foot mountain. More canoes were built while pathways were being cut through the jungle. One of the worst blows was the drowning of Stanley's last white companion, Frank Pocock, while trying to shoot the Massassa Falls. Later the nature of the country changed; thereafter the men marched through a fertile, undulating highland.

By early August the natives informed them that the sea was only a few days' march ahead. So exhausted were the expedition members by now, however, that the entire group practically collapsed. A message sent to Boma, a trading town not far away, resulted in relief porters and food being sent out. On August 9, 1877, exactly 999 days after leaving Zanzibar, Stanley reached an outpost of Europe and was greeted by his first white men. Three months after sailing from Boma, he was back with his black comrades in Zanzibar.

In summarizing the terrible river trip on the Lualaba–Upper Congo, Stanley noted that thirty-two battles had been fought, twenty-eight hostile towns and numerous villages destroyed, fifty-two falls and rapids portaged, thirty miles of roadway cut through the jungle, mountains and high boulders surmounted, and only 115 of his original crew of 356 had survived. The remainder had died or deserted.

The expedition's achievements were little short of phenomenal. Lake Victoria had been circumnavigated and mapped; the entire perimeter of Lake Tanganyika explored; and the Congo traced down to its mouth.

Upon his return to England, Stanley attempted, through discussions, lectures, and conferences, to interest Parliament, bankers, and merchants in the significance of the great river he had conquered. He wanted to see British traders strengthen the empire by opening Africa commercially. Again he was to be disappointed; he met with nothing except scorn and ridicule. A more willing ear, however, was lent by King Leopold II of Belgium. The king had declared his intention to undertake a major developmental plan for Africa whereby, through international cooperation, slavery would be abolished, tribal wars stopped, medical stations and scientific laboratories established, highways and railroads built, and plantations started. For these grandiose purposes, the International African Society was founded.

Stanley was approached by King Leopold's emissaries to assist the plan for the economic exploitation of Africa, particularly the Congo region. Having met with complete indifference in England, he accepted, and together with a number of Belgian businessmen founded a committee for work in the Congo. A few months later he was back in Africa to begin the tremendous task assigned to him, conducting a series of explorations and surveys. Stanley's work there

Henry M. Stanley

secured the Congo for King Leopold and Belgium, leading ulti-mately to the setting up of the Congo Free State, a vast tropical empire more than a million square miles in extent under Leopold's sovereignty. For five-and-a-half years, except for one brief interlude, Stanley's energy and administrative ability were devoted to the construction of roads and to the establishment of permanent stations on the Congo.

It should be noted that, when it was almost too late, England, Germany, and other European powers awakened to Africa's great potentialities and the general scramble to grab pieces of territory began.

Back in England after his arduous labors in the Congo, Stanley thought that his services would be enlisted for the British Empire, but nothing developed. Books and lectures occupied his time and made him a man of means. A year after his return, his book *The Congo and the Founding of Its Free State* (1885) appeared.

Stanley's last journey into Africa was for the rescue of the Egyp-tian governor of Equatoria, Edward Schnitzer, a German, better known as Emin Pasha, who had been cut off by an uprising led by a fanatical Sudanese named Mahdi. Supposedly, Stanley was em-ployed by the khedive of Egypt for the relief mission, though his real concern was the establishment of a British protectorate in East Africa. The expedition added little to Stanley's reputation. Emin was saved, but nearly fifty percent of Stanley's men died from starvation, fever, and attacks by hostile tribes. Still, the operation was not lacking in substantial achievements. Lake Edward, 830 square miles in area, was discovered in East Africa, and the highest peaks in the Ruwenzori Mountains were named. The political importance of the expedition was the agreements made by Stanley with various chiefs in favor of Great Britain, subsequently exploited by the East Africa Company. The expedition was described by Stanley in his *In Darkest Africa* (1890).

After his final return to England, Stanley settled down to the life of a country gentleman. He again became a British citizen, married the daughter of a British member of Parliament, in 1895 was himself elected as a Liberal-Unionist member of Parliament (an institution that he hated), and four years later was knighted. He died in 1904, plagued in his last years by fevers and other ailments incurred in Africa.

Stanley's personal appearance and personality were handicaps. Queen Victoria wrote: "I have this evening seen Mr. Stanley, who discovered Livingstone, a determined, ugly little man—with a strong American twang." Byron Farwell's excellent biography, *The Man Who Presumed,* describes Stanley: "Standing only five feet five inches high and weighing a hundred and sixty-five pounds, he had a broad chest and short legs on which were stuck a pair of large feet. His hair was black above a round, florid face in which were perched a pair of gray, boyish eyes that were strangely penetrating." When Stanley set a goal for himself, he never lost sight of it, and was fully prepared to sacrifice himself or anyone else in order to reach it; there was a streak of ruthlessness in his character. He was, when the occasion demanded it, a pitiless taskmaster and driver of men. In England, his fellow countrymen criticized him for his free use of the whip in controlling rebellious natives, and for shots fired at hostile cannibals. Certainly, Stanley's methods fell far short of being humane, and yet they frequently made the difference between death and survival. His determination to succeed always remained unshakeable.

By continuing Livingstone's work as an explorer, Stanley filled in the last great blank spaces on the map of the Dark Continent and was the first to cross Africa from east to west by way of the Congo. In geographical discoveries, he accomplished more than any other African explorer.

Henry M. Stanley

19
Lone Voyager

Joshua Slocum's Sailing Alone around the World,
1896—1898

The literary critic Hamilton Basso rates Captain Joshua Slocum's *Sailing Alone around the World* as "the most exciting factual sea story" he knew, with Thor Heyerdahl's *Kon-Tiki* coming in a close second. Van Wyck Brooks, another perceptive critic, described the book as "a nautical equivalent to Thoreau's account of his life in the hut at Walden."

Stories of man's battle against the sea are innumerable—Magellan, James Cook, Columbus, Vespucci, Darwin, Vancouver, Scott, Dana, Vasco da Gama, Balboa, Drake, Ross, Heyerdahl, and so on, ad infinitum. Few voyages were more daring or appealing to the imagination than Slocum's one-man circumnavigation of the earth at the end of the nineteenth century, the only man on record to have made the circuit alone by sea up to that time.

Slocum was a native of Nova Scotia, born in 1844, a cold, hard man from the Bay of Fundy. He left school at the age of eight and ran away from home at twelve to earn his living doing odd jobs among the fishermen of the Bay of Fundy. His first ocean voyage was made at the age of sixteen, shipping as a cook on a fishing schooner.

Later, at eighteen, on a voyage from Liverpool to the East Indies, Slocum was promoted to second mate and soon became chief mate. In that capacity, he twice sailed around the Horn on British ships, carrying coal to sell going out and bringing back grain between Liverpool, Cardiff, and San Francisco. He decided to make San Francisco his home port and became an American citizen. The next few years were occupied in shipbuilding, salmon fishing on the Columbia River, and hunting sea otters near Vancouver Island. His real ambition was command of a ship, a goal he achieved in 1869 at the age of twenty-five, when he became captain of a coastal schooner plying between San Francisco and Seattle.

Slocum moved on to other commands. First was the bark *Washington*, 332 tons, which sailed from San Francisco for Sydney, Australia, in 1870, with a general cargo. He married while in Australia, and only his wife accompanied him on the 6,000-mile return voyage across the Pacific. They returned by way of Alaska to engage in salmon fishing, but the *Washington* dragged her anchors in a gale and was stranded on shoals 200 miles from Kodiak. The ship's owners gave Slocum another command, the barkentine *Constitution*, running between San Francisco and Honolulu. Captaincies of a variety of other vessels followed: the *B. Aymar*, a full-rigged, single topsail, East Indies trader, sailing from Sydney to Amoy; the *Amethyst*, a full-rigged ship built for the Philippines-China timber trade; and the *Northern Light*, a three-masted wind-jammer of 1,800 tons register, which according to Slocum was "the finest American sailing ship afloat."

But the age of steam was fast approaching, and sailing ships were becoming outmoded. By the 1890s, Slocum discovered that his type of expert navigation was no longer wanted. He was supremely qualified to command a wind-driven ship under all conceivable conditions. As Bruce Catton comments in his *Prefaces to History*: "He was a master mariner in sail at a time when nobody had any work for master mariners in sail." Unwilling to concede defeat, Slocum invested his savings in the purchase of a 326 ton bark, the *Aquidneck*—an unwise investment in a sailing ship when masters and owners were turning to steam. The *Aquidneck* engaged in trade along the South American coast, but in 1887 was wrecked on a Brazilian sandbar. From the wreckage, Slocum built a thirty-five foot sailing canoe which he named the *Liberdade*, and sailed with his family back to New York.

Thus, with a rich background of voyages to exotic ports in all kinds of sailing vessels, Slocum was prepared to start on his supreme adventure. It is uncertain when or how he got the idea of sailing around the world alone. He was well equipped by a lifetime of nautical experience, of course, and possessed the disposition to undertake such an expedition. Originally he had anticipated making some money from the venture by writing and syndicating travel letters, but that plan fell through.

An unlikely vessel was obtained by Slocum for his daring voyage. At Fairhaven he found a derelict hulk, an ancient oyster sloop named *Spray*. She was said to be a century old, and for the past seven years had been beached high and dry in a pasture beside the Acushnet River. Slocum set about rejuvenating the dilapidated ship, rebuilding most of it; of the original, all that remained was the model. Old timbers were removed and new planks fitted in. Thirteen months were required to finish the job; at the end a craft of "questionable build and almost distressing plainness" was launched into the river, where Slocum thought she "sat on the water like a swan." The *Spray* was thirty-seven feet long, fourteen feet wide, and had a gross tonnage of thirteen tons. She was not designed in the first place for sailing around the world, or even for sailing alone. Her mainsail and gaff were almost too much for a man to raise by himself, and overall she was a large boat for one man to handle. She had the virtue, however, of being able to steer herself, with the tiller lashed, while the captain remained below, cooking, reading, mending his clothes, or sleeping; he did not need to be constantly standing or sitting at the wheel. For a tender, Slocum carried a dory sawed in half, to save space; it also served as a tub for laundry or bath.

Equipment for a long voyage was another matter. One of the first things Slocum thought of was books. A sizable seagoing library was assembled; the captain apparently had broadly catholic tastes, and included a well-rounded selection of science, history, and literature. From his earlier voyages as a merchant captain he had his charts, compass, sextant, rifles, revolvers, and medicines. Well-wishers supplied him with the latest patented taffrail log for measuring speed and distance. Another friend gave him money to buy a two-burner lamp, which he used as a lamp by night and a stove by day. A tin clock was bought for a dollar at Yarmouth, serving as his timepiece throughout the voyage. As he needed $15 to clean and repair his chronometer, this instrument was eliminated. A paint firm gave him a supply of copper paint and he proceeded to apply two coats of it to prevent fouling of the ship's bottom.

For food supplies, Slocum took a barrel of potatoes; two barrels of ship's bread or "pilot bread," a large, thick, hard bread of coarse quality, meant to keep indefinitely when sealed in cans; baking powder, salt, pepper, sugar, and curry powder; salt beef, salt pork, ham, and salt codfish; condensed milk, butter packed in brine to avoid its becoming rancid, and eggs (immersed in hot water for a minute to keep them from spoiling) ; and six barrels of water. The captain knew the importance of eating the right foods while at sea, and he survived in good health on this diet for seventy-five days, his longest passage without touching land.

When he was finally ready to depart, Slocum headed for Gloucester, where he spent two weeks in final outfitting. He had hoped to have the *Spray* carried across the Isthmus of Panama by train, but was informed that it could not be done. An alternative was to go through the Strait of Magellan, after proceeding down the South American coast. Instead, he went east to Nova Scotia and visited his birthplace, which he had not seen in thirty-five years. At last, on July 2, 1895, he left America to face the "boisterous Atlantic." Eighteen days later he arrived in the Azores, where the natives supplied him with quantities of fresh fruits. Under way again, Slocum made a meal of white Pico cheese and plums, a combination which left him lying on the cabin floor, ill with cramps and fever and delirious. He remained in that condition for two days while the *Spray* steered herself; the remaining plums were thrown overboard.

At the next port of call, Gibraltar, the captain was given a hero's welcome. The admiral on duty replenished the ship's larder with fresh milk and vegetables and Slocum, whose funds were down to $1.50, was given a $50 loan. Three leisurely weeks were spent at Gibraltar, after which it was Slocum's intention to sail across the Mediterranean, through the Suez Canal and the Red Sea. The British naval officers, however, urged him not to follow this route because of danger from pirates. That way, they warned him, would be extremely hazardous for a man alone. Two possibilities remained: to sail around Africa, which would involve a long passage between the Cape of Good Hope and Australia; or to return across the Atlantic and navigate around South America and Cape Horn. Slocum elected to take the latter course.

Shortly after he sailed from Gibraltar on August 26, the *Spray* was spotted by Moorish pirates lying off the coast of Morocco, and they gave chase. Slocum crowded on sail to try to outrun them. It appeared that he had lost the race when a squall snapped his ship's main boom, and he was snatching up his rifle and revolvers for defense when he noticed that the pirate craft had lost its mast. "I felt almost a disappointment," the captain reported.

After making the necessary repairs, the *Spray* was carried across the Atlantic by trade winds until she hit the doldrums which, as described by the captain, "are the baffling winds, light air, and heavy rain squalls from all directions," that for a ten-day period slowed Slocum's ship down to an average speed of a mile and a quarter an hour. Forty days out of Gibraltar, he dropped anchor in Pernambuco harbor, Brazil, where the *Spray* was refitted. Another 1,200 miles of sailing brought him to Rio de Janeiro, where he arrived on November 5. The hardest part of his global circumnavigation lay immediately ahead.

Slocum sailed from Rio on November 28. While cruising off the coast of Uruguay a few days later, the *Spray* ran aground on hard sand. In his efforts to free her, the captain was almost drowned; amazingly, he had never learned to swim. As he explained it, he had been reared in Newfoundland where the water was too cold for comfort; furthermore, he added, he did not expect to fall overboard when his ship was in port, and if he fell over in mid-ocean he might as well drown first as last. In any case, with the help of several men nearby, the *Spray* was refloated and got under way again, though somewhat damaged by the pounding she had taken while lying on the sand.

At Montevideo, Slocum was given a royal welcome, including free dockage; free repairs, a stove for the cold, wet weather ahead; a liberal gift of money; and the painting of his dory. He was becoming famous. An excursion was made to Buenos Aires, where Slocum's first wife, Virginia, had died about twelve years earlier and was buried.

Continuing down the coast of Patagonia, the captain had a narrow escape. While making her way through a storm, a tremendous wave came racing down upon the *Spray*. A mountain of water, masthead high, broke over the vessel. Slocum held fast to the rigging and was saved from being swept overboard.

The eastern entrance of the Strait of Magellan was reached in February of 1896. Ordinarily it would have been the most favorable season of the year, but Slocum was met by fierce currents and sudden squalls. In black night a southwest gale, the terror of Cape Horn, struck and kept on blowing hard for thirty hours.

At Sandy Point, a coaling station, Slocum was advised that he might have to fight off Indians farther west in the Strait, and he kept his guns loaded for that eventuality. In addition, a fellow mariner, a Captain Pedro Samblich, presented him with a bag of carpet tacks as a way of keeping his deck clear of intruders at night. When Slocum left Sandy Point, February 20, on his fifty-second birthday, the *Spray* encountered the terrible squalls called Williwaws, described as "compressed gales of wind." Days were spent bucking against windstorms and strong currents. When fair weather came, he found that he was being chased by canoes manned by savages. Several shots fired across their bows, however, sent them scurrying back to shore. Later, when he was able to anchor in a quiet cove, exhausted by the storms, he went to bed, taking the precaution of sprinkling the deck with tacks, sharp ends up. About midnight, two canoe loads of savages came on board.

What followed next was graphically described by the captain: "Now, it is well known that one cannot step on a tack without saying something about it . . . a savage will howl and claw the air, and that was just what happened that night about twelve o'clock, while I was asleep in the cabin, where the savages thought they 'had me,' sloop and all, but changed their minds when they stepped on deck, for then they thought that I or somebody else had them . . . they howled like a pack of hounds, jumped pell-mell, some into their canoes and some into the sea." Slocum fired several guns "to let the rascals" know that he was home, but was disturbed no more.

The ordeal of trying to steer a vessel through the terrible weather conditions commonly prevailing through the straits, especially at night, was vividly told by Slocum. As he approached Cockburn Channel, one of the many arms of the strait, he wrote:

Joshua Slocum

Night closed in before the sloop reached land, leaving her feeling the way in the pitchy darkness. I saw breakers ahead before long. At this I wore ship and stood offshore, but was immediately startled by the tremendous roar of breakers again ahead and on the ice bow.... In this way, among dangers, I spent the rest of the night. Hail and sleet in the fierce squalls cut my flesh till the blood trickled over my face.

When daylight came, Slocum found that it was the white breakers of a huge sea over sunken rocks which had threatened to engulf the *Spray* through the night. "It was Fury Island that I had sighted and steered for. God knows how my vessel escaped."

Varied adventures with weather and Fuegian natives further enlivened passage through the strait. Slocum made six attempts to reach the Pacific and each time was driven back by adverse winds. Eventually, the *Spray* anchored at Port Angosto, at the west entrance to the strait, "a dreary enough place," but a safe haven where the captain could refit and clean up his boat. He arrived at the port in a snowstorm; the snow fell thick and fast until the *Spray* "looked like a white winter bird."

On April 13, 1896, Slocum sailed into the Pacific, more than two months after first entering the strait. The English geographer W. S. Barclay suggested that of the hundreds of passages that have been made through the Strait of Magellan, three are most memorable: the first by the discoverer, Ferdinand Magellan; the second by Francis Drake; and the third by Joshua Slocum. The last-named both navigated and sailed. His principal biographer, Walter M. Teller, adds: "At the western entrance he survived a Cape Horn equinoctial storm. He passed an entire night cruising and tacking in one of the worst death traps of the Seven Seas. Finding his own way to re-enter the Strait, he sailed west again, thus skirting the most perilous triangle a mariner can imagine."

As he headed west on the Pacific, Slocum's first destination was Juan Fernandez Island, about 400 miles west of Chile, sometimes called Robinson Crusoe Island. Alexander Selkirk, the original of Daniel Defoe's hero Robinson Crusoe, lived on the island from 1704 to 1709. Fifteen days out, on April 26, the island loomed ahead. As Slocum recorded his reactions, "the blue hills of Juan Fernandez, high among the clouds, could be seen about thirty miles off. A thousand emotions thrilled me when I saw the island, and I bowed my head to the deck." He offered the natives Yankee hospitality by serving them coffee and doughnuts, the latter fried in tallow and a novelty to the islanders. A visit was paid to Alexander Selkirk's retreat, the captain seeing some analogy between himself and Robinson Crusoe. Ten leisurely days were spent on shore, some of the time with the island's children gathering wild quinces, peaches, and figs, later to be preserved.

Now began the longest leg of the voyage—seventy-three days and nights to Samoa. It appears that never in such long stretches, during which he heard or saw no other human being, did Slocum suffer any serious feeling of loneliness. At first he used his voice often, calling out orders as though to crew members, but he concluded that "my voice sounded hollow on the empty air and I dropped the practice." He liked to sing, however, and he sang the songs of the sea merchant service and hymns. Actually, he noted that "there was no end of companionship; the very coral reefs kept me company, or gave me no time to feel lonely, which is the same thing, and there were many of them now in my course to Samoa." Elsewhere he commented: "My time was all taken up those days—not by standing at the helm—I did better than that, for I sat and read my books, mended my clothes, or cooked my meals and ate them in peace. I made companionship with what there was around me, sometimes with the universe and sometimes with my own insignificant self, but my books were always my friends, let fail all else." During the entire time crossing the South Pacific between Juan Fernandez and Samoa, no ship was sighted.

Among the incidents reported by Slocum as he sailed the Pacific was a narrow escape from a collision with a great whale, which was "absent-mindedly plowing the ocean at night while I was below. The noise from his startled snort and the commotion he made in the sea, as he turned to clear my vessel, brought me on deck in time to catch a wetting from the water he threw up with his flukes. The monster was apparently frightened." The captain also observed that "hungry sharks came about the vessel often when she neared islands or coral reefs. I own to a satisfaction in shooting them as one would a tiger. Sharks, after all, are the tigers of the sea. Nothing is more dreadful to the mind of a sailor, I think, than a possible

Joshua Slocum

encounter with a hungry shark." Throughout his travels, Slocum never shot at anything except men and sharks. Even in the dreadful Tierra del Fuego area, when he could have replenished his food supply by shooting wild ducks, he never raised his gun. "In the loneliness of life about the dreary country," he remarked, "I found myself in no mood to take one life less, except in self-defense." The flying fish landed on deck, he ate; otherwise, he "seldom or never put a hook over during the whole voyage." Crossing the Pacific, birds were constant companions, sometimes perching on the mast of the *Spray*.

On July 16, Slocum's vessel cast anchor at Apia, in the kingdom of Samoa. Instead of going ashore at once, he sat until late in the evening "listening with delight to the musical voices of the Samoan men and women." When he landed, he was warmly greeted by Mrs. Robert Louis Stevenson, who had accompanied her husband on his voyages. After a month in this "summer-land," Slocum took off for his next goal, a forty-two day voyage, "mostly of storms and gales," to Newcastle, New South Wales. It had been a year and a half since he left Boston and he was now halfway around the world. He had become famous and gala receptions were being held for him as he proceeded from place to place.

Also, Slocum seemed to have a remarkable talent for making friends along the way. As Teller points out: "Any man who shows unrelenting purpose attracts admirers and supporters. The unusual voyage appealed to all sorts of people; many wanted to help." Time flew by for the captain. For more than six months he wandered from port to port in Australian and Tasmanian waters. Crowds came to see the *Spray,* and Slocum was widely entertained.

In June of 1897 the captain left Australia and the Great Barrier Reef behind and sailed for the Indian Ocean. A stop was made in the palm-covered Cocos Islands, 600 miles southwest of Java, where Slocum stayed several weeks. On Christmas Day, 1897, he wrote that the *Spray* "was trying to stand on her head" in a gale as she was rounding the Cape of Good Hope peninsula. He finally dropped anchor in the bay off Capetown, and settled down in South Africa to spend three months touring the goldfields and traveling around the country by rail. On March 26, 1898, the *Spray* sailed from South Africa bound for home.

There was a ten-day stopover in St. Helena, about 1,200 miles off the Angolan coast of Africa. Among the gifts received when he departed was a goat, which he was told would be as companionable as a dog. The animal turned out to be an extreme nuisance, which "threatened to devour everything from flying-jib to stern-davits ... there was not a rope in the sloop proof against the goat's awful teeth." The most serious loss was the West Indies charts chewed up by the beast, later handicapping navigation through that area. Slocum and the goat parted company at Ascension Island, the next port of call. The goat was the last of several fellow travelers or stowaways on the *Spray*, including a spider, a tree-crab, a rat, a centipede, and a pair of crickets. The captain concluded that there was no room for pet animals on his craft, not even a small dog (he had an inordinate fear of hydrophobia).

Without further serious incident, after four years of wandering and covering 26,000 miles, Slocum and the *Spray* returned to New England, dropping anchor in his home port of Fairhaven, Massachusetts, on July 3, 1898. In justification for his great adventure, the captain wrote:

> If the *Spray* discovered no continents on her voyage, it may be that there were no more continents to be discovered; she did not seek new worlds, or sail to powwow about the dangers of the seas. The sea has been much maligned. To find one's way to lands already discovered is a good thing, and the *Spray* made the discovery that even the worst sea is not so terrible to a well-appointed ship. No king, no country, no treasury at all, was taxed for the voyage of the *Spray*, and she accomplished all that she undertook to do.

Sailing Alone around the World, Slocum's own account of his voyage, was first published monthly in *Century* magazine in 1899–1900, and then brought out in book form by the Century Company. Within a year it had sold 10,000 copies.

Slocum's subsequent career was anticlimactic. For several years he wandered up and down the Atlantic coast in the *Spray*, dreaming up various schemes which came to nothing substantial. At age sixty-five, in November of 1909, he began planning another sensational voyage. He would sail to South America, up the Orinoco River, and into the Rio Negro, and from there to the head of the Amazon River. From the Amazon, he would sail home. On November 14 he took the *Spray* to sea and vanished, never again to be seen or heard from.

Various theories were offered as to what may have happened. One is that the strains of long sea-voyaging may have been too much for the *Spray* and her master. Since green timber was used in the ship's construction, she would have a shorter life than one built of well-seasoned wood, causing her to disintegrate. The *Spray's* ancient seams apparently opened up in some heavy sea. Slocum was not declared legally dead until 1924.

Joshua Slocum's great adventure was duplicated in 1966–67 by an Englishman, Francis Chichester, who also sailed solo around the world in his sixty-foot ketch, *Gipsy Moth IV*. The route followed and many of the adventures experienced were similar to Slocum's. For his feat, Chichester was knighted by Queen Elizabeth II. A full account of his voyage is contained in Chichester's book *Gipsy Moth Circles the World* (London: Hodder and Stoughton; New York: Coward-McCann, 1967).

A feature story distributed by the Associated Press in November of 1977 reviews similar daring attempts to circumnavigate the world by single sailors or by families, using a variety of crafts. Some have succeeded; others, the report states, "sink from sight, literally victims of storms, reefs or pirates."

20
Farthest North

Robert E. Peary's The North Pole, 1908—1909

Few men in history have shown such single-minded dedication to achieving one objective as Robert Edwin Peary. Early in his career he determined to become an Arctic explorer, with the ultimate aim of reaching the North Pole. As he expressed himself to Theodore Roosevelt in 1906, after the failure of his next-to-last expedition, "To me the final and complete solution of the Polar mystery— is the thing which should be done for the honor and credit of this country, *the thing which it is intended that I should do, and the thing that I must do!"*

After the success of his heroic mission, Peary summarized his feelings:

> My lifework is accomplished. The thing which it was intended from the beginning that I should do, the thing which I believed could be done, and that I could do, I have done. I have got the North Pole out of my system after twenty-three years of effort, hard work, disappointments, hardships, privations, more or less suffering, and some risks. I have won the last great geographical prize, the North Pole, for the credit of the United States. This work is the finish, the cap and climax of nearly four hundred years of effort, loss of life, and expenditures of fortunes by the civilized nations of the world, and it was been accomplished in a way that is thoroughly American.

As Peary noted, numerous Arctic explorers had preceded him in attempts to reach the North Pole. No region of the earth has

Part of Peary's expedition party crossing a ridge

produced more tales of heroism and stoic endurance, of narrow escapes and tragedies, than the Arctic. Examples are John Davis, one of the most remarkable of Elizabethan seamen who, in 1588, reached a point 1,128 miles from the pole; and, several centuries later, David Buchan, another Englishman who, in 1818, sailed with instructions to reach the Sandwich Islands by way of the North Pole and to return, if possible, by the same route. Far short of his goal, Buchan concluded that the task he had been assigned was hopeless.

Other nineteenth-century expeditions—by Ross, Austin, Franklin, McClure, Greely, Nares, Markham, and Nansen—followed each other in rapid succession. It was finally conceded that there was no northern passage across the pole, after which the prime aim became attainment of 90° north latitude, that is, the pole itself, a goal which required nearly a century to achieve. All the explorers prior to Peary had to admit defeat and many failed to return. A noteworthy effort was made by Sir Edward Parry in 1827 and described in his book *Narrative of an Attempt to Reach the North Pole in Boats Fitted for the Purpose,* published in London in 1828. Parry tried to reach the pole from Spitbergen using sledge boats; he attained 82°45' north latitude, a record not broken until 1876. Parry's plan was to use boats shod along their keels with iron strips and dragged by British sailors; on ice the boats were sledges, on water they became boats again. The expedition was still 445 miles short of the pole when Parry abandoned the struggle.

Records were made to be broken. A new one was established in 1875 by Sir George Nares, who went three miles farther north than Parry. Nares was followed by J. B. Lockwood and D. L. Brainard of A. W. Greely's U.S. Army expedition, who exceeded Nares's record by four miles in 1882. In the winter of 1895 Fridtjof Nansen and Frederik Hjalmar Johansen sledged northward to 86°12', breaking the Greely record by 186 geographical miles; five years later, a party of Italians under the Duke of Abruzzi sledged from a Franz Josef base to 86°34'.

Robert Peary poured a lifetime of rugged conditioning and experience into preparation for his drive to the North Pole. He had grown up in Maine, received an engineering degree from Bowdoin College in 1877, and became a naval officer in 1881. During the

Robert E. Peary

years 1884–88 he was associated with and part-time engineer-in-chief of a Nicaraguan canal survey. He went on his first Arctic expedition, to Greenland, while on leave from the navy in 1886. From 1891 until the end of his naval career he was engaged in Arctic explorations more or less continuously.

Peary's second northern expedition, 1891–92, established headquarters at McCormick Bay on the western coast of Greenland. From there, he made extensive sledge excursions; ascended the summit of the great ice cap which covers the interior of Greenland, 5,000 to 8,000 feet in elevation; pushed northward for 500 miles over a region previously unvisited by any white man; and on July 4, 1892, discovered Independence Bay. A broken leg was Peary's only injury on these strenuous travels.

Peary soon became convinced that the Eskimo had much to teach the white man in the matter of polar expeditions. In this important respect, his work was revolutionary. Without the Eskimos, it is extremely doubtful that Peary could ever have reached the North Pole. In early polar explorations, travel was undertaken during the summer because of dread of the northern cold and winter. Edward Parry's men, for example, had practically hibernated, digging themselves in during the fall and emerging in the spring. It was known that the Eskimos drove their dogs and sledges over the snow, but Parry had waited for the snow to melt and then dragged carts through the mud.

Robert Peary rejected these ideas. He completely adopted Eskimo ways. Instead of summer he made full use of winter travel, insisting that serious northern journeys should begin in midwinter and end before the spring thaws. Instead of carrying heavy and burdensome tents, Peary built snow houses or igloos, Eskimo fashion. When trained in the art, four men could build an igloo in an hour's time, using strong snow-sawing knives. Another advantage of the snow houses; an explorer, on the return journey, could usually find the igloos built on the outward journey still intact.

Peary's sledges were also of the Eskimo type, though built with superior materials and lengthened to make them safer for crossing breaks in the ice or in traveling on thin ice. Hauling power was supplied by Eskimo dogs working in Eskimo harness, hitched in

the Eskimo manner. Futhermore, Peary's clothes were of Eskimo
cut, made of local skins, and worn Eskimo style.

Food was a crucial consideration for Peary, as it had been for
all Arctic explorers. Supplies of fresh meat were available from
caribou, Arctic deer, musk-oxen, and occasional polar bears. Certain basic provisions necessary for survival, however, had to be
carried along, and on this subject Peary held strong views: "On
a serious northern sledge journey," he declared, "only four tried
articles—pemmican, tea, condensed milk, and hardtack—are necessary. Of all the items which go to make up the list of supplies for a
polar expedition, the one which ranks first in importance is pemmican. With pemmican, the most serious sledge journey can be
undertaken and carried to a successful issue in the absence of all
other foods."

Pemmican, as made up for Peary's expeditions, was an American
Indian invention consisting of lean meat dried, pounded fine, and
mixed with melted fat, a mixture to which Peary added a few raisins
per pound for flavoring. Milk and sugar in hot tea were also used
for flavor and variety, rather than dietetic value. A pound of biscuit
or hardtack per day was considered important for bulk.

At age fifty-two, Peary realized that his seventh attempt to reach
the North Pole would probably be his last. His preparations for
the expedition, therefore, were made with extraordinary care. For
a 1906 try, he had designed and constructed the *Roosevelt,* a boat
built to withstand the crush of masses of ice. The *Roosevelt* was
a three-masted steamship, built entirely of white oak, with walls
up to thirty inches thick. Her heavy bow was backed by twelve
feet of solid deadwood, and the stern was reinforced by iron and
had a long overhang to protect the rudder from ice. The rudder
itself could be lifted out of the water when jammed or entangled.
The ship was completely overhauled in readiness for the 1908
expedition.

In July 1908, the Peary party sailed from New York. At Etah,
an Eskimo settlement in northwest Greenland, a number of Eskimos
were taken aboard. The tribe from which these natives came was
known variously as the Whale Sound tribe, the Polar Eskimos, or
the Arctic Highlanders. Their dialect, customs, and traditions were

somewhat different from Eskimos in other areas, an indication of an isolation of many centuries. There were about thirty-five families in the tribe and all were well known to Perry through previous contacts. He was also familiar with their language.

The *Roosevelt* pushed steadily northward, through the Kennedy and Robeson channels, the vessel picking its way between ice floes. The voyage was hazardous in the extreme. There was a strong tidal current, which created a moving pack of chaotic ice floes and icebergs in midstream. For days the channel was frozen solid, and the *Roosevelt* had to find a sheltered cove until the way was again clear. At times gigantic floes, an acre or more in size, surged towards the ship, threatening to crush it. A charging iceberg smashed the bulwark. But three weeks later the Arctic Ocean came in sight. Peary's aim was to reach Cape Columbia on the north coast of Grant Land; the ice pack, however, made any progress beyond Cape Sheridan impossible. On the first day of September the *Roosevelt* anchored in a snug harbor under the protection of Cape Sheridan and the crew went into winter quarters. Not until February, when the first gray light of the approaching dawn began to break through the darkness, could the dash to the pole begin. Several hunting trips were arranged to pass the time and to provide the party with a plentiful supply of fresh meat during the winter.

On February 28 and March 1, 1909, Peary's men, divided into several groups, set out. The party was composed of twenty-four men (six whites, one Negro, and seventeen Eskimos) and 133 dogs. All headed straight north for the pole, 413 nautical miles away. Advance groups broke trail, while Peary brought up the rear. The greatest problem throughout the arduous trek, and the cause of frequent delays, was "leads," channels of water running through the ice, which had to be crossed with the sledges. For lack of supplies, the last trailbreaking group was sent back to the base camp on April 1. That left Peary with a supporting group of five men for the final drive—four Eskimos and Matthew Henson, a Negro, his long-time valet and companion, who was also a skilled dog driver. The best dogs, forty in number, had been reserved for the final march, pulling five sledges. All were in excellent condition.

As the party, now much reduced in size, pushed north it continued to encounter many cracks in the ice. The sledges had to charge across from one ice cake to another as though they were leaping across a series of swaying stepping-stones. On one occasion Peary fell in the water, but since his clothes were watertight, he scraped off the ice and proceeded. Despite the obstacle course they were pursuing—open leads and massive hummocks of ice to avoid—the picked party was able to travel fast. The distance covered during the last five marches averaged twenty-six miles daily.

The pole was reached on the morning of April 6, 1909. To make certain of the exact location, different observations of the sun were taken and marches made ten miles in every direction, to allow for any slight error in computation. Afterward, flags were raised on a heap of snow and a record left of the expedition. Peary spent thirty hours at the pole and photographed the desolate, snow-swept scene in all directions. The return journey was begun after a short sleep in an igloo.

Of scientific interest are the soundings which Peary made in the polar area. Five miles from the pole itself, the depth was found to be 1,500 fathoms, or 9,000 feet, without touching bottom. A sounding in 1937 reached bottom near the pole at 13,200 feet. The pole, as discovered by Peary, lies in an ocean, 391 geographical miles from the nearest land.

Peary was delighted, of course, with his conquest of the North Pole:

> For more than a score of years that point on the earth's surface had been the object of my every effort. To its attainment my whole being, physical, mental and moral, had been dedicated. Many times my own life and the lives of those with me had been risked. My own material and forces and those of my friends had been devoted to this object. This journey was my eighth into the Arctic wilderness. In that wilderness I had spent nearly twelve years, out of the twenty-three between my thirtieth and my fifty-third year, and the intervening time spent in civilized communities during that period had been mainly occupied with preparations for returning to the wilderness. The determination to reach the Pole had become so much a part of my being that, strange as it may seem, I long ago ceased to think of myself, save as an instrument for the attainment of that end.

The extraordinary speed which the Peary party made in reaching

Robert E. Peary

the pole was exceeded in the journey home. "Our return from the Pole was accomplished in sixteen marches," Peary wrote. "It had been, as a result of our experience and perfected clothing, an amazingly comfortable return, as compared with previous ones." In order to avoid the danger of the spring tides, which would cause many breaks in the ice, Peary had decided the return must be speeded up and he planned double marches for the entire return trip. A continuous threat was the possibility that a gale might break up the ice, separating the floes by stretches of open water, and accelerate the drift eastward toward the Atlantic, melting the solid ice from beneath the explorers. On April 23, 1909, Peary and his party were back at Cape Columbia. One of the Eskimos was heard to mutter in his own language, "the Devil is asleep or having trouble with his wife, or we should never have come back so easily."

A few days later Peary reached the *Roosevelt* at Cape Sheridan. There he received the sad news that a young engineer, Ross Marvin, had broken through thin ice on the return to Cape Columbia and drowned—the only casualty during the entire expedition.

The *Roosevelt* reached the Labrador coast in early September. A message was relayed from there to Peary's sponsors, the Peary Arctic Club: "Stars and Stripes nailed to the pole. Peary." When the message was sent, Peary was unaware that a week earlier the triumph which he was announcing had been claimed by another American. Dr. Frederick A. Cook, who had once been associated with Peary, asserted that he, traveling with two Eskimos, had reached the pole on April 21, 1908, a year ahead of Peary. Cook spread his story over the civilized world before Peary's message was sent. Many believed him and he was given receptions, balls, the freedom of cities, and other honors.

Peary reacted in fury. In several telegrams to news media, he denounced Cook as a liar, basing his statement on what Cook's own Eskimos had said, that they had never been out of sight of land. In a dispatch to the *New York Times,* Peary stated: "Cook has not been to the Pole on April 21, 1908, or at any other time. He has simply handed the public a gold brick." Almost all authorities soon came to agree that Cook's story was a hoax, because he was unable to offer any scientific evidence to support his claim. But Cook was a popular favorite, and Peary was viewed as arrogant and unsportsmanlike. Some persons even challenged Peary's own account of having reached the pole. The controversy dragged on until the beginning of World War I, when more serious matters diverted the public's attention. The whole affair, unfortunately, had the effect of tarnishing Peary's great achievement and cast a shadow over the remainder of his career.

Racial prejudice was involved in one criticism of Peary. Why had he taken a black and four Eskimos on the last lap of his race for the pole, and no white men? The answer was obvious in the case of the Eskimos. In defense of Matthew Henson, Peary pointed out: "In this selection I acted exactly as I have done on all my expeditions for the past fifteen years. He has in those years always been with me at my point farthest north. Moreover, Henson was the best man I had with me for this kind of work, with the exception of the Eskimos, who, with their racial inheritance of ice technique and their ability to handle sledges and dogs, were more necessary to me as members of my own individual party than any white man could have been." Also important was Henson's influence with the Eskimos; he persuaded them to travel over the heaving and splitting ice for the first time in the history of the tribe and prevented a mutiny on the way to the pole.

Another Cook exaggeration, his claim to have ascended to the peak of Mt. McKinley in Alaska in 1906, was proved false. Fourteen years after the North Pole imbroglio, Cook suffered a greater defeat. In 1923, at Fort Worth, Texas, he was sentenced to more than fourteen years in prison for mail fraud in connection with an oil promotion.

A comparison of Peary's expedition to the North Pole and Roald Amundsen's conquest of the South Pole illustrates several important differences in exploratory techniques. In Peary's view, the South Pole was relatively easier to reach. Among significant dissimilarities pointed out by Peary are that the Arctic is a sea encompassed by lands, while the Antarctic is a continent surrounded by an ocean; the Antarctic pole lies on a plateau two miles high while the Arctic pole is in a sea two miles deep. A further handicap for the Arctic explorer, stressed Peary, is that in trying to reach the North Pole the traveler must sledge at the coldest time of year, in order to take advantage of frozen-over water, while in aiming for the South Pole

Robert E. Peary

travel is at the warmest period of the year, the ice is firm, resting on land, and there is no open water. Another great advantage over southern as contrasted with northern conditions, Peary stated, is the food supply. Going south, caches can be set up on the forward march and picked up when homeward bound. In the Arctic, on the other hand, the northward journey is over moving ice and the possibility of finding a deposit on the return march is remote. There is also the likelihood of having a depot plundered by polar bears and foxes, for "a polar bear can and will tear asunder practically any sort of package." An Antarctic depot is completely safe, however, for three reasons: it cannot float away because the land is stable; it cannot spoil, for there is neither rain nor decay; and it cannot be destroyed by wild life—there is none.

Amundsen, the discoverer of the South Pole, would doubtless have maintained that the problems of Antarctic exploration might be different in kind but not in technical difficulties than those encountered in the Arctic region. As noted in chapter 21, on the exploration of the South Pole, there was frequent danger of losing a sledge with its load and men into a bottomless crevasse, although Peary held that this hazard was considerably less than the risk of losing life or load in the turbulent movement of the drifting Arctic ice pack.

The great Arctic explorer Vilhjalmur Stefansson commented on this issue: "Peary's forecast of the relatively easy attainment of the South Pole was destined to be confirmed within three years. It took hundreds of years of search to find the Antarctic mainland, but it was only sixteen years (1895–1911) from the first placing of human feet upon the shore of the southern continent until the first men stood at the southern Pole."

Perhaps no better tribute to Peary and his achievements can be found than was written by Stefansson: "Those before Peary pursued explorations with a heroic frame of mind. They did not set out to adapt themselves to difficulties; their whole purpose was to do or die in their attempt. Peary first set out to find how he could overcome the conditions of living in the Arctic. His great contribution to polar discovery lay in the fact that he introduced common-sense methods."

In belated recognition of Peary's feat, two years after the North Pole was attained, the U.S. Congress in 1911 adopted the following resolution:

Your committee believe that in view of his long distinguished service in the Arctic regions in ascertaining the northern boundaries of Greenland, his soundings and tidal observations; his ascertainment of facts concerning the northern Arctic Ocean; the general information he has obtained by living over 12 years within the Arctic circle; and finally having successfully followed a carefully laid out plan resulting in his reaching on April 6, 1909, and bringing back to civilization the conditions existing at the North Pole, that Robert Edwin Peary has performed a most remarkable and wonderful service, that he has attracted the favorable attention of the civilized world; and that, therefore, the American people, through its Congress, shall render him thanks, and bestow upon him the highest rank of the service which he adorns.

Peary was retired in the same year as a rear admiral. He became an aviation enthusiast and predicted the coming importance of air power in warfare. After his death in 1920, Peary Land, a peninsula in northern Greenland that he explored extensively, was named for him.

Robert E. Peary

21
Intrepid Norsemen

Roald Amundsen's The South Pole, 1911

Robert Peary's expedition to the North Pole in 1909 undoubtedly spurred competition among Arctic explorers to be first to reach the earth's opposite extreme, the South Pole. In fact, less than three years elapsed between the two discoveries.

As Roald Amundsen pointed out in a historical sketch introducing his account, *The South Pole,* navigators since early times had attempted to establish the existence of a great frozen continent to the south. Motivating forces were various: politics, trade, religion, science. Captain James Cook crossed the Antarctic Circle for the first time in 1773 and, in the course of his most southerly navigation of the globe, showed that there was no connection between the mysterious Antarctica and the northern continent of South America. Later, "the boldest voyage known in Antarctic exploration," as Amundsen called it, was undertaken by Admiral Sir James Clark Ross who, with two specially fortified vessels, crossed the Antarctic Circle on New Year's Day in 1841, plowed through dangerous ice packs, and emerged four days later after a rough passage in the open water to the south, now known as Ross Sea. Another epoch-making expedition was under the command of the whaling captain Leonard Kristensen who, in January of 1895, was the first to set foot on the sixth continent, Antarctica.

One of the most famous names associated with Antarctic exploration and discovery was that of Sir Ernest Shackleton. In 1908–9 he led an expedition in search of the South Pole. For draft animals, Shackleton depended mainly on ponies. His party of four men, four sledges, four ponies, and provisions for ninety-one days started on October 29, 1908. By the time latitude 84° was reached all the ponies were dead, and the men had to draw the sledges themselves up the difficult ascent of Beardmore Glacier to reach the high plateau surrounding the pole. On January 9, 1909, they were compelled to return because of bad weather and shortage of provisions when within ninety-seven miles of the pole—the farthest point south reached up to that time. Amundsen described "Shackleton's exploit" as "the most brilliant incident in the history of Antarctic exploration."

Amundsen himself may be said to have been preparing for his greatest feat from early boyhood. Born on a farm near Oslo, Norway, he had led a rugged life, trained for endurance and fortitude. The young lad became an expert skier and slept with open windows in the most severe winter weather. He read everything that he could find on polar exploration, and during the summers of 1894–96 signed on as a crew member of a sailing ship cruising in the Arctic. From 1897 to 1899 he served as first mate on a Belgian ship, the *Belgica,* the first to winter in the Antarctic. From 1903 to 1906 Amundsen commanded the *Gjöa* in the first complete navigation of the Northwest Passage between the Atlantic and Pacific oceans.

His first major achievement behind him, Amundsen began to plan a far more important and spectacular one—an attempt to reach the South Pole. This objective was also the goal of Captain Robert Falcon Scott, whose reputation had been established by his discovery of the Ross Ice Shelf and King Edward VII Land in the Antarctic.

No military tactician could have planned the logistics of his campaign any more carefully or methodically than did Amundsen. His aim was to leave nothing to chance. In order to avoid newspaper publicity and charges of unfair rivalry, his South Pole plans were prepared in secret. When his ship, the *Fram,* left Norway in August of 1910, not even the crew knew her real destination. They had been mystified by the presence on board of ninety-seven Greenland sledge-dogs and a large sectional hut. Not until they reached Madeira were they informed where the ship was headed.

A critical decision for Amundsen involved the location of his base camp. A vertical wall of snow and ice from 150 to 300 feet in height, the "Ross Barrier," formed an almost insurmountable obstacle for hundreds of miles. From the beginning, however, Amundsen was favored by good fortune. At the Bay of Whales, explored by Ross some seventy years before, the Amundsen party discovered that, instead of being confronted by a fearsome ice-cliff, the barrier at that spot was about twenty feet high, and the junction between it and the sea ice was completely filled up with driven snow. The barrier was easily surmounted on New Year's Day, 1911.

After landing the selected shore party of nine men, materials for a house, equipment, and provisions for two years, the *Fram* departed, with the understanding that she would return to the Bay of Whales in October to pick up Amundsen and his men.

Amundsen considered that his choice of a site for the base camp was a prime factor in his success. The air currents in the Antarctic region make the weather far more severe on the land than on the ice. "At best the climate in the Antarctic is about the worst in the world," Admundsen pointed out, "chiefly because of the terrific intensity of the gales which blow almost incessantly in these regions. These gales are of almost unbelievable velocity." The Amundsen camp on the ice was favored with comparatively good weather, and at no time were the men there subject to serious discomfort. The location on the Bay of Whales had several advantages in trying to reach the pole; it was somewhat nearer to the pole than Scott's camp, and the path southward turned out to be easier to travel.

The expedition hut was soon erected: the "Framheim," as it was called, had foundations sunk four feet into the ice, and the roof was anchored by hawsers. The many tons of provisions, supplies, and equipment, amounting to 900 cases, which had been unloaded from the *Fram*, were safely stored. A shelter was also built for the 120 dogs now running loose.

The ice was teeming with life. In every direction were large herds of seals, and the landing party began to accumulate a vast store of blubber and seal meat for the winter. Amundsen estimated that at least 250 seals were shot without appreciably reducing the size of the herds or discouraging the seals from remaining at the Bay of Whales. Among species, the Weddell seal was by far the most common. This seal grew to a great size; a full-grown bull was almost as large as a walrus and weighed close to 800 pounds. Huge schools of whales were frequently observed in the bay, chiefly finners and blue whales.

Amundsen stressed the wisdom of his choice of dogs as draft animals. His earlier experience had convinced him that these were the only work animals that could withstand the intense cold of the Arctic winter. They were capable of pulling heavy sleighs over ice and snow, and proved to be an essential element in his successful drive to the pole. According to Amundsen, the dogs were "quick, strong, sure-footed, intelligent, and able to negotiate any terrain that man himself can traverse." Captain Scott, on the other hand, apparently disliked dogs and, following Shackleton's example before him, relied on Manchurian ponies, a factor in his party's disastrous fate. The ponies were unable to endure the frigid atmosphere and froze to death or had to be killed.

As there were a number of bitches in the pack, the number of dogs began to increase before the *Fram* landed. Each female and her pups had to be housed separately; otherwise, the pups would be eaten. The young ones appealed particularly to Amundsen. Their coats were surprisingly thick, and they easily stood the cold. In fact, they were more hardy than the older animals. "While the grown-up dogs were glad to go into their tents in the evening," Amundsen observed, "the little ones refused to do so; they preferred to sleep outside. And they did so for a greater part of the winter."

Another advantage possessed by the Amundsen party over Scott and his men was that they were expert skiers. "I am not giving too much credit to our excellent ski," Amundsen wrote, "when I say that they not only played a very important part, but possibly the most important part of all, on our journey to the South Pole." The Norwegians were practically born and bred with skis on their feet. Those worn on the South Polar expedition were made of hickory, eight feet long, and narrow. Speed and a large bearing surface on both yielding snow and the thin crust bridging crevasses were thus secured. Without the skis, in Amundsen's opinion, he and his men would have landed in some bottomless crevasse. "Many a time we traversed stretches of surface so cleft and disturbed that it would have been an impossibility to get over them on foot."

Dress was another element credited with considerable importance

Roald Amundsen

by Amundsen. Here he learned from the Eskimos. Woolen under-clothing and windproof outer garments favored by Captain Scott were worn only in moderate temperatures, as woolen clothing becomes soaked with perspiration and stays wet. In extreme cold Amundsen used fur clothing. Reindeer-skin garments made in Eskimo fashion had been prepared for the expedition before leaving Norway. Such clothing allowed free circulation of air to keep the body dry, and the skin dried much faster than with wool. The explorers were warm and comfortable from the time the skin clothing was put on and, further, the skins were absolutely windproof.

The Framheim camp on the Bay of Whales was set up and functioning as a lively community two months or more in advance of winter. The explorers had a great deal to accomplish before the long period of darkness and extreme cold set in, and before the actual start of the polar expedition. Between January 14 and April 11 accommodations had been erected for nine men for several years, if needed; fresh meat provided for nine men and 115 dogs for half a year (including sixty tons of seal meat), and three tons of supplies stored in depots in the direction of the pole.

A key element in Amundsen's plan was the depot idea, demonstrating a remarkable ability to foresee and develop a method to meet the difficulties of the journey. Obviously, no party could carry sufficient food and fuel on the sleighs for the trip of more than 1,800 miles to the pole and back. As stated by Amundsen, "our method of attacking the Pole was to make repeated trips from the permanent camp southward, setting up shelters and making caches of provisions one after the other at several days' travel apart, so that we should be able to make the return trip from the pole without having to carry all our supplies there and back." The wisdom of this scheme is shown by the fate of Captain Scott and his companions, who died of starvation on their return trip.

Before the winter season commenced Amundsen and his men had laid depots at latitudes 80°, 81°, and 82°. Typical of each cache were the following supplies: 5,300 biscuits, 412 rations of dogs' pemmican (dried meat), 30 bags of dried milk, chocolate, and biscuits, and 86 rations of men's pemmican. The total weight, carried on four sledges, was about 2,670 pounds of food.

As another safety factor, in case the depots should be missed on the return trip, Amundsen had cairns of snow built, surmounted by signals, for a distance of five kilometers on either side and at distances a kilometer apart. To insure further that no depot would be overlooked later, he did not place his sole reliance on the lateral cairns, but also set up snow beacons six feet high along his line of march, each with a bamboo pole or a dried fish at the top, first at intervals of nine miles, then at every five miles, and finally at each three miles. A total of 150 beacons were built and 9,000 blocks of snow were used in their construction.

These preliminary preparations were barely completed before the onset of winter. On April 21 the sun disappeared and, as Amundsen graphically commented, "the longest night began which had ever been experienced by man in the Antarctic." The daylight gave way to twilight and the twilight was gradually absorbed by the darkness in the long polar night. But Amundsen and his men were ready; they were well equipped with sufficient provisions for years and occupied a comfortable, well-ventilated, well-situated and protected house. For five months the temperature ranged under fifty-eight degrees below zero, and on one occasion in mid-August dropped to minus seventy-four degrees.

The waiting time was utilized by the men to overhaul their equipment. All sleds were discarded as too heavy and unwieldly, and the rebuilt sledges were reduced in weight from 165 to only 48 pounds, which meant that an additional 117 pounds of food could be carried on each sledge. Clothing, boots, and skis had to be fitted, tested, and broken in.

An example of Amundsen's meticulous planning was the equipment provided for beard trimming and tooth extraction. He explained that "as the beard has to be kept short to prevent ice accumulating from one's breath, a beard-cutting machine which we had taken along proved invaluable. Another article taken was a tooth extractor, and this also proved valuable, for one man had a tooth which became so bad that it was absolutely essential that it should be pulled out, and this could hardly have been done without a proper instrument."

With the sun's reappearance in late August, everything was made ready for departure. The first start, on September 8, however, was

Roald Amundsen

aborted. Instead of the weather remaining favorable, as it had appeared to be at the outset, the temperature dropped to seventy degrees below and after two days' march the expedition returned to Framheim. Two men had frozen their heels.

It was not until October 19 that the party of five men with four sledges drawn by thirteen dogs each set out from the Bay of Whales. This time there was no turning back. Amundsen was accompanied by Helmer Hanssen, Olav Bjaaland, Sverre Hassel, and Oscar Wisting.

Rapid progress was made in the beginning, with 90 miles traveled the first day. The terrain, however, was dangerous. The region between the eighty-first and eighty-second parallel brought them into a veritable labyrinth of crevasses, extremely hazardous to cross. The crevasses zigzagged in all directions like a huge plane of broken glass. Visibility became poor and the light more and more deceptive. Snow began to fall, blowing and drifting before the wind. Bjaaland's sled fell into one of the numerous crevasses, but at a critical moment the other members of the party came to the rescue; a moment later the sledge and its thirteen dogs would have disappeared in the seemingly bottomless pit. Another exciting occasion involved Hanssen, who had driven his sledge across a crack about a yard wide. The dogs were across and the sledge was spanning the abyss when Hanssen caught his ski in one of the traces and fell down. The dogs began to fight among themselves, while the sledge was in danger of going over the brink and taking the driver with it. One of the other drivers leaped across the crevasse with his whip to straighten out the dogs, while another threw Hanssen a rope by which he was pulled out of danger. Wisting fell into another bottomless crevasse, but saved himself by spreading out his arms as he fell and catching himself.

Beyond the eighty-third parallel, the route ahead began to rise. "From now on," Amundsen wrote, "the landscape changed more and more from day to day; one mountain after another loomed up, one always higher than the other. Their average elevation was 10,000 to 16,000 feet." In describing the mountains, Amundsen allowed himself one of his few passages of almost poetic language: "Their crest line was always sharp; the peaks were like needles. I have never seen a more beautiful, wild, and imposing landscape. Here a peak would appear with somber and cold outlines, its head buried in the clouds; there one could see snow fields and glaciers thrown together in hopeless confusion."

The peculiar light conditions of the Ice Barrier had long mystified the men. Mountains which were miles away appeared to be immediately in front of them and at other times they would be stumbling over rough spots of the trail that had appeared far off a moment before. These strange phenomena were the result of the reflection of the rays of light from the great crystal mass of the barrier. Another curious natural phenomenon involved rumbling noises that seemed to be alarmingly near, which wakened the men at night; the sounds were produced by the settling of the snowfields as the surface gave way and fell to a new level.

The ascent over a series of steep glaciers took the exploring party to an altitude of more than 10,000 feet. Amundsen wrote that "the effect of the great and sudden change of altitude made itself felt at once; when I wanted to turn round in my bag, I had to do it a bit at a time, so as not to get out of breath." His comrades were similarly affected.

The last great obstacle confronting Amundsen was the "Devil's Glacier," which took three days to climb. By December the men had left this glacier behind, with its crevasses and deep pits, and were at an elevation of 9,350 feet above sea level. Before them was an ice plateau, resmbling a frozen lake, quickly named the "Devil's Ball Room." Storms and snow flurries occurred daily, reducing visibility to zero. The floor on which the men were walking was hollow beneath them. On December 6 the highest point was reached, 11,024 feet; from here the interior plateau remained level and at nearly the same elevation on to the pole.

Before climbing the high plateau, from which it would be comparatively easy sailing to the pole, Amundsen and his men had reached an agreement—one which the squeamish and especially dog lovers must find little short of horrifying—a decision for which Amundsen was severely criticized upon his return home. The vast flat land reached by the party was, in a way, the home stretch. Amundsen described the plan being put into effect as follows:

Roald Amundsen

We now had forty-two dogs. Our plan was to take all the forty-two up to the plateau; there twenty-four of them were to be slaughtered, and the journey continued with three sledges and eighteen dogs. Of these last eighteen, it would be necessary, in our opinion, to slaughter six in order to bring the other twelve back to this point. As a number of dogs grew less, the sledges would become lighter and lighter, and when the time came for reducing their number to twelve, we should have only two sledges left.

The gruesome executions were duly carried out by a firing squad and for some days thereafter the men and the remaining dogs feasted on dog meat. The decision to reduce the number of animals was an exceedingly difficult one for Amundsen, but he and his companions had agreed to shrink at nothing in order to reach their goal. From this point on the extra dogs would have been a burden. With the arrival on the plateau their added strength was no longer needed to draw the sledges, and the food for so many would have made a heavy load. If turned loose they would have starved. The ravenously hungry animals had little hesitation in turning cannibal when offered fresh meat.

After passing the eighty-seventh meridian the weather improved and the pole was in easy striking distance. Shackleton's farthest point south at 88°28' was passed. On December 14, 1911, the Norwegian flag was raised over the South Pole—a month before the arrival of Scott's British expedition. To remove any doubt that the pole had been reached, men were sent out in three directions with instructions to travel twelve and a half miles, plant a flag, then return. A pedestal of solid snow was erected at what was judged to be the actual pole.

A three-day camping stay at the pole rested the Amundsen party for the return trip, begun on December 17. They were favored by what Amundsen described as "splendid weather" which enabled them to get an excellent view of the mighty mountain range. Now and again they lost the trail and had to steer by compass. All the depots in which they had stored provisions were found again, giving a superabundance of food for men and dogs. On one of the glaciers, immense avalanches were seen.

The men found the light of the sun so trying on their eyes during the day that they began to travel only at night. Even wearing snow goggles, there was danger of snow blindness. At this time of year there was, of course, no difference between day and night at the South Pole except that at night the sun was behind the Amundsen party. Also, they now had the wind at their backs instead of having to face it continually as they had done on their way out. Their frozen faces had a chance to heal and breathing was easier.

After an absence of 99 days, the winter quarters at Framheim were reached on January 25. The party came back with two sledges and eleven dogs. Except for frostbitten faces, all the men were in top physical condition. They had traveled a distance of 1,860 miles in their round-trip to the South Pole. The *Fram* was waiting in the Bay of Whales to provide transportation to Norway.

Another noted explorer, Fridtjof Nansen, writing of the Amundsen expedition, stated: "The victory is not due to the great inventions of the present day and the many new appliances of every kind. . . . But *everything*, great and small, was thoroughly thought out, and the plan was splendidly executed. It is the *man* that matters, here as everywhere."

Captain Robert Scott's expedition, so closely linked with Amundsen's in objective and timing, met with a far different fate. He and his four-man team reached the pole about January 16, 1912, more than a month after the Amundsen party. Blizzards, cold, and illness brought disaster on the return trip to the base camp. The entire party perished. Scott and two of his men pushed to within eleven miles of the safety of their supply camp before dying of hunger and exposure. Their bodies were found by a search party the following November.

Roald Amundsen

22
The River of Doubt

*Theodore Roosevelt's Through the
Brazilian Wilderness, 1913*

Of all American presidents who preceded or follow him, Theodore Roosevelt most exemplified the strenuous life. "TR" glorified in constant and vigorous action, whether competing for the light heavyweight boxing championship at Harvard, climbing the Matterhorn in the Alps, ranching in the Dakota Badlands, leading his Rough Riders up San Juan Hill in Cuba during the Spanish American War, hunting big game in East Africa, or exploring an unknown river in the Brazilian jungle.

Roosevelt's first major safari was undertaken in 1909, a few months after leaving the White House. During an extended hunting and naturalist expedition, described in his *African Game Trails*, Roosevelt toured a region comprising Kenya, Uganda, Tanganyika, Nyasaland, and Mozambique, in the course of which the "great conservationist" killed an incredible number of elephants, lions, zebras, rhinos, giraffes, leopards, buffalos, cheetahs, hippos, antelopes, and other wild game.

His successful African adventures whetted Roosevelt's appetite for further travel and exploration. His second, far more rugged, expedition, begun late in 1913, took him into the heart of Brazil's wildest, most remote, and least known region. The stated object was to obtain animal, bird, and plant specimens from the central plateau of Brazil, an area lying between the headwaters of the Amazon and Paraguay rivers. Originally, the plan was for an expedition to travel up the Paraguay as far as possible, from there cross to one of the Amazon tributaries, and then return to civilization.

A portage crossing on Roosevelt's journey. (From a photo by Kermit Roosevelt)

Theodore Roosevelt

When the colonel reached Rio de Janeiro, however, the Brazilian minister of foreign affairs proposed a more ambitious venture. He pointed out that through the immense wilderness of western Brazil, known as the Mato Grosso, flowed a great river whose course and destination geographers had never traced. The Brazilians called it the Rio da Dúvida, the River of Doubt. It was suggested that Roosevelt should join with Colonel Candido Mariano da Silva Rondon, a famous Brazilian explorer, to follow the course of this vast stream, thereby advancing the causes of both geography and natural history. Roosevelt eagerly assented.

Prior to the Expedição Scientifica Roosevelt-Rondon, as it was officially entitled by the Brazilian government, South America had been studied by many eminent naturalists, notably Alexander von Humboldt, Charles Waterton, Richard Schomburgh, Alfred Russel Wallace, Richard Spruce, Henry Walter Bates, Louis Agassiz, and Charles Darwin. Humboldt, Waterton, and Schomburgh had been mainly concerned with the northern rim of the continent; Wallace, Bates, Spruce, and Agassiz with the tropical rain forest of the Amazon basin; and Darwin the eastern and western coasts south of the equator. Until the Roosevelt expedition, no naturalist had penetrated deep into the great central region of Brazil, the divide between the mighty Amazon and La Plata systems.

At the outset, Roosevelt apparently had little conception of the perils and hardships to which he and his party would be exposed during their nine hundred mile trek through a tropical jungle. The nature of the expedition changed, from one that had been strictly zoological to one of geographic exploration. Roosevelt described it as "a zoogeographic reconnaissance."

Weeks of travel preceded the Roosevelt party's arrival at its predetermined starting point. The expedition actually got under way on December 9, when the group boarded a small river steamer and began the ascent of the Paraguay River. The Brazilian border was crossed three days later. At first the river ran through an extensive, level plain. Farther on the whole region became a great swamp. As higher elevations were reached, the country became heavily forested. A remote village called Tapirapoan was the last outpost; from it the party began a forty-four day trip across the Paraguay-Amazon divide to the headwaters of the River of Doubt. Gradually the Roosevelt party left behind the dense, almost impenetrable forest as it reached higher ground. On February 23 it came to the Papagaio River, a tributary of the Tapajoz, itself one of the mightiest tributaries of the Amazon. Three weeks later a small stream feeding into the River of Doubt was reached. Six miles from there, the Roosevelt expedition launched its hazardous drive into the unknown.

The hardy crew assembled for this arduous trek was composed of Roosevelt, his twenty-four-year-old son Kermit, Colonel Rondon, George K. Cherrie (a naturalist sent by the American Museum of Natural History), Lieutenant João Lyra, a surveyor, and Doctor Cajazeira, a physician. Quite indispensable were sixteen camaradas, or native paddlers. As Roosevelt described the camaradas:

> They were expert rivermen of the forest, skilled veterans in wilderness work. They were lithe as panthers and brawny as bears. They swam like water-dogs. They were equally at home with pole and paddle, with axe and machete. They looked like pirates . . . one or two were pirates. They were white—or, rather, the olive of southern Europe—black, copper-colored, and of all intermediate shades.

Roosevelt noted that provisions were carried for fifty days, though not full rations, for it was hoped that in part the men could live off of the country, on fish, game, nuts, and palm tops. Personal baggage was reduced to the bare limit. Such necessities as medicine, blankets, a light tent, firearms, and instruments for determining altitude and longitude were also included.

The seven canoes in which the party traveled left much to be desired. All were dugouts. According to Roosevelt's description, "one was small, one was cranky, and two were old, water-logged, and leaky. The other three were good." Several failed to survive the trip, in part because of being too heavily laden.

The Roosevelt expedition began at the height of the rainy season and the swollen river was swift and brown. The height of the water was an advantage, in part, as most of the snags and fallen trees were well beneath the surface. But sometimes, Roosevelt wrote, "the swift water hurried up toward ripples that marked ugly spikes of sunken timber, or toward uprooted trees that stretched almost across the stream." He went on to note that "the lofty and matted forest

Theodore Roosevelt

rose like a green wall on either hand. The trees were stately and beautiful. The looped and twisted vines hung from them like great ropes."

Most hazardous and troublesome for the voyagers were the numerous rapids. It was flood season, and more of the land was under than above water; for miles the water stood or ran among the trees, and dry camping spots were difficult to find. Soon after embarking, the party found that the current quickened, became faster and faster "until it began to run like a mill-race and we heard the roar of rapids ahead." This stretch of river was more than a mile in length, with many whirlpools and several drops of at least six feet. At one point the river narrowed to less than two yards between bare rock walls. "It seemed extraordinary, almost impossible," the colonel commented, "that so broad a river could in so short a space of time contract its dimensions to the width of the strangled channel through which it now poured its entire volume." It took the expedition two and a half days to make a portage around these first rapids. The heavy, cumbersome dugout canoes were moved with the aid of several hundred small logs used as rollers.

The treacherous rapids, added to overloading, brought disaster to the dugouts on a number of occasions. One of the boats was damaged during the portage, and when launched again below the rapids filled with water and sank to the bottom; hard labor was required to raise it. During the night of the tenth day, two of the older canoes filled with water in the rising river, sank, and were broken apart by boulders along the river bottom. Time out was taken for four days to make a new dugout.

A greater disaster occurred shortly after travel was resumed on March 15. Again, "the roar of broken water announced that once more our course was checked by dangerous rapids." Kermit was in the lead canoe with two camaradas, a pet dog, and a week's supply of boxed provisions. While searching for a possible passage, Kermit found his canoe caught in a whirlpool and carried broadside into the rapids. The camaradas, João the helmsman and Simplicio the bowsman—both Negroes, and "exceptionally good men in every way"—attempted to turn the boat's head. The water came abroad, wave after wave, as they raced down. The men reached the bottom of the rapids with the canoe upright, but so full as barely to float, the paddlers struggled to bring it to the shore. They had nearly reached the bank when another whirlpool tore them away and carried them back to midstream. João managed to swim ashore. Simplicio appeared to have been pulled under, however, and never rose again, nor was his body ever recovered. Meanwhile, Kermit had climbed on the bottom of the upset boat. In a minute he was swept into a second series of rapids and whirled away from the rolling boat. The water drove him below the surface, and when he rose he was almost drowned. With his last ounce of strength, he swam toward an overhanging branch and barely managed to pull himself out on the land. It was a narrow escape.

Further misfortunes struck the following day. In attempting to pass more rapids, the new canoe, which was very large and heavy, was lost along with the rope and pulleys used for portages, while one of the steersmen, Luiz, was nearly drowned. The loss of the rope and pulleys meant that it would be physically impossible to pull big canoes along hilly or rocky land. Time was lacking to build new dugouts, since the expedition had already been gone eighteen days and over a third of the food had been consumed. The four remaining canoes could not carry all the loads and all the men. Loads were drastically reduced and twelve men walked in single file along the bank. As more rapids were reached, the supplies were carried overland while the empty canoes were run down through the least dangerous channels among the islands in the river.

Another disaster to the canoes was narrowly averted. The roaring of big rapids had been heard in the distance the previous day. When they were reached the following day, the canoes were run down empty. Even so, two were almost lost, the pair lashed together in which Roosevelt usually rode. "In a sharp bend of the rapids," the colonel wrote, "between two big curls, they were swept among the boulders and under the matted branches which stretched out from the bank. They filled, and the racing current pinned them where they were, one partly on the other." Heroic efforts by the entire crew separated the boats, hauled them out of the water and baled them, after which two paddlers took them down to safety.

On March 19, the party halted for three days to construct two

Theodore Roosevelt

new canoes, built of lighter wood to ride higher in the water, and easier to handle than the heavy dugout lost in the rapids. Now, with six dugouts, all could ride. By this time, half of their original supply of food was gone and the men reduced themselves to two meals a day. Only when some large bird, monkey, or fish was caught was there enough food. For twenty famished men, the discovery of some Brazil nuts and wild pineapples, or the capture of a few birds and fish, did little to alleviate their hunger. The lack of food and the tremendous physical labor were beginning to tell on the strength and spirits of the party. Some of the men had fever, and serious illness was prevented only by repeated doses of quinine. The rapids grew more and more continuous and the spaces of open water between them shorter and shorter.

Ferocious insects made the lives of the men miserable. There was no rest by day or night from swarms of flies, gnats, mosquitoes, ants, bees, and other malignant creatures. As described by Roosevelt, "the little bees were in such swarms as to be a nuisance. Many small stinging bees were with them, which stung badly. We were bitten by huge horse-flies, the size of bumblebees. More serious annoyance was caused by the pium and boroshuda flies during the hours of daylight, and by the polvora, the sand-flies, after dark. The boroshudas were the worst pests; they brought the blood at once, and left marks that lasted for weeks. I did my writing in head net and gauntlets. . . . The termites got into our tent on the sand flat, ate holes in Cherrie's mosquito net and poncho, and were starting to work at our duffel-bags when we discovered them."

On one occasion, while hunting in the forest, Roosevelt grasped a branch and inadvertently shook down a shower of fire ants; he was bitten by one of the giant ants, which stung like a hornet and pained for several hours. The camaradas generally went barefoot or wore only sandals; their ankles and feet were swollen and inflamed from the bites of the boroshudas and ants, some men being actually incapacitated for work. "All of us suffered more or less," wrote Roosevelt, "our hands and feet swelling slightly from the boroshuda bites; and in spite of our clothes we were bitten all over our bodies, chiefly by ants and the small forest ticks." No one, however, was bitten by a venomous serpent, a scorpion, or a centipede, though all three were killed within camp limits.

A particularly annoying specimen was the carregadores ants. **243**
At one camp they completely devoured Dr. Cajazeira's undershirt, ate holes in his mosquito net, and ate the strap of Lyra's gun case. On another night Roosevelt thought that he had put his clothing out of reach, but both the termites and carregadores ants got at them, ate holes in one boot, ate one leg of his underwear, and riddled his handkerchief; by then he had nothing to replace anything destroyed. Other members of the party were amused, though not Roosevelt.

Early in April, a terrible tragedy struck the expedition. Of the sixteen original camaradas only one had proved worthless. Julio, a huge, surly man of European blood, was constantly shirking tasks and had been caught stealing food on several occasions. One evening Paishon, a Negro corporal, described by Roosevelt as "one of our best men," caught Julio in the act of theft and struck him. The next day Julio picked up a carbine and followed Paishon down the portage trail. A minute later a shot rang out and several of the men ran back to say that Julio had killed Paishon and disappeared into the forest. The colonel and the doctor tried to find the killer, but soon lost his trail in the dense undergrowth. Paishon was quickly and simply buried along the portage trail, and the expedition proceeded. Three days later Julio appeared along the bank and called out that he wished to surrender. While Roosevelt and Rondon were debating whether or not to allow him to return, the canoes swept on past Julio. He disappeared once more into the wilderness, and was never seen again.

It was a surprising fact that the Roosevelt party glimpsed not a single Indian during their long river trip, though there were evidences of their presence. At one point an Indian village was discovered, apparently inhabited only during the dry season. Marks on the trees showed that these Indians had axes and knives, and there were old fields in which maize, beans, and cotton had been grown. Later, Colonel Rondon was strolling with a dog into the forest while a portage was being made. Running on ahead the dog, one of three carried on the expedition, was suddenly felled by two Indian arrows. Colonel Rondon had heard a kind of howling noise which he thought was made by spider monkeys, and then heard his dog Lobo yelp with pain as the arrows struck him. It seemed

Theodore Roosevelt

probable that the Indian was howling to lure the spider monkeys toward him. A feared Indian attack on the Roosevelt party, however, did not materialize.

Well before the end of their arduous trek the health of the crew became an urgent problem. Roosevelt himself was in the most serious condition. Jumping in the water to help with an overturned dugout, he had bruised a leg which soon became infamed. In fact, he developed what his son called "a veritable plague of deep abscesses." At the same time he had a sharp attack of fever which completely disabled him for the next forty-eight hours. So desperate was his state and loss of hope that Roosevelt called Kermit and Cherrie to his side and asked them to proceed without him, feeling that he was only a burden on the party. This drastic idea was, of course, rejected.

Meanwhile, Kermit was having an attack of fever and Cherrie and Lyra were afflicted with dysentery. But, according to Cherrie, it was Kermit who, at this point, held the expedition together—working nearly naked in the water with the canoes, his legs cut and bruised and swollen with insect bites, while suffering from fever himself. At least half of the crew was too ill and weak to do hard labor.

In part, the poor physical condition of the men was due to semi-starvation. Monkeys, more than any other animal, saved the expedition. The deep forests through which the men passed were remarkably lacking in game, and time after time monkeys provided the only fresh meat. A close second was the fierce piranha fish, a bloodthirsty creature, bony but well flavored. An occasion for celebration was the catching one day of a huge catfish, over three and a half feet long, with the usual huge head and enormous mouth. This one contained the nearly digested remains of a monkey, a fact which astonished the Americans who had never heard of a catfish preying on a monkey.

April 15 turned out, quite unexpectedly, to be a red-letter day for the expedition. The previous day the party had observed what looked to be cuttings of rubber trees. A short time later, a newly built house was seen in a planted clearing and everyone cheered. No one was home, but within an hour a second house was sighted and there Roosevelt and his men were welcomed by "an old black man who showed the innate courtesy of the Brazilian peasant." It had been forty-eight days since the explorers had embarked on the River of Doubt. From here on they would be following a river known to the men of the wilderness. "It was time to get out," Roosevelt wrote, "our adventures and our troubles alike were over." A rubber grower was hired as guide and, even though more rapids lay ahead, "it was child's play compared to what we had gone through."

The Dúvida turned out to be what the frontier rubber men called the Castanho, a branch of the Aripuaña, which eventually flowed into the Madeira and then into the Amazon. An April 27, two full months after entering the River of Doubt, the Expedição Scientifica Roosevelt-Rondon reached the hamlet of São João. From there river steamers carried the party to Manãos and then to Belém for the departure home.

What did the Roosevelt expedition into the heart of the Brazilian wilderness accomplish? Up until 1912, large-scale maps of South America showed a great blank space, terra incognita, in the center of the continent. It was this huge, unknown area that Roosevelt had traversed, in the course of which he had explored a new river nearly a thousand miles long. In his honor, by action of the Brazilian government, the Dúvida became the Roosevelt River.

From a zoological point of view, too, the results were gratifying. Some 2,500 birds and 500 mammals had been collected, plus a large number of reptiles, amphibians, fish, and insects. A number of species brought back were previously unknown to science, greatly enriching the resources of the American Museum of Natural History.

On the other hand, the South American trip was a calamity from the standpoint of Roosevelt's health. Roosevelt wrote to a friend that "the Brazilian wilderness stole away ten years of my life." A member of the expedition commented that by the time Roosevelt arrived at the port of embarkation for home, he "had wasted to a mere shadow of his former self." He was thin, gaunt, and never thereafter wholly free from recurrent attacks of the terrible jungle fever. His health was permanently impaired and his death hastened. Yet, as Roosevelt once remarked, "I am always willing to pay the piper when I have a good dance; and every now and then I like to drink the wine of life with brandy in it."

Theodore Roosevelt

Summing up the case for Roosevelt's narrative, *Through the Brazilian Wilderness,* one of his biographers, Paul Russell Cutright, predicted that this "spirit-stirring account of the River of Doubt" would long be read: "A better record of adventure by rapids and cataracts, through impenetrable and unknown forests, it would be hard to find."

23
Stone Age Voyage

Thor Heyerdahl's Kon-Tiki: Across the Pacific by Raft,
1947

Anthropologists and historians of the American Indian are in general agreement that Amerindians came from Asia by way of the Aleutian Islands or Bering Strait. The first such aborigines may have arrived on the American mainland between twenty and forty thousand years ago.

Far more recent, it is believed, was the settlement of people on the widely scattered islands of the central Pacific, known as Polynesia. Archeological evidence indicates that there were two migrations into the islands, one perhaps around 500 A.D. and the second about 1000 A.D. A question that has long puzzled anthropologists, however, is the origin of the Polynesian people. Undoubtedly they came from either America or Asia, and specialists have inclined to the view that their origin was Asiatic.

The debate was enlivened in 1947 by a young Norwegian scientist and explorer, Thor Heyerdahl, who was convinced that the Polynesians originated on the American side of the Pacific. His somewhat heretical ideas were derived from an extended stay in the South Pacific area. After leaving the University of Oslon in 1937, he made a zoological-ethnological survey of the Marquesas Islands and visited Tahiti and the Tuamotu Archipelago. The problem he had originally set out to study was how animals got to these remote islands, risen from the ocean without ever having been linked to any of the large land masses. Shortly, however, Heyerdahl's zoological interests turned toward anthropology. "What I found," he wrote, "led me to suspect that an influence from early

Kon-Tiki in the harbor at Callao, Peru. (Courtesy Rand McNally and Allen & Unwin)

Central or South America had somehow preceded the present Polynesian culture in this area."

The inspiration for the theory came by chance. As Heyerdahl tells it, he was lying on a beach in the Marquesas, looking towards America, watching the breakers thundering upon the shore, and the easterly trade winds rustling through the palm tops, while he listened to an old native relating the legends of his forefathers and the exploits of Kon-Tiki, the god chieftain who had founded his race by arriving with the sun from the east. This last survivor of an extinct tribe on the Marquesas spoke of giant statues on the islands, reminding the young Norwegian zoologist of the great monoliths of the South American Andes. Reinforcement for the idea came later when Heyerdahl read of the sun god Con-Ticci Viracocha, the legendary hero who, according to Inca tradition, had left Peru and sailed out into the Pacific with his followers. Now the Polynesians' chief god, son of the sun, was called Tiki.

In seeking an answer to the enigma of the ancient culture of Polynesia, Heyerdahl believed that two facts were essential and stood out. First, there was a Stone Age race of bearded white men with aquiline profiles who carved and erected colossal images in Peru, and were wiped out by the Incas. Second, about the same time, again according to Polynesian folklore, men of the same type began to carve the same gigantic stone figures on Easter Island and many other South Sea islands. All the evidence—stones and men, language and legend, history and archeology—merged to support the theory that Kon-Tiki, or some men like him, floated themselves across the Pacific from Peru to Polynesia; they, in turn, were subdued and submerged by an immigration of the dark-skinned people who now inhabit the eastern Pacific islands. The feasibility of the migration from Peru is supported by the fact that a floating object placed in the water there would drift by the Humboldt and South Equatorial currents in a tremendous arc to the Marquesas or Low Archipelago, 4,000 miles away.

Heyerdahl documents his case further by noting that South Sea coconuts probably originated in South America. The sweet potato, which originated in South America, is also found in Polynesia, and is called *kumara* in both. The runic tablets on Easter Island bear ancient names relating them to Peru. The Swedish ethnologist Baron Erland Nordenskjöld listed forty-nine such parallels, in fact, between Oceania and South America.

Whatever their origin, there is no doubt that the Polynesians traveled to the islands from some other land by sea. Assuming that Kon-Tiki and his people indeed sailed across several thousand miles of trackless sea, what was their means of conveyance? Heyerdahl determined that they used rafts constructed of lightweight balsa

Thor Heyerdahl

wood. To prove his point he proposed, if money could be raised and a crew recruited, to obtain balsa logs, bamboo, and hempen rope; to make an exact copy of such an ancient craft; and attempt to sail it across the Pacific. Funds were contributed by adventurous-minded individuals in the United States, and approval for the expedition secured from American, Peruvian, and Norwegian officials. With these preliminaries concluded, Heyerdahl proceeded to Ecuador and Peru, where balsa trees grow.

Heyerdahl's crew numbered six, including himself. In his short letter of invitation to the men selected, he wrote, "Am going to cross Pacific on a wooden raft to support a theory that the South Sea islands were peopled from Peru. Will you come? I guarantee nothing but a free trip to Peru and the South Sea islands and back, but you will find good use for your technical abilities on the voyage. Reply at once." All accepted. The five men who volunteered to accompany Heyerdahl on what all recognized as a hazardous venture were: Herman Watzinger, a technical engineer who directed the building of the balsa raft, guided by detailed accounts and sketches left in the earliest records after the conquest of Peru; Erik Hesselberg, an artist, who would assume responsibility for plotting the raft's drift; two radio operators, Knut Haugland and Torstein Raaby, both famous for their sabotage activities during World War II; and Bengt Danielsson, the lone Swede, who had just returned from an expedition in the Brazilian jungles, an ethnologist from the University of Uppsala. None of the six was a seaman. The crew's ages ranged from twenty-five to thirty-two.

The first problem encountered by Heyerdahl and his men after their arrival in South America was to find suitable balsa timber for their raft. In its dry state the wood is lighter than cork and thousands of trees had been felled for aircraft construction. The balsa tree grows in Peru, but only beyond the mountains in the Andes range. The seafarers in Inca times therefore went up along the coast to Ecuador, where they could drop their huge balsa trees right down to the edge of the Pacific. Heyerdahl hoped to do the same. The matter was not that simple, however, and it was necessary to go deep into the heart of the Ecuadorian jungle to find present-day balsa trees that would match the dimensions of the prehistoric rafts.

Nine giant trees were cut down, during the rainy season, and bound together with tough lianas that hung down from the tops of jungle trees. This temporary raft was pushed into the water and Heyerdahl and his men climbed aboard for a hair-raising ride down a jungle river to the Pacific coast.

With the blessings of the president of Peru and his naval minister, the "prehistoric" craft was built in the main naval harbor of Callao. The nine balsa logs were lashed together side by side with many separate pieces of hemp rope. The bow of the raft had an organ-pipe design, with the largest log in the center measuring forty-five feet and projecting beyond the others in front and in the stern. In the rear, a large separate piece of balsa held tholepins for a steering oar. The oar was hardwood, nineteen feet long and with a leverage of fifteen feet. The logs were more than half submerged in the water, but nine smaller crossbeams of light balsa covered with bamboo lifted the highest portion of the deck (including the floor of the open hut upon which the men slept) eighteen inches above the sea. The craft was completed with the little plaited bamboo and banana-leaf hut with thatched roof; two hardwood masts side by side, with a square sail; and five centerboards two feet wide and six feet deep, inserted at irregular intervals between the logs.

Dire warnings came from every side about the unseaworthiness of the primitive raft. It was predicted that the nine logs of porous balsa wood were too fragile and would break up in the heavy coastal swells or, more likely, would become waterlogged and sink long before the 4,000 miles to Polynesia were covered. The bamboo hut, which offered the only shelter, would place the crew at the constant mercy of high waves and would probably be lost in the first storm. Other gloomy critics insisted that the tropic sun and seawater would cause the ropes to disintegrate, and because no nails, pegs, or wire were used in the construction, the raft would be torn to pieces as soon as the constant movement of the logs started to rub against the hempen lashings. And finally, even if the raft should prove seaworthy, it could not be navigated with its clumsy square sail and single steering oar.

The predictions were almost completely erroneous, for reasons cited by Heyerdahl himself:

Thor Heyerdahl

The secret of the safety and seaworthiness of the unprotected balsa raft, in spite of its negligible freeboard, was primarily its unique ability to rise with any threatening sea, thus riding over the dangerous water-masses which would have broken aboard most other small craft. Secondly, it was the ingenious wash-through construction which allowed all water to disappear as through a sieve. Neither towering swells nor breaking wind-waves had any chance of getting a grip on the vessel, and the result was a feeling of complete security which no other open or small craft could have offered.

Records left by the ancient Peruvians also gave Heyerdahl confidence in the survival of his crude raft. In early times long voyages were made in similar vessels; there are many reports of Indian balsa rafts, carrying women and children aboard, often staying out at sea for weeks on end. Some of the rafts seen by early Europeans carried merchants and their families and tons of cargo, while others were used for army transportation and fishing expeditions of long duration. Ample supplies of food and water were taken along on such voyages.

Before embarking on the journey, which Heyerdahl estimated might last as long as four months, the supply problem was given careful thought. Heyerdahl comments that "we did not mean to eat llama flesh or dried *kumara* potatoes on our trip, for we were not making it to prove that we had once been Indians ourselves. . . . Our native forerunners would certainly have managed to live on dried meat and fish and *kumara* potatoes on board, as that was their staple diet ashore." For his crew Heyerdahl settled on simple field service rations as he had known them during the war. He was interested in finding out whether additional supplies of fresh fish and rain water could be obtained while crossing the sea. A good quart of water was allowed per man daily, an amount that proved fully adequate. Later, on hot days when salt was craved, it was found that twenty to forty percent of salt seawater could be added to the fresh water ration without ill effects. After two months, the fresh water aboard the raft was no longer palatable, and was replenished with rain water. A ton of water was consumed on the journey. Also included in the supplies were 200 coconuts to provide refreshing drinks and to exercise the men's teeth.

Preparations were finally completed, and the *Kon-Tiki,* named for the mythical sun king of the pre-Incas, set sail on April 29, 1947. A Peruvian naval tug towed the raft out into the Pacific from the Callao, Peru, port. For the 101 days of the voyage, the crew was not to see other human beings again until reaching the Polynesian islands. They would be crossing a vast span of little-known ocean, outside all the usual shipping lanes. At the request of the U.S. Weather Bureau, continuous observations were made and reported via the amateur radio network.

Heyerdahl and his mates were going to sea in a sieve which they had not learned to steer. The craft could not be steered many degrees off wind, it could not turn back, and it could not stop. The first weeks at sea were enormously difficult. One man was seasick for several days and confined to the hut. Within forty-eight hours of their departure, they were experiencing the worst of what was ahead, as they rode through the rough Humboldt Current. Great waves doused the crew with tons of water. Two men at a time held the clumsy oar, but the craft steered like a wild bull. Even so, the southeast trade wind and the Humboldt Current were pushing them along so rapidly that their daily average was fifty-five to sixty miles.

Heyerdahl calculated that in an ordinary calm sea, with about seven seconds between the highest waves, the raft took in about 200 tons of water astern in twenty-four hours, hardly enough to notice as it disappeared between the logs. But in a heavy storm more than 10,000 tons of water poured on board in a day's time, breaking over the craft like a "deafening thunder clap," leaving the helmsman standing in water up to his waist.

After the first few weeks the raft came into calmer seas, with long rolling swells. As described by Heyerdahl, "the great blue ocean was dotted with whitecaps, and trade wind clouds drifted across the blue sky. We had soft days with swimming and rest, and we traveled along in comfort. Our drift turned from northwest to west as we left the green and cold Humboldt Current and entered the blue and increasingly warm South Equatorial Current."

The ropes were a matter of concern from the outset. The *Kon-Tiki* was held together by about 300 separate lengths of hemp rope. In heavy seas, the balsa logs rubbed against one another, and there were constant creaking and groaning noises. Would the ropes grad-

Thor Heyerdahl

ually wear through and cause the raft to fall apart? A close examination when far out to sea revealed no sign of wear on the ropes. The explanation was that the balsa wood was so soft that, in case of friction, a rope would soon work itself into the waterlogged surface of a log and there remain protected. Fear that the balsa logs would become so heavy and sodden they would sink was also groundless. The surface became waterlogged, but the wood remained dry an inch or so below.

Strange creatures of the sea dominate many pages of *Kon-Tiki*. The first large monster encountered was the whale shark, some forty-five feet in length. Heyerdahl wrote: "Accompanied by a shoal of pilot fish, this giant among all fishes slowly caught up with us from astern, and the water splashed around its enormous, white-speckled back as though on a small reef. The fish bumped into the steering oar and placed its huge frog-like head, with tiny eyes and a five-foot mouth, right up against the raft." The whale shark followed for several hours, but disappeared when harpooned by one of the crew. On another occasion, at night, three whale sharks swam in circles around the raft, then vanished.

Whales were common visitors. Often small porpoises and toothed whales played around in large schools on the surface of the water. From time to time giant sperm whales, much longer than the raft, appeared singly or in small schools. One such specimen came within two yards of the *Kon-Tiki*, and the men could hear its "blowing and puffing, heavy and long drawn . . . an enormous, thick-skinned, ungainly land animal that came toiling through the water, as unlike a fish as a bat is unlike a bird." The monster glided under the raft, lay there dark and motionless for a time, then disappeared from sight. None of the whales showed any inclination to attack the raft.

For sport the men caught sharks by the tail. As graphically described by Heyerdahl,

> to get hold of a shark we first had to give it a real tidbit. When it turned quickly to go under again, its tail flickered up above the surface and was easy to grasp. The shark's skin was just like sandpaper to hold on to, and inside the upper joint of its tail there was an indentation which might have been made solely to allow of a good grip. If we once got a firm grasp there, there was no chance of our grip not holding. Then we had to give a

jerk, before the shark could collect itself, and get as much as possible of the tail pulled in tight over the logs. After a few desperate jerks, during which we had to keep a tight hold of the tail, the surprised shark became quite crestfallen and apathetic, and at last completely paralyzed.

The raft's most constant companions were dolphins and pilot fish. Almost from the moment the *Kon-Tiki* left Callao, it was joined by dolphins, and there was not a day on the whole voyage when large dolphins were not swimming around. Possibly, Heyerdahl comments, they were feeding on "our kitchen garden of seaweed and barnacles that hung like garlands from all the logs and from the steering oar. It began with a thin coating of smooth green, but then the clusters of seaweed grew with astonishing speed, so that the *Kon-Tiki* looked like a bearded sea-god as she tumbled along among the waves." Tiny fish and crabs stowed away inside the green seaweed.

The nearer the *Kon-Tiki* came to the tropics, the more common flying fish became. If a little paraffin lamp was set out at night, they were attracted by the light and shot over the raft. Every morning, the cook could count on finding at least a half-dozen on deck for breakfast. Flying fish were the dolphins' favorite food.

One morning about four o'clock a creature came hurtling on board, knocking over the paraffin lamp and landing on one of the sleeping men. It turned out to be a long thin fish, some three feet in length, which wiggled like an eel. It was slender as a snake with dull black eyes, a long snout, and a greedy jaw full of sharp teeth. The strange creature was identified as a snake mackerel, theretofore known only through a few skeletons found on the South American coast and the Galápagos Islands.

About 600 miles southwest of the Galápagos the raft was twice visited by giant sea turtles. One was under constant attack by a dozen angry dolphins which tried to snap at the turtle's neck and fins. When men from the *Kon-Tiki* attempted to capture the turtle, it swam away.

Ants were the most unwelcome stowaways on board. Small black ants lived in some of the logs; when the raft got to sea, the damp began to penetrate into the wood, and the ants swarmed out and

Thor Heyerdahl

into the sleeping bags. They bit and tormented the crew almost beyond endurance. As it became wetter out at sea, however, the ants began to vanish and only a few were left at the end of the voyage.

Heyerdahl wanted to discover whether primitive man would have been able to renew his supply of food and water while drifting at sea for weeks at a time. Judging by the *Kon-Tiki*'s experience, there would have been no problem. Dolphins were sporting fish to catch and, when freshly caught, their flesh was firm and delicious to eat, like a combination of cod and salmon. Edible barnacles and seaweed grew all over the huge logs and could be picked like garden greens. The men found that with sievelike nets they could harvest plankton in unlimited quantities and survive on the myriad microscopic animals that comprise this sea crop. Heyerdahl expresses the belief that "in good plankton waters there are thousands in a glassful. Some day in the future, perhaps, men will think of harvesting plankton from the sea to the same extent as now they harvest grain on land. Plankton tasted like shrimp paste, lobster or crab. If it was mostly deep-sea ova, it tasted like caviar and now and then like oysters."

The *Kon-Tiki* crew engaged in a variety of generally leisurely activities. One man struggled with the long steering oar; Bengt spent much time reading the small library of sociological books he had brought aboard; Herman was busy with meteorological observations. Knut and Torstein kept their little radio station going and sent out reports and weather observations to be picked up by chance radio amateurs; Erik was usually occupied with patching sails, splicing ropes, and using a sextant to keep track of distance covered; and Thor used his time writing reports, maintaining the logbook, collecting plankton, fishing, and filming.

When the sea was not too rough, the men were often out in their little rubber dinghy taking photographs. It was always hazardous, however, to undertake such trips, for though they never went far, if the wind and sea were higher than anticipated, they had to row for their lives to catch up with the raft. The primary thought in every man's head was that they must not be separated. The *Kon-Tiki* could never stop and wait or turn around and come back. "Once overboard always overboard" was a lesson constantly in their minds.

A failure to heed the lesson led to a near tragedy and the most dramatic episode in the whole voyage. Herman, trying to catch a sleeping bag blown overboard, took a rash step and fell over the side. Torstein and Heyerdahl rushed to the nearest lifesaving gear. Herman missed the end of the logs and the steering oar as he tried to grasp them sliding by. Knut plunged into the sea head first, with a life belt in one hand. The two men in the water swam to meet each other and both hung onto the life belt's line. The four men on board hauled with all their strength and soon had the swimmers safe on board.

On the ninety-third day at sea the blue haze of land was outlined against a reddish sky. It was the tiny atoll of Pukapuka, but wind and current would not permit the raft to turn or stop. On the ninety-seventh day another island loomed up out of the ocean. From the top of the mast, it was observed that "a roaring reef was twisted like a submerged snake all around the island, blocking the approach to the palm-clad beaches beyond." When they sighted the *Kon-Tiki,* Polynesians in small outrigger canoes slid through a passage in the reef and swarmed aboard. All efforts to land were in vain. A strong wind blew up and drove the raft on. The friendly natives jumped into their canoes and returned to their island.

On the hundred and first day at sea, the watchman at the top of the *Kon-Tiki* mast saw an enormous reef spanning the entire horizon ahead. It was the treacherous fifty-mile reef of Raroia Atoll. "With white spray shooting high into the air," Heyerdahl writes, "the surf battered the endless reef in fury." The men knew that the *Kon-Tiki* would have to stop in her own way. She took the tremendous pounding of the surf and piled herself up on its inner edge. Tons of crashing water tore up the deck, flattened the hut, broke the hardwood mast, and splintered the steering oar and stern crossbeams. A tremendous wave lifted the *Kon-Tiki* free of the water and tossed it high up on the reef. While the crew hung on to the raft, other waves pushed it closer to shore, until they could jump off and wade the shallow coral reef to a tiny uninhabited coconut island. Valuable cargo had been placed in watertight bags lashed to the raft, and so was saved.

A week later, natives from an island six miles away found Heyerdahl and his men and they were given a royal welcome party. Their battered raft was towed to Tahiti by a French government schooner

Thor Heyerdahl

sent to pick up the crew. From Tahiti the *Kon-Tiki* was carried back to the Norwegian Museum of Navigation in Oslo.

Heyerdahl concludes the account of his epic expedition with this statement:

> My migration theory, as such, was not necessarily proved by the successful outcome of the Kon-Tiki expedition. What we *did* prove was that the South American balsa raft possessed qualities not previously known to scientists of our time, and that the Pacific islands are located well inside the range of prehistoric craft from Peru. Primitive people are capable of undertaking immense voyages over the open ocean.

Critics have attacked Heyerdahl's general thesis and conclusions. James Michener, for example, maintains that "the weight of evidence remains heavily in favor of an Asiatic origin. Linguistically, ethnologically, and culturally, the Polynesian appears to be of Asiatic descent." Nevertheless, due to Heyerdahl, the idea of pre-Columbian voyages westward into the Pacific is widely accepted. The evidence is strong that there were contacts between Polynesians and American aborigines.

Thor Heyerdahl's dramatic account of his daring exhibition, in *Kon-Tiki,* attracted a worldwide audience. The stirring tale has been translated into not less than fifty-three languages—probably a record for a travel book.

24
Eight Thousand Meters Plus

Maurice Herzog's Annapurna, 1950

For three years, until the conquest of Mount Everest in 1953, two French alpinists held a unique record; they had reached the summit of a mountain exceeding 8,000 meters (about 26,000 feet) in altitude.

Previous mountain climbers had gone higher in altitude than Maurice Herzog and Louis Lackenal when they reached the top of the Himalayan peak Annapurna in 1950, but no other had attained the summit of a higher mountain. In 1924 and again in 1933 climbers came within a thousand feet of Everest's 29,141. Nanga Parbat (26,620), Kanchenjunga (28,146), and K2 (28,500) had *almost* been climbed. But in each case the mountain won, for diverse reasons: sheer walls of rock and ice, a sudden onslaught of impossible weather, or physical and mental exhaustion—and the climbers had turned back.

During World War II and for several years following, high mountaineering was in a suspended state. The road to Everest was through Tibet, and Tibet had been denying admission to all large expeditions. India and Pakistan had been in a state of ferment since winning their independence from Britain. Kashmir was in the midst of virtual civil war. The great opportunity for the French came in 1949. Nepal, on India's northern border, had long been sealed from the outside world, but the French envoy to Katmandu had become a close friend of the maharajah. A request for permission to undertake an expedition received royal approval.

The word was received back in France in the fall of 1949. Plans

A Sherpa below Camp 4 on Annapurna. (Courtesy E. P. Dutton and Federation Française de la Montagne)

for launching a major expedition were started immediately. A third of the funds required was provided by the French goverment and the rest was raised by the French Alpine Club and other mountaineering organizations. Supplies and equipment were provided by the French army and numerous manufacturers and merchants.

Hundreds of ambitious mountain climbers applied to join the team, to be selected by a committee set up by several climbing clubs. The leader chosen was thirty-one-year-old Maurice Herzog, by profession an engineer, by avocation an experienced alpinist, a veteran of World War II, who for four years had commanded a company of Alpine troops. Five other men, all outstanding among the postwar French mountaineers, were Louis Lackenal, Lionel Terray, Gaston Rébuffat, Jean Couzy, and Marcel Schatz. To round out the party, three specialists were named: Dr. Jacques Oudot as physician, Marcel Ichac as photographer, and Francis de Noyelle as transport officer. All members of this strong, well-balanced team played key roles in the expedition's success, indeed in its survival.

The explorers left Paris by air on March 30, 1950, and two weeks later, traveling by way of New Delhi and Lucknow and narrow-gauged railway, reached the Nepal border. Ahead of them lay the highest mountains on earth; eight of fourteen or more Himalayan peaks exceeding 26,000 feet in height are in Nepal.

The overpowering nature of the Himalayas staggers the imagination. A German writer, Hermann Keyserling, commented, in 1914: "Never have I found myself in the presence of such immense power. One would say that the frozen moon had transfixed itself onto the green earth, so supernatural is their impact, so out of proportion their grandeur to the usual aspects of this planet. They are a pyramid of formation upon formation, flora upon flora, fauna upon fauna. A tropical world transforms itself, little by little, into an arctic world; the kingdom of the elephant gives way to the kingdom of the bear, and that in turn to the kingdom of the snow leopard. It is not until one has reached the top of this world that the Himalaya proper begins."

Before departing from France, the Herzog expedition had agreed to consider alternative goals: first Dhaulagiri, at an altitude of 26,795 feet in central Nepal, or, if that was found impossible, to aim for a slightly lower peak, Annapurna, at 26,493 feet.

Maurice Herzog

An arduous preliminary journey preceded an actual ascent. In his account, Herzog describes the daily travels through a hot, steamy jungle in the lowlands and the dirty villages of Nepal; the hiring of Sherpas, the native semiprofessional mountain climbers essential to the success of any Himalayan adventure; the hiring of coolies, along with pack animals, to carry four tons of equipment and supplies; and the slow advance upon the mountains.

The gigantic peaks which were their objective began to appear and disappear in the distant clouds. A major difficulty was to find their bases. No available map was of any value. The Nepalese who lived in the valleys knew practically nothing about the uplands. Highly superstitious, they believed that the mountains were inhabited by gods and demons. And so the Herzog party was reduced to searching for a feasible route. It climbed up and down, zigzagged and backtracked through unexplored wilderness of ridges, gorges, blind valleys, and across swollen torrents.

The explorers were always aware of the need for speed. They knew that the only time an assault was even possible on the highest mountains was from the time the winter snows began to melt to the coming of the summer monsoon. It was now the end of April and the beginning of the monsoon rains was predicted for early June.

When a place called Tukucha was reached, a decision had to be made as to the target mountain. Members of the group went off in various directions for reconnaissance. The final report indicated that Dhaulagiri was insurmountable—an immense tapering pyramid, shaped like the Matterhorn in the Alps, but almost twice as high, too formidable for Herzog's party to attempt. Thereafter all thought was concentrated on Annapurna. Here, too, problems were encountered. No one knew definitely where the mysterious mountain was located. It was not shown on maps. Eventually, of course, it was found, and plans for an attack on it began to take shape.

At first, an approach over the northwest spur seemed feasible, but a climb to its top revealed that the spur led nowhere. As the climbers circled the great mountain, through a frightening world of rock and ice, the southern, eastern, and western sides were found impregnable. All faced the men with impossible, sheer rock walls or ice cliffs that were continually breaking off and starting tremendous avalanches. In the end, a way was found on the northwest

Annapurna

flank of the mountain. A base camp was set up at 14,500 feet; Camp 1 at 16,750; Camp 2 at 19,350; Camp 3 at 21,650; Camp 4 at 23,500; and Camp 5 at 24,600 feet. The task of establishing the chain of higher camps was backbreaking. Most of the food supply consisted of French army field rations, and enough had to be packed up to meet any emergency. For days, the climbers and porters accustomed to high altitudes moved up and down the mountainside in relays, carrying forty-pound loads with food, tents, sleeping bags, extra clothing, spirit stoves, and all the other gear requisite for survival. Two vertical miles of snow and ice, wind and cold, had to be overcome. It was now mid-May and the monsoon was a mere three weeks ahead.

Herzog and his men caught their first full view of Annapurna on May 23. When coming out of their tents in early morning, they were almost blinded by the glare. As Herzog describes the scene: "For the first time Annapurna was beginning to reveal its secrets. The huge north face with all its rivers of ice shone and sparkled in the light. Never had I seen a mountain so impressive in all its proportions. It was a world both dazzling and menacing; the eye was lost in its immensities." But for the first time, as Herzog notes with satisfaction, "we were not being confronted with vertical walls, jagged ridges and hanging glaciers which put an end to all hopes of climbing."

It is difficult for the nonprofessional mountaineer to comprehend the hazards and problems of climbing at such extreme altitudes, and the Himalayas offer obstacles unique among the world's great mountains. The bitter winds, the sudden blinding snows, the sheer precipices, the frequent avalanches breaking loose hundreds of tons of ice and snow, and the shortage of oxygen, making breathing almost agonizing, together with such technical matters as proper use of climbing ropes, the sinking of pitons (spikes driven into rock or ice surfaces as supports), and the cutting of handholds or footholds in the ice—all caused endless complications. Nevertheless, Herzog and his companions maintained steady progress upward, establishing camps, caching equipment, doubling back to bring up more supplies, and operating a continuous human belt from one camp to the next.

During the first days, as preparations were made for the final

Maurice Herzog

attempt, the weather was good, and no serious climbing difficulties were met. The chief danger was from the avalanches crashing down the mountainside, and there were several narrow escapes; but by choosing routes and camp sites carefully, the climbers kept out of the paths of the great snowfalls. Terray and his porters led an advance, reconnoitering party. Typical of the problems is this excerpt from his report: "At Camp 3: My two porters and I spent a terrible night, for I couldn't find the second tent that was supposed to have been left there in a bag. Even worse, avalanches were crashing down all night to the left and right of our single tent, in which we were huddled one on top of another."

Before Camp 4 could be established the weather worsened. Fog began to cover the mountainside and snow fell every day. Even the usually optimistic Herzog felt gloomy, remarking that "all our efforts will be wasted if the snow doesn't stop falling at least for two days." Fortunately the snow let up, and Camp 4 was established on a huge, curving arch of cliffs that supported the snow dome of the summit. Meanwhile, word was received by radio at the base camp far below that the monsoon, crossing the Indian Ocean, had already reached Calcutta.

Throughout the ascent it was the practice of the climbers to work in teams of two. When time came for the final drive, Herzog and Lackenal became the first team. The last camp was to be set up as near the summit as possible. A row of steep cliffs cut off direct access to the top, and the pair veered to the left to find a passage-way. After hours of climbing, every foot a major effort, Camp 5 was set up against what seemed hopeless odds at 24,600 feet. Herzog and Lackenal had hoped to find a flat ledge for their tent, but no flat surface could be found in any direction. They therefore dug out a spot against a curve of the rock. A storm broke in the evening, blowing so fiercely that it threatened to rip the small tent from the mountainside.

When morning came, the two men were ready for the last move. They were still 2,200 feet from the summit; between them and the top appeared to be gently rising snow. At daybreak on the third of June, Herzog and Lackenal crept from their sleeping bags; pulled on their boots, which were frozen stiff; placed tubes of condensed milk, some nougats, extra socks, and first aid equipment in sacks, and were off. Lightweight crampons, or climbing irons, bit deep into the steep slopes of ice and hard snow during the first stage of the climb. Sometimes the hard crust would bear the climbers' weight; at others they broke through and sank into soft powder snow, making progress exhausting. They took turns in leading, in order to share equally the strain of opening up the track. The cold was penetrating despite the special eiderdown clothing they were wearing. "The going was incredibly exhausting," Herzog writes, "and every step was a struggle of mind over matter." Both men feared that frostbite had begun to set in. Should they give up and turn back? Herzog answered:

> A whole sequence of pictures flashed through my head; the days of marching in sweltering heat; the hard pitches we had overcome, the tremendous efforts we had all made to lay seige to the mountain, the daily heroism of all my friends in establishing the camps. Now we were nearing our goal. In an hour or two, perhaps, victory would be ours. Must we give up? Impossible! My whole being revolted against the idea. I had made up my mind, irrevocably. Today we were consecrating an ideal, and no sacrifice was too great.

The day was fair and the climbers were almost blinded by the glaring light of the tropical sun. Sometimes clouds of snow whipped into their faces. The raw, thin air supplied only a fraction as much oxygen as needed, and they stopped again and again to breathe. But Herzog described the scene around them in almost poetic terms: "This diaphanous landscape, this quintessence of purity—these were not the mountains I knew; they were the mountains of my dreams. The snow, sprinkled over every rock and gleaming in the sun, was of a radiant beauty that touched me to the heart. I had never seen such complete transparency, and I was living in a world of crystal. An enormous gulf was between me and the world. This was a different universe—withered, desert, lifeless; a fantastic universe where the presence of man was not foreseen, perhaps not desired."

As the hours passed and Herzog and Lackenal struggled on, they came at last to a final rock ledge directly beneath the summit dome. A cleft split the center of the rock wall and through this break, the last barrier, they dragged themselves, step by step, to the top, where

Maurice Herzog

"a fierce and savage wind tore at us." They had surmounted Annapurna's 8,075 meters, 26,493 feet, the first "8,000-er" ever climbed. The summit was a corniced crest of ice and the precipices on the far side plunged vertically down, "terrifying, unfathomable."

The weather was changing rapidly by now and the two men began an immediate descent. On the way, Herzog dropped his gloves and saw them slide down the mountain out of sight—a mishap for which he paid a high price. The sky was covered with clouds and an icy wind spring up. At Camp 5, Rébuffat and Terray were waiting for them. But in a moment it was noticed that Herzog's fingers had turned violet and white and were hard as wood—frozen. Lackenal, who had plunged ahead on the way down, slipped on the icy slope 300 feet below his companions and was lying on the wind-hardened snow, suffering from a concussion after his tremendous fall. He was in a state of collapse, with no ice axe or gloves, and only one crampon. Terray, a first-class skier, managed to reach him and cut steps for the two of them to drag themselves back up to a tent. Terray and Rébuffat rubbed, slapped and beat Herzog and Lackenal's frozen hands and feet until feeling began to return.

Outside the tents, the storm howled and snow was still falling. The mist grew thick and darkness came. Only by clinging to the poles could the men prevent the tents being carried away by the wind. "The night was absolute hell," Herzog wrote. "Frightful onslaughts of wind battered us incessantly, while the never-ceasing snow piled up on the tents."

The worst was just beginning. No sooner had the four men started their descent the next morning than the storm burst in full fury. All landmarks were blotted out and they groped and stumbled along, lost in the thick snowfall and mist. Herzog's feet and hands were beginning to freeze again. It was found later that the group had passed within thirty yards of Camp 4, which would have been their salvation. Night had fallen and they knew that if they remained on the slope, they would all be dead before morning.

Suddenly, Lackenal fell into a crevasse, which turned out to be a sort of twisting tunnel, quite steep, and about thirty feet long. "This shelter was heaven-sent," and all four dropped into the minute grotto to spend the night. The enclosing walls of ice were damp and the floor a carpet of fresh snow, but they were protected from the wind. Boots were taken off, since to leave them on would have meant certain frostbite. A single sleeping bag provided some protection for their feet, and the men lay practically one on top of another to generate such warmth as they could. At dawn, a new misfortune struck. An avalanche of new snow came down, spreading over the cavern, and nearly burying them. Rébuffat and Terray had been stricken by snow blindness—the penalty for having taken off their glasses the previous day to lead the others down.

At daybreak the four men struggled to the surface, after more than an hour of frantic searching for their boots, packs, and climbing equipment buried under the white tons of snow. The storm had passed and there was bright sunshine. "The mountains were resplendent," Herzog commented; "never had I seen them look so beautiful—our last day would be magnificent." They were definitely lost. Their legs could scarcely support their weight and they were forced to keep their eyes shut against the glaring sun. Marcel Schatz was credited with their rescue. While waiting for Herzog and Lackenal at Camp 4, he had spotted the four ghostly looking figures blind and crippled above him. Schatz climbed up and led them down.

With Schatz and Couzy leading and Sherpa porters assisting, the descent from Camp 4 to Camp 2 was made in one day. Just above Camp 3, however, the gods of the mountain made one last attempt at revenge for the climbers' temerity. An avalanche came hurtling down, almost carrying Herzog, Rébuffat, and two Sherpas to their deaths. At the last moment, Rébuffat managed to leap from its path. Herzog was swept off his feet, but fortunately became wedged against the side of a small crevasse and was able to hold the porters on a rope. Toward evening, the whole exhausted party limped and crawled into Camp 2.

Annapurna had been conquered, in a manner of speaking, at a high price. The descent was far more hazardous than the ascent— a nightmare unsurpassed in the history of mountaineering. On the slow, painful journey down the mountain under the monsoon rains, Herzog suffered delirium and extreme pain. Part of the time he was carried on a stretcher and again in a sort of litter. Every movement was torture. He lost his will to live. The expedition proceeded regardless, on down the mountain and through the valleys of Nepal.

Maurice Herzog

Herzog and Lackenal had to be carried every step of the way, over steep ridges, swollen rivers fed by the monsoon, and finally through the underbrush of the lowland jungles. Dr. Jacques Oudot kept both patients under sedation, and they were given massive doses of penicillin to control infection. By the time the journey was over, Herzog had all his toes and fingers amputated and Lackenal had lost all his toes.

In the second week of July, Katmandu, the Nepalese capital, was reached. Herzog refused to leave the country until a call was made on the maharajah who had granted permission for the expedition. He was carried on a chair into the palace, where he was received in a ceremony full of oriental pomp and ancient ritual. The maharajah greeted him with a declaration, "You are a brave man, and we welcome you here as a brave man." Then Herzog and his companions flew back to France, heroes to their fellow countrymen and to the world.

Did the victory justify such a harrowing experience? Herzog's belief was strongly affirmative. From the American hospital at Neuilly, the year after his return, he wrote:

> In overstepping our limitations, in touching the extreme boundaries of man's world, we have come to know something of its true splendor. In my worst moments of anguish, I seemed to discover the deep significance of existence of which till then I had been unaware. I saw that it was better to be true than to be strong. The marks of the ordeal are apparent on my body. I was saved and I had won my freedom. This freedom, which I shall never lose, has given me the assurance of serenity of a man who has fulfilled himself. It has given me the rare joy of loving that which I used to despise. A new and splendid life has opened out before me.

The conquest of Annapurna is beyond question one of the great adventure stories of modern times. As another mountain climber, Justice William O. Douglas, remarked of Herzog's book *Annapurna,* "to read it is to be the companion of greatness."

25
Top of the World

Sir John Hunt's The Conquest of Everest, 1953

For more than thirty years Everest, the world's highest mountain, remained an unconquered challenge to mountain climbers of all nations. Ten expeditions, each having at its goal the summit of Mt. Everest, preceded the first successful attempt, and each ended in defeat, frustration, and sometimes death. In the thirty-two year period between 1920 and 1952, seven major expeditions went forth to conquer the great mountain. Every one was well equipped, led and manned by superbly qualified mountaineers, and supported by large contingents of porters. The several parties threw everything—all available resources, skills, the limit of human endurance, and even lives—into their campaigns, before conceding defeat.

Sir John Hunt, leader of the British Everest Expedition which finally achieved its objective, analyzed the peculiar problems confronting even the most skilled mountaineers in the ascent of Everest. He noted that Alaska's Mt. McKinley, for example, demands more actual climbing, as it rises 19,000 feet above its lowland base, while Everest is only 12,000 feet above its 17,000-foot Tibetan plateau. The winds of Everest are fierce, but those in the Scottish Highlands, battered by North Atlantic hurricanes, are as terrible. The crags and crevasses of Everest offer no more severe technical difficulties than certain Alpine peaks. The temperature on Everest can drop to forty degrees below zero in summer, but in Arctic and subarctic zones exploreres have lived through weather seventy or eighty degrees below.

The answer, in Hunt's judgment, is that a variety of factors unite to cause Everest to be the most difficult and hazardous of all the world's mountains to climb. "What makes Everest murderous," he points out, "is the fact that its cold, its wind, and its climbing difficulty converge upon the mountaineer at altitudes which have already robbed him of resistance. At 28,000 feet a given volume of air breathed contains only a third as much oxygen as at sea level. . . . Since a man inhales his air cold and dry and exhales it warm and moist, the stress on his parched lungs and respiratory passages becomes appalling."

Without a prolonged period of acclimatization, a climber exposed to the low atmospheric pressure of Everest's upper reaches would quickly become unconscious and die. For that reason, a climber must spend a month or more at altitudes of 15,000 to 20,000 feet in repeated ascents to adapt his body to survive. His bone marrow will then produce more oxygen-carrying red corpuscles, his heart muscles will adjust to the new strain put upon them, and his lungs will become more accustomed to rapid respiration. Even with such rigorous advance training, however, Hunt comments that "above 25,000 feet the climber's heavy legs seem riveted to the ground, his pulse races, his vision blurs, his ice ax sags in his hand like a crowbar." Another Himalayan veteran, Frank Smythe, adds: "On Everest it is an effort to cook, an effort to talk, an effort to think, almost too much of an effort to live."

Another nearly insuperable obstacle to climbing Everest is the weather. There is virtually no hope of a successful ascent except for a few days in late spring and a brief spell in the autumn. In winter the mountain's flanks are bare of snow, but the high winds are intolerable, while in summer the deep snows deposited during the monsoon season are treacherous, causing fatal slips or avalanches.

The world's tallest mountain, 29,002 feet above sea level, stands in a range of giant peaks, many of them 26,000 feet or more. The peak of Everest rests mainly between two colossal members: the northern ridge, which drops gradually for 1,000 feet and then dips precipitously downwards, and the northwestern ridge, which descends sharply from the summit and stretches far away below. Until 1951 all approaches to the mountain had been from the north.

It was not until 1920 that the Tibetan government granted permission for the first serious attempt to climb Everest. After two years of preparation, an expedition sponsored by the British Alpine Club and Royal Geographical Society got under way. A group composed of 13 Englishmen, 60 Nepalese and Northern Indian hillmen, over 100 Tibetan coolies, and more than 300 animals set out from Darjeeling, 250 miles from the mountain's base. A well-conceived plan provided for proceeding by leisurely stages within striking distance of the summit, acclimatizing the whole party by degrees, and conserving the energies of the climbers selected to make the final assault. A camp was set up at 23,000 feet, 6,000 below the summit. Two parties, with two Englishmen in each and supporting Sherpas, were chosen for the final struggle to reach the top. The first, buffeted by high winds and snowstorms, turned back at 27,000 feet—a new altitude record. The second party also encountered winds of gale force and all the strength of its members was needed to prevent their tent being blown away with themselves inside of it. At 27,300 feet, a half-mile from the summit, they reached the limit of their strength and turned back. An avalanche struck before the men could return; miraculously, the English climbers survived, but seven porters were swept away and lost.

The first explorers who reached lofty heights on Everest found wildlife at high altitudes. Wolves were seen at 19,000 feet and a fox, a hare, and wild sheep at over 20,000 feet. Birds flew to even greater heights; the lammergeier reached nearly 25,000 feet and the jackdaw more than 26,200. Stories about the Yeti or Abominable Snowman were traditional among the Sherpas, though this creature was as elusive as the Loch Ness Monster. As described by those who claimed to have seen him, "Big Foot," as he was nicknamed, was about five feet high and covered with reddish hair.

One useful piece of information learned by the first men who attempted to climb Everest was the need for supplementary oxygen. Those who carried extra oxygen to breathe made far more rapid progress at high altitudes than those without it.

Expeditions that followed the aborted 1922 climb had similar experiences. The second major attempt, made in the spring of 1924, was again manned by British mountaineers. As they were ready to start their ascent, a blizzard was raging, snow penetrated everything, it was appallingly cold, and a number of men were ill of frostbite, throat trouble, and even pneumonia. Two Sherpas died.

Sir John Hunt

Eventually a camp was set up at nearly 25,000 feet altitude, and later at 26,800 feet—a magnificent achievement. Two men, T. H. Somervell and E. F. Norton, pressed on, but Somervell gave up, overcome by a throat problem. Norton went on alone and reached a height of 28,128 feet—a record which remained unbeaten for some years—before having to admit defeat so close to his goal and turning back. Unwilling to concede that it was a lost cause, two other members of the expedition, George Mallory and Andrew Irvine, made a last attempt. They were lost and their fate has always remained uncertain. Unanswered questions were: Had they died in an accident? Did they freeze to death? Did they reach the summit before they disappeared?

Having failed to surmount Everest from ground bases, the British now decided to fly over the mountain to photograph the mysterious South Face. At the current state of aviation development, no plane was capable of flying at such a height. Two Westland biplanes were fitted with an extra-powerful engine and a modified fuselage, however, and arrangements were made for them to fly from the Indian plain a few miles from the Nepal frontier. It was expected that Everest could be reached in two hours. The flights took off on April 3, 1933. Flying over the hollow of the South Col from Everest, the planes were caught in a down-current and dropped nearly 1,700 feet. Altitude was regained. The planes rose above the mountain, and circled for a quarter of an hour, despite being buffeted by furious gusts of wind and hit by particles of ice. The numerous photographs brought back from this venture and a second airborne expedition two weeks later unfortunately yielded little useful information for mountain climbers.

In the same year, 1933, another British expedition was organized. A camp was set up at 27,550 feet—650 feet higher than in 1924. After various perilous experiences, though without loss of life, the indomitable climbers had to turn back when within a thousand feet or so of the goal.

Three misguided individuals attempted to climb Everest alone, without a large supporting expeditions. One, a former British Army captain, Maurice Wilson, froze to death in his tent high on the slopes of the North Col in the spring of 1934. Later, in 1947, a Canadian named Denman managed to reach a height of 24,000 feet before cold and poor equipment forced him to give up. Then, in 1951, a Danish mountaineer, R. B. Larsen, secretly reached the Tibetan side of the mountain by crossing Nepal, and made his way up the North Col. The accompanying Sherpas refused to make camp because of Larsen's inadequate equipment and the whole party turned back.

Still another British expedition, made up mainly of veterans of previous climbs, was ready to try its luck in the spring of 1936. The monsoon season came early, winds rose to gale force, and the venture nearly had a catastrophic ending when some of the men were caught in an avalanche and escaped death by sheer luck. None of the party climbed to more than 21,000 feet. A smaller party, also composed of experienced Britishers, set out in May 1938 and remained near the mountain for nearly two months; its maximum climb was 27,200 feet.

From this time successes began to outnumber failures. During the World War II period, Everest was left undisturbed. But then, in 1951, the Himalayan Joint Committee, which had initiated the first expedition in 1922, decided to send out a reconnaissance party to explore a different approach to Everest. The party was directed by Eric Shipton, who had played an active role in the 1933, 1935, 1936, and 1938 attempts.

Up until this date, the North Col had been the accepted approach to Everest. Shipton's assignment was to explore the possibilities of the southwestern approach, through Nepal. After the many disappointments, even disasters, experienced on the North Col side, it was considered possible that more favorable conditions of snow, sun, and wind might be found on the mountain's other flank. Almost nothing was known of the South Face and of the western side of the South Col except that the approach lay through a steep icefall and a narrow defile constantly threatened by ice avalanches from the hanging glaciers above. At 20,000 feet altitude, Shipton and his party could look across to the North Peak and the North Col; Everest's whole northwest face was visible. It appeared that here lay a way to the mountain's peak.

The Shipton expedition was the first to photograph footprints of the Abominable Snowman, a legendary Himalayan creature, though no one in this party or any other Westerner is reputed to have seen the humanoid itself.

Sir John Hunt

Before the next British expedition could be mounted, following up on the knowledge acquired by Shipton, the Swiss had a go at Everest. For a time it appeared that a keen contest was shaping up between the Swiss and the 1953 British expedition: a race to the top of Everest. A team of first-rate Alpine climbers was assembled by the Swiss Foundation for Alpine Research, permission for the climb was obtained from the Nepalese government, and early in April of 1952 the expedition set out from Katmandu. The carefully developed plan was: first, to set up a base camp on the 16,500-foot Khumbu glacier facing the icefall guarding the approaches to the mountain; second, to negotiate the six miles of crevices at the beginning; third, to cross the snow-covered plateau leading to the southeastern ridge; and then begin the final assault. The expedition possessed the best available equipment: lightweight oxygen apparatus, isothermic tents lined with swansdown, insulated pneumatic sleeping bags, reindeer-skin climbing boots, and climbing suits that gave almost perfect protection against cold.

After crossing the dangerous icefall safely, the Swiss set up a succession of camps: at 21,150 feet; 22,630 feet; 25,840 feet; and 27,550 feet. The pair chosen to make the final assault was Raymond Lambert and the Sherpa Tensing. Slowly they fought their way up to 28,210 feet, only 800 feet from their goal, and the highest any man had yet climbed. Then, completely exhausted and ready to collapse, they returned to Camp Five at 22,630 feet. A second team took up the challenge, but reached no higher than Camp Six, at 25,840 feet. A second Swiss expedition in the fall of 1952 met with disaster. Struck by an avalanche, a young Sherpa was killed instantly and three others fell 600 feet down the slope, but suffered only broken bones and bruises. Still another attempt was made; after climbing to 26,575 feet, the climbers were forced back by the wind and bitter cold.

The British now had the field to themselves. Eric Shipton's preliminary reconnaissance in 1951 paved the way. His exploration of the southwestern side of the mountain discovered a route that might succeed where the others had failed.

The leader of the 1953 expedition was Colonel John Hunt, a first-rate climber, an able organizer, and a natural leader, forty-two years old. Accompanying him were twelve Britons and one Sherpa,

Tensing, who had already taken part in five Everest expeditions. Included in the group, too, was a young New Zealander, Edmund Hillary, who was to play a key part in the dramatic conclusion of the venture. Probably no military campaign in history, with a single-minded aim, had ever been planned with more precision than this British effort to overcome thirty years of frustration and defeat. New clothing, equipment, and oxygen apparatus were tested by members of the party, the lessons of previous climbs were virtually memorized, and every detail of the operation planned with meticulous care.

In March, the party began gathering at Katmandu, capital city of Nepal. Seven and a half tons of baggage, representing 350 loads for the Sherpa porters, were assembled. Fifteen days out of Katmandu, the party climbed the last ridge overlooking the village of Namche Bazar, where suddenly the solid mass of Everest loomed up. Years before George Mallory, seeing the mountain for the first time from the north, had called it "a prodigious white fang excrescent from the jaw of the world." It was an awesome sight.

From the village the Hunt expedition climbed to the monastery of Thyangboche, described by Hunt as "surely the most magnificent grandstand ever provided for mountain scenery," at 13,500 feet altitude. There followed a three-week period of acclimatization and practice with the oxygen sets. A number of 19,000- and 20,000-foot peaks in the area were surmounted for practice. Some of the Sherpas were trained in oxygen use and the men learned to maneuver among the ice pinnacles of nearby glaciers.

By April 13 the expedition was ready for its next move: reconnaissance of the Khumbu Icefall. Edmund Hillary led a fifty-man party of climbers, Sherpas, and porters over an incredible route of shaky ice towers, yawning blue crevasses, and up sheer glazed passages to come upon a comparatively open plateau, where Camp III was established.

Now Hunt's basic plan began to emerge: the transportation of three tons of supplies by way of Camp III at the top of the icefall to an advance base, at Camp IV, high up in the cwm (a Welsh word meaning an enclosed valley on the flank of a mountain); from here begin the crucial carry past Camp V, up Lhotse's glacier to Camps VI and VII, and the long traverse across the face to Camp VIII

Sir John Hunt

on the South Col, an altitude of 25,800 feet. Burning temperatures at midday and subzero temperatures at night slowed progress. Nevertheless, despite blizzards, cold, the debilitating effects of altitude, and a furious west wind, the men pushed on.

It had been agreed that two separate assault parties, each consisting of two men, would attempt the final drive for the summit. Tom Bourdillon and Charles Evans would lead off, while Edmund Hillary and Tensing, who had proved a very strong team of climbers, were to serve as a second wave of attack. Each pair would be backed up by a close support team.

At first, Bourdillon and Evans made excellent progress, climbing about 1,000 feet an hour, a rate which would have taken them to the summit with time to spare. During the next two hours, however, they went up barely 700 feet; fresh snow covered the rock ledges, providing little for their crampons (spiked boots) to grip. At the 28,000-foot snow shoulder up the South Peak, the canisters in their oxygen sets were found near exhaustion and were changed. Climbing slowly, the men stood upon the South Peak, at an altitude of 28,700 feet, a new record.

At this point, unfortunately, Bourdillon and Evans reached an impasse. The knife-edged ridge soared upward at a sharp angle. On the left, it fell away to rocks, a sheer 8,000 feet below; on the right was an even steeper precipice falling more than 10,000 feet into Tibet and overhung with huge, treacherous cornices of snow. The men estimated that they would need another three hours to reach the summit and two hours to return to the peak on which they stood, after which they would have to descend 3,000 feet to safety. Their oxygen would last only a fraction of that time. There was no question of going on. They turned back and barely averted disaster on the return.

Though the first team had been unable to go all the way, they could give Hillary and Tensing the benefit of their experience; they had surmounted the South Ridge, studied the problem of climbing the final ridge, and cached extra oxygen bottles.

On May 28, Hillary and Tensing, with a strong support team, worked up to 27,900 feet before deciding to camp. The support team returned to the South Col, leaving the two principals on their own. A tent was set up on a narrow strip of ground; at times tremendous gusts of wind threatened to sweep it over the edge of the precipitous slope. The men drank a good deal of lemon juice, ate sardines on biscuits, tinned apricots, dates, biscuits, jam, and honey. They had only enough oxygen to give them four hours' sleep, and so at four A.M. on May 29 they were up, ready for the final drive. The weather was perfect. Hillary had to take time out to thaw his frozen boots on the little Primus stove. The upward climb began over deep, powderlike snow, which often broke through under them. By nine o'clock they had reached the South Summit. There they were confronted by the fearsome ridge leading up to the earth's highest summit.

The only hope of getting on top of the ridge was to cut steps in the snow along the edge, between the overhanging cornices and the precipices. Hillary and Tensing took turns hewing lines of steps forty feet long, belaying one another with loops of rope round their ice axes. Frozen exhaust tubes in their oxygen apparatus posed a crucial problem and had to be cleared before proceeding. After an hour's step-cutting, the men came up against their most formidable obstacle yet—a vertical rock face, forty feet high.

Here was the most critical stage of the entire 29,000-foot climb— the difference between success and failure. Hillary decided there was one chance: along one side of the rock was a vast ice mass and between it and the rock was a narrow crevice. Hillary squeezed into the cleft facing the rock, and as he described it, "taking advantage of every little rock hold and all the frictions of knee, shoulders and arms I could muster, I literally cramponed backwards up the crack, with a fervent prayer that the cornice would remain attached to the rock." He rose inch by inch, panting and with his limbs feeling like lead, and eventually got to the top. Tensing was pulled up and the pair went on cutting steps in slope after slope still facing them. The end came suddenly when Hillary realized that the ridge on which they were standing was no longer rising but dropped sharply before them; "a few more whacks of the ice-axe in the firm snow, and we stood on the summit."

The two men shook hands, slapped each other on the back, and felt a great sense of relief and exultation. Tensing, a devout Buddhist, buried a bar of chocolate, biscuits, and sweets in the snow, as an offering to the gods, while Hillary took photographs.

Sir John Hunt

Afterwards it was a race against time and a nearly exhausted oxygen supply to retrace their steps. They reached the South Col camp as a gale was blowing, too exhausted to respond to an enthusiastic welcome, and collapsed into their sleeping bags. Everest had been conquered.

In view of the later controversy that erupted over whether Hillary or Tensing deserved greater credit for the final triumph, Sir John Hunt's comment is relevant: "The Sherpas were magnificent, their cooperation beyond praise. . . . The tasks of Sherpas and Sahibs [Britishers] were identical. All were sharing the same burdens, all equipped with the same aids, were sharing the difficulties of the climb and the height." In assessing the reasons for the expedition's success, Hunt listed these factors: lessons learned from all who had climbed on Everest before; the careful planning and other preparations; the excellence of the equipment; the Sherpas; and favorable elements.

Travel in Fact and Fancy

The literature of travel is immense. Any large general library holds tens of thousands of volumes classified under the headings of travel, geographical exploration, and discovery. For example, in the relatively narrow field of polar exploration Vilhjalmar Stefansson's library, now in the Dartmouth College Library, contains 25,000 volumes and 10,000 pamphlets relating to the Arctic, the Antarctic, and their subregions.

The earliest known work of travel in the English literature is said to be *Itinerary through Wales* by Gerald of Wales (c.1146–1220), ecclesiastical scholar, geographer, and historian. The account of his journey, taken in company with Archbishop Baldwin, who was preaching on behaf of the Crusades, describes the Welsh countryside. Since that time, 800 years ago, travelers and explorers have left virtually no corner of the earth uninvestigated and have now begun probing outer space.

Space, in fact, is the new frontier in travel. The possibility of exploring outer space has intrigued mankind's imagination for centuries. The Greek satirist Lucian, in the second century A.D., wrote two accounts of voyages to the moon. Entitled *True History*, the book, according to the author, contains nothing but lies from beginning to end. The translation of this work into English in 1634 inspired a number of English writers. The celestial voyage was also not unknown in medieval literature, and tales of magic voyages through the air are found in the *Arabian Nights*. Ariosto's *Orlando Furioso* (1516) features the character Astolfo ascending to the moon by means of a chariot drawn by four coursers; upon arrival, he finds the moon much greater in size than he had imagined and is struck by its similarities to earth.

A great astronomer, Johannes Kepler, left in manuscript form at the time of his death an imaginative work entitled *Somnium* (1634), since published in German and English. In this book mortals were able to travel to the moon through the aid of demons. Kepler's scientific spirit is revealed when he considers the effect of gravity upon the human body forced away from the earth. He also discusses distances; sizes of objects; heights of mountains; depths of valleys; and the climatology and mineralogy of the lunar world, whose inhabitants he pictures as monstrous creatures, grotesque in shape.

Another scientist, John Wilkins, in the second edition of his book *Discovery of a New World in the Moone* (1640), looks at a possible conveyance to the moon and the prospect of finding inhabitants there. The first English voyage to the moon, however, is believed to have been Francis Godwin's *The Man in the Moone, or a Discourse of a Voyage Thither by Domingo Gonsales* (1638); the hero is borne upward by trained wild swans which were accustomed to hibernate in the moon.

In 1751 appeared *A Narrative of the Life and Astonishing Adventures of John Daniel Taken from His Own Mouth by Mr. Ralph Morris*. The highly descriptive subtitle reads: "Containing, the Melancholy Occasion of His Travels. His Shipwreck with One Companion on a Desolate Island. Their Way of Life, His Accidental Discovery of a Woman for His Companion. Their Peopling the Island. Also, A Description of a Most Surprising Engine, Invented by His Son Jacob, on Which he Flew to the Moon, with Some Account of Its Inhabitants. His Return, and Accidental Fall into the Habitation of a Sea Monster, with Whom He Lived for Two Years," etc. This is one of the earliest published descriptions of a flying machine, though Leonardo da Vinci's sketchbooks, more than two centuries earlier, showed a parachute, a helicopter, and an ornithopter (man-propelled flying machine).

Cyrano de Bergerac wrote, in a satirical vein, a *Voyage to the Moon* in 1656 and *Voyage to the Sun* in 1662. In 1703 appeared David Russen's *Iter Lunare; or, A Voyage to the Moon, Containing Some Considerations on the Nature of That Planet. The Possibility of Getting Thither. With Other Pleasant Conceits about the Inhabitants, Their Manners and Customs.* A short time later, Daniel Defoe tried his hand on a lunar theme in his *A Journey to the World in the Moon* (1705).

Marjorie Nicholson, in an article on "Cosmic Voyages" (*ELH, a Journal of Literary History,* June 1940), suggests that "The moon-voyages and cosmic voyages of the seventeenth and eighteenth centuries played their small part in popularizing the conception of a plurality of worlds, the possibility of many inhabited worlds."

More recent writers have continued to be fascinated by and allowed their imaginations to roam freely throughout outer space. A famous example is Jules Verne's *From the Earth to the Moon* (1865). Comparable to Verne was H. G. Wells's early science fiction, such as *The Time Machine* (1895), picturing time as the fourth dimension through which the Time Traveler journeys into the far future; and *The First Man in the Moon* (1901), dealing with space travel.

A later writer, Edgar Rice Burroughs, creator of Tarzan, produced a series of novels about life on Mars that achieved wide popularity. Subsequently, moden science fiction writers have proliferated space travel fiction.

A curious work in the opposite direction is the Danish-Norwegian author Louis Holberg's *Niels Klim's A Journey to the World Under-Ground. Being a Narrative of His Wonderful Descent to the Subterranean Lands; Together with an Account of the Sensible Animals and Trees Inhabiting the Planet Nazar and the Firmament* (1741), written in poetic form. Klim, the hero of the tale, is transported to the world under ground, where he meets with surprising adventures and encounters many strange creatures. Jules Verne used a similar idea in his *Journey to the Center of the Earth* (1864).

While generally remaining earthbound, many other fictional creations relating to imaginary travel have been written. Philip Babcock Gove, in his *The Imaginary Voyage in Prose Fiction,* records 215 imaginary voyages from 1700 to 1800. Several of the most celebrated will be reviewed here.

Most famous of all is Daniel Defoe's *The Life and Strange Surprizing Adventures of Robinson Crusoe, of York, Mariner; Who Lived Eight and Twenty Years, All Alone in an Un-inhabited Island on the Coast of America, Near the Mouth of the Great River of Oroonoque; Having Been Cast on Shore by Shipwreck, Wherein All the Men Perished but Himself. With an Account How He Was at Last as Strangely Deliver'd by Pyrates* (1719; 3 volumes). The tale was inspired by the adventures of Alexander Selkirk, a Scottish sailor who was marooned and lived alone for more than four years on the Juan Fernandez Islands early in the eighteenth century.

Defoe's prolific pen produced a number of similar, though less well-known accounts, such as his *The Life, Adventures, and Pyracies, of the Famous Captain Singleton: Containing an Account His Being Set on Shore in the Island of Madagascar, His Settlement There, with a Description of the Place and Inhabitants; of His Passage from Thence, in a Paraguay, to the Main Land of Africa, with an Account of the Customs and Manners of the People; His Great Deliverance from the Barbarous Natives and Wild Beasts,* etc. (1720), and *Madagascar; or, Robert Drury's Journal, during Fifteen Years Captivity on That Island,* etc. (1729).

A few years after *Robinson Crusoe* came Jonathan Swift's *Travels into Several Remote Nations of the World. By Lemuel Gulliver* (1726). *Gulliver's Travels* is of interest to adults because of its satire on man and his institutions, and to children because of its fantasy. In the beginning Gulliver is shipwrecked on the island of Lilliput, whose inhabitants are no more than six inches high; next he finds himself in Brobdingnag, a race of gigantic men. Part three, about Laputa, ridicules scientists and philosophers, who have lost any common sense and engage in all sorts of foolish pursuits. The last part of the book relates Gulliver's visit to the land of the Houyhnhnms, a race of intelligent horses who are served by a depised, filthy, and degenerate human race known as Yahoos.

Contemporary with Defoe and Swift was William Rufus Chetwood, several of whose works went through multiple editions. Best known are his *The Voyages, Dangerous Adventures, and Imminent Escapes of Captain Richard Falconer; Containing the Laws, Customs, and Manners of the Indians in America; His Shipwrecks,* etc. (1720), and *The Voyages and Adventures of Captain Robert Boyle, in Several Parts of the World* (1726).

Isaac Bickerstaffe is the supposed author of *The Life, Strange Voyages, and Uncommon Adventures of Ambrose Gwinett* (1770), who voyaged to the West Indies, was captured by Spaniards, taken by pirates, condemned to the galleys, carried into slavery, and after many other handships returned to England.

The New World has produced its share of or provided the background for imaginary travel accounts. The noted American bibliographer, Henry R. Wagner, traced the history of numerous such stories in his articles "Some Imaginary California Geography" and "Apocryphal Voyages to the Northwest Coast of America" (*Proceedings of the American Antiquarian Society*, April 1926 and April 1931).

A real character, long recognized as a champion prevaricator, was Baron Munchausen, whose lies and incredible stories were first recorded in Rudolf Erich Raspe's *Baron Munchausen's Narrative of His Marvelous Travels and Campaigns in Russia* (1785). The work is a kind of caricature of the exaggerated reports of travelers returning from foreign lands. The original of the hero was Baron Karl Friedrich Hieronymus von Manchausen, of Göttingen, who was accustomed to entertain his guests with outrageously improbable tales.

A nineteenth-century book that has remained popular with children and many adults since its publication is *The Swiss Family Robinson* (1813), by J. R. Wyss. The Swiss author records the amazing adventures of a minister, his wife, and four sons after they are shipwrecked and cast upon a desert island. Some indispensable items are salvaged from the ship, but for the most part the family survives by the ingenious use of everything found on the island. The close kinship with Robinson Crusoe is obvious.

The father of science fiction is almost indisputably Jules Verne, whose writings forecast with remarkable accuracy the submarine, dirigible, airplane, automobile, and other modern technological developments. His novels have provided the basis for widely popular motion pictures, television shows, and other forms of entertainment to the present day. In addition to his *From the Earth to the Moon* and *Journey to the Center of the Earth*, previously mentioned, Verne was the author of *Twenty Thousand Leagues under the Sea* (1869), a work which introduced the submarine to literature, and *Around the World in Eighty Days* (1873).

A notable name in American literature, Herman Melville's early

Travel in Fact and Fancy

fame was based on travel narratives. His first five books are auto-biographical adventure novels. *Typee* (1846) and *Omoo* (1847) are stirring tales of two heroes who live among South Sea cannibals, escape, and ship on an Australian whaler on a trip off Japan. *Redburn* (1849) and *White Jacket* (1850) deal with life aboard ship. Melville's *Moby Dick* (1851), sometimes called "The Great American Novel," has all the elements of an epic sea adventure, as the *Pequod* cruises across the length and breadth of the Pacific in Captain Ahab's mad search for the great white whale, Moby Dick.

The sea stories of Joseph Conrad are classics of the genre, written against the background of the author's intimate knowledge of the sea and of maritime life. His *Typhoon* (1903) contains an unforgettable description of a storm at sea. *The Nigger of the Narcissus* (1897) is a somewhat allegorical novel about life and death at sea. Other Conrad works relating to the sea include *Mirror of the Sea* (1906), a novel of maritime reminiscences; *The Shadow Line* (1917), based upon the author's experiences as commander of the *Otaga*; and *Twixt Land and Sea* (1912), a collection of short stories. Conrad's writing is remarkable for vivid descriptions of exotic scenes and in depicting the effects of tropical surroundings and of contacts with Asiatics on European sailors and traders.

Collecting travel accounts has been a favorite pastime of anthologists and editors from Richard Hakluyt and Samuel Purchas in the sixteenth and seventeenth centuries until the present time. Hakluyt, an English geographer, historian, and clergyman, published in 1582 his *Divers Voyages Touching the Discovery of America and the Islands Adjacent,* a work that encouraged further English exploration, colonization, and foreign trade. His major opus, however, was the collecting and editing of more than 100 accounts of voyages and explorations as told by ordinary civil servants and seamen and by such adventurers as the Cabots, Frobisher, Drake, and Raleigh. The first edition was issued in 1859 under the title *The Principal Navigations, Voyages, Traffics, and Discoveries of the English Nation;* an enlarged, three-volume edition appeared in 1598–1600.

To continue Hakluyt's endeavours, the Hakluyt Society was founded in London in 1846 to publish rare works of travel and exploration. Since then the society has been engaged in a continuous program of publication. As of 1976, it had issued 288 volumes.

Another English compiler of works of travel and discovery was Samuel Purchas (1575?–1626). His major publication, a continuation of Hakluyt's *Principal Navigations,* came out in 1625 under the title *Purchas His Pilgrimes, Contayning a History of the World in Sea Voyages and Lande Travels, by Englishmen and Others,* in four volumes. An expanded edition of Purchas was published in 1905–7 in twenty volumes.

The examples set by Hakluyt and Purchas were emulated early in the nineteenth century by, for example, E. D. Clarke's *Travels in Various Countries of Europe, Asia and Africa* (1816–24, in eleven volumes) and John Pinkerton's *Voyages and Travels in All Parts of the World* (1808–17, in seventeen volumes).

Modern anthologies of travel are numerous. Among the best of the species are the following:

Baker, John N. L. *A History of Geographical Discovery and Exploration*

Brendon, John A. *Great Navigators and Discoverers*

Cary, Max. *The Ancient Explorers*

Crowe, Gerald R. *The Explorers; An Anthology of Discovery*

Greely, A. W. *Explorers and Travelers*

Hale, John R. *Age of Exploration*

Herrmann, Paul. *The Great Age of Discovery*

Key, Charles E. *The Story of Twentieth-Century Exploration*

Mallory, Richard D. *Masterworks of Travel and Exploration*

Newton, Arthur P. *The Great Age of Discovery*

Rugoff, Milton. *The Great Travelers*

Stefansson, Vilhjalmur. *Great Discoveries and Explorations*

Synge, Margaret B. *A Book of Discovery*

Wright, Helen, and Rapport, Samuel. *The Great Explorers*

And so, authors and anthologists of travel, exploration, and discovery continue to keep printing presses busy and to maintain the popularity of this fascinating branch of literature.

Bibliography

AMUNDSEN, ROALD (1872–1928)
The South Pole: an Account of the Norwegian Antarctic Expedition in the "Fram," 1910–1912, translated from the Norwegian by A. G. Chater. London: J. Murray; New York: Lee Keedick, 1912. 2 v.

BARTRAM, WILLIAM (1739–1823)
Travels through North and South Carolina, Georgia, East and West Florida, the Cherokee Country, the Extensive Territory of the Muscogulges, or Creek Confederacy, and the Country of the Chactaws. Philadelphia: James and Johnson, 1791.

BORROW, GEORGE (1803–81)
The Bible in Spain; or the Journeys, Adventures, and Imprisonments of an Englishman, in an Attempt to Circulate the Scriptures in the Peninsula. London: J. Murray, 1843. 3 v.

BURTON, RICHARD FRANCIS (1821–90)
Personal Narrative of a Pilgrimage to El-Medinah and Meccah. London: Longman, 1855. 3 v.

COOK, JAMES (1728–79)
An Account of a Voyage round the World. London: Richard Phillips, 1809. 7 v. (Includes accounts of Cook's first, second, and third voyages.)

DANA, RICHARD HENRY, JR. (1815–82)
Two Years before the Mast: a Personal Narrative of the Sea. New York: Harper, 1840.

288   DARWIN, CHARLES, (1809–82)
Journal of Researches into the Geology and Natural History of the Various Countries Visited by H.M.S. Beagle. London: H. Colburn, 1839.

FUKUZAWA YUKICHI (1834–1901)
The Autobiography of Fukuzawa Yukichi, translated by Eiichi Kiyooka. Revised and authorized edition. Tokyo: Hokuseido Pubs., 1948.

HERODOTUS (c.484–425 B.C.)
History of the Persian Wars. First English edition: London: Thomas Marche, 1584. First printed edition: Venice: Jacobus Rubeus, 1474. First Greek edition: Venice: Aldus Manutius, 1502.

HERZOG, MAURICE (1919–   )
Annapurna: First Conquest of an 8,000-Meter Peak. Translated from the French by Nea Morin and Janet Adam Smith. New York: Dutton, 1953.

HEYERDAHL, THOR (1914–   )
Kon-Tiki: Across the Pacific by Raft. Translated from the Norwegian by F. H. Lyon. Chicago: Rand McNally, 1950.

HUMBOLDT, ALEXANDER VON (1769–1859)
Personal Narrative of Travels in the Equinoctial Regions of the New Continent during the Years 1799–1804. London: Longman, 1818–29. 7 v.

HUNT, JOHN (1910–   )
The Ascent of Everest. London: Dutton, 1953. American edition entitled *The Conquest of Everest.* New York: Dutton, 1954. See also: Edmund Hillary (1919–   ). *High Adventure.* London: Hodder, 1955. New York: Dutton, 1955.

LEWIS, MERIWETHER (1774–1809) and CLARK, WILLIAM (1770–1838)
History of the Expedition under the Command of Captains Lewis and Clark to the Sources of the Missouri; Thence across the Rocky Mountains and down the River Columbia to the Pacific Ocean, Performed during the Years 1804–5–6, by Order of the Government of the United States. Philadelphia: Bradford and Inskeep, 1814. 2 v.

PARK, MUNGO (1771–1806)
Travels in the Interior Districts of Africa Performed under the Direction and Patronage of the African Association in the Years 1795, 1796, and 1797. London: W. Hulmer, 1799. A modern reprint was issued by Arno Press and the *New York Times* in 1971.

PARKMAN, FRANCIS (1823–93)
The California and Oregon Trail: Being Sketches of Prairie and Rocky Mountain Life. New York: Putnam, 1849.

PEARY, ROBERT EDWIN (1856–1920)
The North Pole; Its Discovery in 1909 under the Auspices of the Peary Arctic Club. New York: Stokes, 1910.

PIGAFETTA, ANTONIO (1491–1534?)
Le Voyage et Navigation Faict Par les Espagnoles. Paris, 1524. *The First Voyage around the World by Magellan,* translated by Lord Stanley of Alderley. London: Hakluyt Society, 1874. *Magellan's Voyage, a Narrative Account of the First Circumnavigator,* translated by R. A. Skelton. New Haven: Yale Univ. Press, 1969 (the only complete edition in English).

POLO, MARCO (c.1254–1324)
The Most Noble and Famous Travels of Marcus Paulus into the East Partes of the World. London: Newbery, 1579 (first English edition). First Italian edition: Venice: Baptista da Sessa, 1496.

ROOSEVELT, THEODORE (1858–1919)
Through the Brazilian Wilderness. New York: Scribner, 1914.

SCHOOLCRAFT, HENRY (1793–1864)
Narrative Journal of Travels through the Northwestern Regions of the United States, Extending from Detroit through the Great Chain of American Lakes to the Sources of the Mississippi River, Performed as a Member of the Expedition under Governor Cass in the Year 1820. Albany, New York: Hosford, 1821.

SLOCUM, JOSHUA (1844–1909?)
Sailing Alone around the World. New York: Century, 1900.

290   STANLEY, HENRY MORTON (1841–1904)

Through the Dark Continent, or, the Sources of the Nile, around the Great Lakes of Equatorial Africa, and down the Livingstone River to the Atlantic Ocean. New York: Harper, 1878.

VESPUCCI, AMERIGO (1451–1512)

Lettera di Amerigo Vespucci. Florence: Pietro Pacina da Pescia, 1505–6. First edition in Italian of four voyages. Various English translations have been published, e.g., *The First Four Voyages of Amerigo Vespucci.* London: Quaritch, 1893; *The Letter of Amerigo Vespucci Describing His Four Voyages to the New World, 1497–1504.* San Francisco: Book Club of California, 1926; *The Letters of Amerigo Vespucci.* London: Hakluyt Society, 1894.

JUN 9 '82	DATE DUE	
B.O.	APR 0 5 1983 · OCT 0 3 1983	
	APR 2 6 1983 · OCT 2 6 1983	
JUN 1 8 82	MAY 1 4 1983 · NOV 2 3 1983	
SEP 3 0 '82	MAY 2 4 1983 · DEC 1 4 1983	
NOV 0 5 '82	JUN 1 6 1983 · JAN 17 1984	
DEC 0 7 '82	JUL 0 5 '83 · MAR 0 8 1984	
DEC 3 0 '82	JUL 2 6 1983 · MAR 2 8 1984	
JAN 18 '83	AUG 1 7 1983 · MAY 0 2 1984	
FEB 1 1 '83	SEP 1 3 1983 · SEP 0 1 1988	
FEB 2 6 1983	SEP 2 0 1983 · FEB 0 3 1999	
MAR 1 0 1983 R	FEB 0 3 1999	